Marketing without Advertising

Routledge Advances in Management and Business Studies

For a full list of titles in this series, please visit www.routledge.com

17 **Strategy Talk**
A Critique of the Discourse of Strategic Management
Pete Thomas

18 **Power and Influence in the Boardroom**
James Kelly and John Gennard

19 **Public Private Partnerships**
Theory and Practice in International Perspective
Stephen Osborne

20 **Work and Unseen Chronic Illness**
Silent Voices
Margaret Vickers

21 **Measuring Business Excellence**
Gopal K Kanji

22 **Innovation as Strategic Reflexivity**
Edited by Jon Sundbo and Lars Fuglsang

23 **The Foundations of Management Knowledge**
Edited by Paul Jeffcutt

24 **Gender and the Public Sector**
Professionals and Managerial Change
Edited by Jim Barry, Mike Dent and Maggie O'Neill

25 **Managing Technological Development**
Hakan Hakansson and Alexandra Waluszewski

26 **Human Resource Management and Occupational Health and Safety**
Carol Boyd

27 **Business, Government and Sustainable Development**
Gerard Keijzers

28 **Strategic Management and Online Selling**
Creating Competitive Advantage with Intangible Web Goods
Susanne Royer

29 **Female Entrepreneurship**
Implications for Education, Training and Policy
Edited by Nancy M. Carter, Colette Henry, Barra Ó Cinnéide and Kate Johnston

30 **Managerial Competence within the Hospitality and Tourism Service Industries**
Global Cultural Contextual Analysis
John Saee

31 **Innovation Diffusion in the New Economy**
The Tacit Component
Barbara Jones and Bob Miller

32 Technological Communities and Networks
International, National and Regional Perspectives
Dimitris G. Assimakopoulos

33 Narrating the Management Guru
In Search of Tom Peters
David Collins

34 Development on the Ground
Clusters, Networks and Regions in Emerging Economies
Edited by Allen J. Scott and Gioacchino Garofoli

35 Reconfiguring Public Relations
Ecology, Equity, and Enterprise
David McKie and Debashish Munshi

36 The Pricing and Revenue Management of Services
A Strategic Approach
Irene C. L. Ng

37 Critical Representations of Work and Organization in Popular Culture
Carl Rhodes and Robert Westwood

38 Intellectual Capital and Knowledge Management
Strategic Management of Knowledge Resources
Federica Ricceri

39 Flagship Marketing
Concepts and Places
Edited by Tony Kent and Reva Brown

40 Managing Project Ending
Virpi Havila and Asta Salmi

41 AIDS and Business
Saskia Faulk and Jean-Claude Usunier

42 The Evaluation of Transportation Investment Projects
Joseph Berechman

43 Urban Regeneration Management
International Perspectives
Edited by John Diamond, Joyce Liddle, Alan Southern and Philip Osei

44 Global Advertising, Attitudes, and Audiences
Tony Wilson

45 Challenges and Controversies in Management Research
Edited by Catherine Cassell and Bill Lee

46 Economy, Work, and Education
Critical Connections
Catherine Casey

47 Regulatory Governance and Risk Management
Occupational Health and Safety in the Coal Mining Industry
Binglin Yang

48 Risk Management and Corporate Governance
Edited by Abolhassan Jalilvand and A. G. Malliaris

49 Careers in Creative Industries
Chris Mathieu

50 Marketing without Advertising
Brand Preference and Consumer Choice in Cuba
Emilio Morales and Joseph L. Scarpaci

Marketing without Advertising

Brand Preference and Consumer Choice in Cuba

Emilio Morales and Joseph L. Scarpaci

Routledge
Taylor & Francis Group
NEW YORK LONDON

First published 2012
by Routledge
711 Third Avenue, New York, NY 10017

Simultaneously published in the UK
by Routledge
2 Park Square, Milton Park, Abingdon, Oxon OX14 4RN

Routledge is an imprint of the Taylor & Francis Group, an informa business

Typeset in Sabon by IBT Global.
Printed and bound in the United States of America on acid-free paper by IBT Global.

Library of Congress Cataloging-in-Publication Data

Morales, Emilio, 1969–
Marketing without advertising : brand preference and consumer choice in Cuba / by Emilio Morales & Joseph L. Scarpaci. — 1st ed.
p. cm. — (Routledge advances in management and business studies ; 50)
Includes bibliographical references and index.
1. Marketing—Cuba. 2. Consumers' preferences—Cuba. 3. Brand choice—Cuba. I. Scarpaci, Joseph L. II. Title.
HF5415.12.C8M67 2011
658.8'343097291—dc23
2011031620

ISBN13: 978-0-415-89698-6 (hbk)
ISBN13: 978-0-203-13414-6 (ebk)

Emilio Morales—
Al tesoro más grande que tengo en mi vida:
mi hijo Emilio Daniel

Joseph L. Scarpaci—
In Loving Memory of Delia Maria Sosa López (1911–2010)
por su sencillez, humildad y abundante cariño

Contents

Figures

Tables

Preface

All Cuban Communist Party Congresses are to take place each five years. The frequency of the meetings harks back to the time of the former Soviet Union and the central role played by the infamous five-year plans. Synchronizing the plans and Congress aimed to make operating the central governmental apparatus more efficient. In Cuba, the Party Congress has only met six times since the 1960s, and is at least four congresses in arrears. Still, the VI Cuban Congress Party met as we completed this book; its previous meeting was 12 years earlier, back in 1997. The Congress will no doubt be remembered as the final era of Fidel Castro, whose government and mandates reigned sovereign for nearly half a century. In theory, the Congress also denotes the beginning of a transition to a market economy of some ilk, and perhaps too it marks the outset of nascent sociopolitical changes whose full features will not be known for years to come. Millions on and off the island hope that these changes portend a more efficient government and economy and, most of all, greater opportunities for all Cubans.

What is novel about things afoot in Cuba is that it was not the fall of the Berlin Wall or the Soviet Union 20 years ago that set change in motion in Cuba. Nor was it a lifting of the U.S. trade embargo, something most Cuban Americans have supported since the 1960s and have been agile in convincing 10 U.S. presidents to hold in force. After 50 years of failed policies both in Washington, D.C., and Havana, we believe that what has changed the economic course of Cuba by 180 degrees is the Revolution's putting up with the free market.

The return to the starting line is now an irreversible process. Both the nature and depth of these reforms leave no doubt that the elements of the 'old' guard of the Cuban Communist Party have been cast aside without any chance of returning to those same 'old' ways. Raúl Castro made it clear that Cuban bureaucracy is on notice: there will be no backpedaling on these new measures. Even the vanguard youth (those under 50 or so) have been excluded from the island's newly reformulated Political Bureau, and leaders cannot hold ranks for longer than two periods of five years each. Twenty-first-century Cuba has undoubtedly embarked on a transition.

Since 1993, the Cuban economy has depended upon three fundamental pillars to sustain itself: Venezuelan oil, tourism and remittances. And it is remittances that, paradoxically, have been the main vehicle of change. They derive from out-migration from the island, which has actually unified relations between Cubans on the island and the Cuban diaspora in exile. This out-migration in the 1960s had the opposite effect: families grew apart and there was little contact, let alone sending dollars back home. At the same time, remittances have been the backbone of small businesses who allowed the Cuban government to avoid a huge economic and political crisis back in the 1990s. We are convinced that these small businesses have been the silent transformer of all aspects of Cuban society. Weaning Cubans away from the 'State' means a search for private solutions, individual choices and new brands and modes of consumption.

In penning these lines we are struck by the wave of change sweeping over the Middle East and Central Asia in what will be labeled as the 'Arab Spring.' It began in Tunisia in December 2010 when a man protested his treatment by police through self-immolation. Pro-democracy protests and rebellions erupted throughout the Middle East (Bahrain, Egypt, Iran, Libya, Saudi Arabia, Syria, Tunisia, and Yemen). Although somewhat disconnected, it not insignificant that Osama Bin Laden was shot by U.S. Navy Seals in Pakistan. The events in Cuba have been much quieter, but no less impressive. We are tempted to enter the old debate about whether economic reforms lead to political freedom or vice versa, but that would be a digression. The key point is that something truly global is murmuring and we are waiting to see where these changes will lead.

For the U.S. government, avoiding something apocalyptic, or at least Arab Spring–like, in a country just 90 miles away remains a strategic foreign policy goal. As Italy, France and Spain cope with displaced Libyans and Tunisians clamoring for work and freedom as refugees, the U.S. can ill afford a repeat of the infamous Mariel boatlift of 1980, which brought over 120,000 Cubans to its shores. Herein lies the pragmatism and—dare we say 'genius'—of the Obama administration's plan towards Cuba. An orderly transition orchestrated by Cuban generals is preferable to a democratic regime without leadership; a 'democracy' that might be weak, anarchical, disorganized and uncertain. Such a wild-card scenario would prove unpredictable and might bring untold consequences to the United States.

We have little doubt that the U.S. is watching Cuba's economic transition favorably; its rather silent observation of the island's changes casts a sort of quiet legitimacy about all of it despite the strong opposition from parts of South Florida's most conservative and ideologically driven sector of the exile community. What is clear, though, is that the conservative sectors of the Cuban American community no longer reflect the majority sentiment; they held that role some 35 years ago. A new demographic, however, has taken root and it consists of second- and third-wave immigrants to the

United States who view rapprochement more favorably than the first-wave members who arrived in the 1960s.

The great majority of the Cuban diaspora outside the island desire change in their homeland, and they express that by traveling to the island to visit family and friends, bringing and sending them money and investing in their new businesses. They are also sharing with them firsthand information about life outside the island. As marketers and individuals who are quite fond of many things Cuban, we believe these exchanges drive a series of behind-the-scenes events on the island, and brand preference and information about the 'world of consumption' (*el mundo del consumo*) is only one part of the information that the exile community delivers. Indeed, these family exchanges neither herald the glories of a consumer society abroad (it is, in fact, full of perils, costly and fraught with risk and the fear of debt) nor carry tales of woe about how bad life on the island will get under the socialist government.

These encounters across the Florida Straits do, however, carry information about the trials and tribulations of starting new businesses, a fact that should gladden the hearts of the most conservative element of the exile community. We speculate on the impact of these Cuban visits, remittances and formal and informal advice in our final two chapters.

The next five years will be of paramount importance in the Cuban transition. New generations will have a chance to build a different society. New measures will allow for the sale of homes and cars and will unleash a dynamism not seen in 50 years. At the same time, an emerging private sector will play a key role in reviving the economy. The future privatization of many public services and products will chart a new course for the island's economy.

The high level of formal training in the current labor force is underutilized. Cubans' ability to quickly adapt to changing technology as well as their accumulated knowledge about the consumption of brands will transform their level of consumption; the past 18 years provides fertile ground upon which this new market will grow in its transition to more market forces.

In the next two years or perhaps even before then, we expect to see a growth in advertising in modern massive communication channels. It will be essential to drive consumption, which the current regime needs to sustain itself economically and politically. At the same time, advertising will grant a certain legitimacy to the market reforms, as would a reduction in barriers to the Internet.

Foreign investment will continue to expand, especially by the exile community. We envision the diaspora playing a key role in supporting, financially or through business acumen, microenterprises in Cuba. We may be forecasting a mini–reverse migration but it would be spurred as much by a desire to reunite with family as one to run a successful and profitable business. Consequently, a middle class will gradually take hold, something essential for strengthening Cuban civil society in the twenty-first century.

In the realm of services marketing, we expect a rise in the number of Cuban and international franchises operating in the island. Franchise development will send a positive signal to international investors: aspects of private property and standardized services sustained by quality control of product and service are possible in Cuba. The tourist sector will be particularly aware of these franchise developments, and their development could be a harbinger for the U.S. tourism sector, which, although it has been banned for purely recreational reasons, has risen considerably in the form of cultural, religious and people-to-people excursions over the past two decades. As a result of increased U.S. travel, it would make sense to a growing U.S. business lobby in Washington, D.C., demanding a greater presence of U.S. products in the island, and a decrease in emerging economy (China, India, South Korea, Taiwan) products. Bit by bit, the pressure to end the U.S. embargo will mount.

Currently, about 700 U.S. companies sell food products in Cuba despite the embargo. This barely scratches the surface of the binational business opportunities that exist. In a new context, U.S. energy, telecommunication, pharmaceutical, biotechnology and other sectors have much to explore in Cuba. A second Obama term could be the time when all this happens, and the older conservative sectors of the Cuban exile community in the United States finally exert a minority opinion over U.S. foreign policy. In their place is emerging a consensus by Cuban immigrants, especially those who arrived after 1980, to end the U.S. trade embargo and allow the market and the 'biological solution' (the natural demise of the islands' leaders) to run their course. In 2007, only 42 percent of Cuban Americans responding to Florida International University's annual poll about all things Cuban said that they opposed the U.S. government's continuance of the trade embargo against their homeland. By 2008, that percentage had increased to 55 percent, which the pollsters interpreted as "a continuing shift in attitudes by Cuban-Americans and reflects a generational rift between those Cuban-Americans who arrived in the U.S. in the 1960s and those who came to the U.S. in the 1980s or later" (Reuters 2008).

Without question, these are exciting and promising times to study Cuban markets, consumers, brands and consumption. April 2011's VI Cuban Communist Party Congress released many of the same tired and ideological pronouncements about Cuban socialism. However, the reality is that a new sphere of consumption is out of the bag and the market implementations prohibit a return to the dogmatic confines of the past. Cuba's future is in the hands of new generations; it is just a matter of time.

Emilio Morales Dopico, Miami, FL
Joseph L. Scarpaci, Blacksburg, VA
June 2011

Acknowledgments

Numerous individuals in the United States and Cuba supported this project in countless ways. We are particularly grateful to the staff at the Hispanic Reading Room of the Library of Congress in Washington, D.C. (Tracy North, Katherine D. McCann and Marisa H. Grijalva), Armando Hugo Portela, Jorge Pérez-López, Roger Betancourt, Osvaldo Villegas Moré, Manuel Orozco, Rolando Castañeda, Arch Ritter, the Inter-American Dialogue and Mauricio Font of the Bildner Center at CUNY.

The Authors

I want to recognize the generous professional help provided by Angel Hernández Gómez (my dear *profe* and friend), Jorge Salazar Carillo, José de la Torre, Carlos Alberto Montaner, Ricardo Puerta, Modesto Arocha and Wilfredo Cancio. I am also grateful for the moral support and encouragement I received throughout the course of the project from my family and friends, especially my parents, dear uncles Fernando Milanes and Ramón Pages, my everlasting friends Dr. Roberto Carlos Fernández-Blay and José Maria González for their exemplary perseverance; they are successful men in the United States who provided help in difficult times. And to my adorable Ileana Domínguez (*mi sol*), who has filled me with energy and the necessary inspiration in the final stretch of this project.

Emilio Morales

Thanks to Eloise Coupey, Jim Littlefield, Joe Sirgy, Elizabeth White Baker, Amy Weinreb, Sarah Blue, Mabel Matamoros, Bob Oliver, Sujatha Fernandes, Mario Coyula, Tomás Robaina, Tim Brothers, Bruce Macdonald and Maria Padrón Hernández for their professional insights at various stages of the work. On the home front, the unwavering Gilda de los Angeles Machín, Michael Joseph and Cristina Alessandra continue to be my Gibraltar.

Joseph L. Scarpaci

All errors and omissions are, of course, our own.

1 Marketing without Advertising
Brand Preference and Consumer Choice in Cuba

The collapse of the former Soviet Union and the fall of the Iron Curtain signaled a clarion call that championed global capitalism. Multinational corporations rushed to position themselves in the utility, manufacturing and service industries that blossomed in Eastern Europe and the USSR. Across the Atlantic Ocean, however, Fidel Castro clung steadfastly to power. In 1993, his government reluctantly instituted a series of limited reforms to compensate for the cessation of foreign aid from Moscow—estimated at approximately $5 million daily—to stop the economic free fall on the island that began in 1989. These policies, part of a series of structural changes referred to as the 'Special Period in a Time of Peace,' ushered in a broad spectrum of national and international consumer products and services previously unknown to islanders. Limited joint ventures, ending limits on remittances sent from the exile community in the U.S. and Europe and a push towards international tourism drove these reforms. In a few short years, Cubans were seeing foreign brands among consumer durables in dollar stores (Plate 1.1) and a broad array of logos brought in by tourists; in 1989, just over 100,000 international tourists visited Cuba, but by the early 2000s, the figure had surpassed two million annually. Three decades of a closed, centrally planned economy reluctantly produced a tepid Cuban-style *perestroika.*

Today, nearly two decades into these limited market reforms, it is curious that no systematic research has explored consumer brand awareness among the 11 million Cubans living just 90 miles from the United States. The paucity of academic research stems from the challenges of conducting public/consumer opinion surveys and the Cuban government's reluctance to share anything but favorable information with the international community. Official state policy contends that consumer wants and needs are satisfied by either a series of generic and Cuban-made brands, or by independent entrepreneurs (*cuentapropistas*) who provide brandless products and services. This book, however, seeks to fill this research gap and challenge official policy interpretations.

Marketing without Advertising: Brand Preference and Consumer Choice in Cuba analyzes the role, narratives and behavior of consumption since 1959. It documents how consumer behavior has changed since

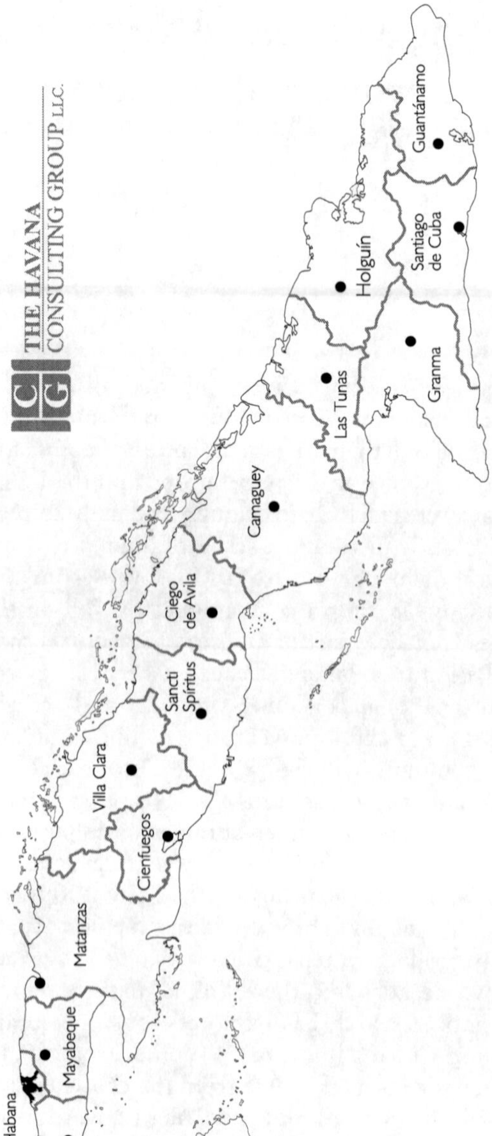

Plate 1.1 Political Map of Cuba, 2011. Courtesy of Armando Portela, The Havana Consulting Group.

the prerevolutionary period, with a special focus on the Special Period in a Time of Peace that began in the early 1990s. The book traces the shift from moral-based rewards in the early years of the Revolution to the rise of material-based incentives. To anchor our study of Cuban consumption empirically, we draw on primary data that analyzes and situates the level of brand awareness and brand values among a national sample of 780 consumers in Havana City and eight other provinces.

In its first English version,[1] our book debunks the notion that Communist Cuba has been able to separate from the minds of Cubans the differences between essential and nonessential consumer goods and services. Cubans have long been exposed to foreign mass media in the form of movies, music videos and limited cable television shown in hotels and tourist centers. Although the Internet is highly regulated and firewalls limit what university and government researchers access, the Cuban diaspora in exile brings back clothing, personal care products, electronic goods and magazines that increase the awareness of brand logos, jingles, products and services.

Our survey findings presented in Chapter 3 reveal that more than 2,000 brands were identified by respondents/informants. Findings also show that McDonald's and Sears garnered 3 percent and 4 percent of all brand responses in the quick-service restaurant and retail categories, respectively, even though the former has never operated on the island and the latter was closed following the 1959 revolution. These and related findings are ripe with marketing implications such as substitution effects, price elasticity, latent demand for certain products and services, and consumer behavior.

The breakdown of unassisted recall responses (top-of-mind awareness) among 32 national and international products and service categories (and the number of respondents identifying said categories in parentheses) is discussed in Chapter 3. These 32 product and service categories are further subdivided by Cuban and foreign brands as well as the likelihood that the consumers would purchase them. Surprisingly, not only did the sample population have a broad knowledge of brands and express strong preferences for particular brands, but also not all of the preferred brands were foreign. We say "surprisingly" because the state subsidies for food and basic goods are specified by the ration book, or *libreta*. Rationed durable and nondurable products often reach the customer as "brandless" objects; toothpaste in a silver tube with no label, condensed milk in a tin with no product information or coffee doled out from large bins into small bags. These practices intentionally work to forge a 'brandless' array of products.

Only a limited number of Cubans with access to hard currency (dollars, euros or the Cuban Convertible Currency [CUC]) can purchase 'named' foreign-made products. Put another way, after 50 years of 'window-shopping,' Cuban consumers exhibit strong preferences in satisfying their wants and needs even though their purchasing power does not allow them to do so. An increase in remittances sent from overseas and a growing number of Cubans working in tourism have enlarged the circulation of hard currency

Figure 1.1 The Cohiba cigar is one of the most iconic Cuban brands and remains one of the premier products on the global market. Photograph by Emilio Morales.

(versus the Cuban peso) across the island. In doing so, a new world of consumer products—previously unavailable—now blurs the lines between the 'moral' and 'material' rewards permitted by the Cuban government. For the Cuban government, exporting iconic Cuban brands (Figure 1.1) through franchising and the removal of the U.S. trade embargo portends considerable revenues in the future.

Our work shows that Cuban consumers, either through hearsay, product placement in the media, viral marketing, window-shopping (*vitriniando*) or firsthand experience, possess sophisticated knowledge about product breadth and depth. Previously, consumer brand awareness was thought to be quite limited. Because just one FM-frequency radio show (called Radio Taino, which is geared towards international tourists) actually carries Spanish-language consumer product advertisements, the normal marketing channels found in other countries do not operate in Cuba. The broadcast, moreover, is confined to limited tourist poles throughout the island (Scarpaci and Portela 2009, chap. 4). Our research indicates that in-store promotion (by store personnel, floor demonstrations, promotional materials, free samples) is the greatest driver in consumer decision-making. This important 'touch point' (a time before, during or after a purchase when a firm, brand, product or service has a chance to influence a customer directly) in future services marketing and retailing should be paramount if firms wish to capitalize on what we regard as fairly savvy 'Communist' consumers. Even though Latin America was an earlier adopter of chain supermarkets than Asia and Africa (McCullough et al. 2008, 48–49), it will simply not be enough to someday build big-box stores or establish internationally recognized brand chains in Cuba if sales personnel are not well informed about product features and Cubans' preferences (Table 1.1). Until a significant consumer population has access to certain products and services, Cuban consumers will likely continue to rely heavily on in-store promotion and word of mouth (WOM) for their decision-making.

Our conclusions indicate that the stigma once associated with certain types of consumption has dissipated. The final chapter speculates on what retailing in a post-Castro era might look like in the not-too-distant future. 'Big-box' stores coming to the island would mark a radical change from the neighborhood-based stores where professional sales staff and consumers appear to have forged a strong bond (Hirt and Scarpaci 2007); high turnover rates of sales staff in chain stores would disrupt that buyer–seller relationship borne out by our research. The Revolution's shift to a limited material-based reward system allows us to revisit the conventional 'Western' branding literature and contextualize it to the case at hand. Our basic-research contribution challenges the conventional assumptions about brand equity, brand extension and brand loyalty because of Cuba's unique marketing conditions. Consumption on the island also appears to fall uniquely between the conspicuous model found throughout the 'developed North' and the more modest levels found in the so-called 'developing South.' We suggest that this tempering of consumption may be one of the lasting contributions of the Revolution on the social and moral fabric of Cubans. Islanders are neither rabid consumers nor ignorant simpletons in a complex world of goods and services.

The applied research value of the book is considerable for American firms wishing to operate on the island in a post-embargo era, and for those actually selling goods there now. This will be a 'must-read' book for

Table 1.1 Selected 'Big-box' Retailers Operating in the Caribbean Basin, Central America and Mexico, 2011

Retailer (stock ticker name)	Headquarters and regional traits
Carrefour (CA.PA)	French-based firm with 1,395 'hyper-markets' globally makes it the second largest retail chain that distributes mainly food, clothing and electronic appliances and equipment. Recent shift to 5,400 sq. meter 'human-scale' stores. Operates in Dominican Republic (5 hypermarkets and 20 convenience stores) and Colombia (with 46 hypermarkets under the cash-and-carry (*cobre y lleve*) wholesale brand Atacado). In Mexico until 2005 when it was purchased by Chedraui. About 14% of its sales and 62% of its revenues come from Latin America (including Argentina and Brazil) and hypermarket stores, respectively. The chain's Argentine slogan *Está bueno para vos* (Its good for you) would have to be altered for the Cuban market to include the second-person singular indirect object pronoun (*tí*) instead of the Argentine vernacular *vos*.

Continued

Table 1.1 Continued

Costco (COST)	The Washington-state based retailer operates an international chain of membership warehouses, mainly under the "Costco Wholesale" name, and has 32 locations in 18 Mexican states.
Home Depot (HD)	The largest U.S. home improvement chain has 70 stores in Mexico. Its slogan, "*Haz más, ahorrando*," (do more, saving) could resonate well with Cubans.
Hipermercado Bicentenario (not traded)	Formerly a French (majority-owned by Saint-Etienne, France-based Casino Guichard Perrachon S.A.)-Colombian chain called Hipermercado Exito, it was expropriated by the government of Venezuelan president Hugo Chávez in 2010 because of allegations of unnecessary price speculation and consumer gouging. With just four stores in Venezuela, President Chávez aims to promote the clothing, food, and electronics offerings by as much as 40% below market prices.[1] Given Venezuela's alliance with Cuba, this could be a model for new retailing in the island.
Jumbo (CENCOSUD)	Chilean-based firm with strong presence in that country and neighboring Argentina. It operates six supermarkets in the Dominican Republic (DR) , where the 2009 opening of its last store was 23,000 square meters (236,806 sq. ft.). At least three stores in Costa Rica. Like Carrefour and WalMart, it sells mainly food, clothing and electronic appliances and equipment. Its Chilean slogan '*Te da más*' (Gives you more) and the DR's '*Lo máxmio*' (The most) would both work in Cuba.
PriceSmart (PSMT)	PriceSmart operates membership warehouse shopping clubs in Central America and the Caribbean (Aruba, Barbados, Dom. Rep., Jamaica, Trinidad, and US Virgin Islands), bringing members brand name food and merchandise Panama. Similar to Costco and Sam's Club in U.S., though store sizes are smaller (50,000-75,000 sq. ft.)
Supermercardos Internacional H-E-B (not traded)	A privately held San Antonio, Texas based supermarket chain operating over 30 supermarkets in Mexico. Its big-box version is called H-E-B Plus but is so far concentrated in Texas. Draws on well-known international brands as in-store tenants even though in Mexico it aims to promote local produce and products.
Wal-Mart (WMT)	The world's largest retailer located in Arkansas opened its Latin American Headquarters in Miami in 2010. Regional director claimed its strategy in Latin America is "focused on the fundamentals of growth, leverage and performance,"[2] Honduras (55 stores under the names País (7), Hiper Paiz (1), Despensa Familiar (41), Maxi Bodega (6)); Nicaragua (58 stores under the names La Unión (6) and Pali (51)); Costa Rica (175 stores under names Maxi Bodega (12), Más X Menos (25), Hiper Más (6), and Pali (132)); El Salvador (77 stores under names Hiper Paiz (2), Despensa Familiar (59), and La Despensa de Don Juan (25);

Continued

Table 1.1 Continued

	Guatemala (171 stores operate under names Paiz (30), Hiper Paiz (7), Despensa Familiar (118), ClubCo (2), and Maxi Bodega (14)); Mexico (1,606 stores under the names Supercenter (182), Bodega Aurerra Express (313), Sam's Club (107); Superama (72), Suburbia (89), Mi Bodega Aurrera (155), and VIPS Restaurants (366).

Note: 'Big box' retailers refers mainly to stores that have at least 80,000 square feet of space, though it is common for them to range from 100,000 to 250,000 square feet (Macdonald 2008, 141). Not all of the subsidiary retailers operate big-box outlets, nor is the big-box model always exportable. Best Buy and Home Depot, for instance retrenched their presence in China because of consumer pushback. In just five years, Best Buy shuttered all nine of its branded stores by 2011 as well as its headquarters in Shanghai. Home Depot purchased local Chinese chain Home Way in 2006, but by 2011, only seven of the 12 stores operate (see Macleod 2011). See Hirt and Scarpaci (2007) for their assessment on the future of big box retailing in Cuba from the perspective of transportation, land use, and cultural factors. Table sources are from company websites unless noted otherwise.

1. Orozco, J. 2010. Venezuela Opens Seized Exito Stores as Bicentenario Outlets (Bloomberg) February 13, 2010, 4:52 PM EST http://www.businessweek.com/news/2010-02-13/venezuela-opens-seized-exito-stores-as-bicentenario-outlets.htmlm Accessed December 18, 2010

2. WalMart Latinoamérica Opens New Regional Office in South Florida, Introduces New Regional President and CEO Eduardo Solórzano, http://walmartstores.com/pressroom/news/9663.aspx, Accessed December 18, 2010

Cubanologists as well as foreign firms operating in Cuba or entrepreneurs considering franchising options who need to know more about Cuba's iconic brands. The latter, especially firms in European Union nations and

Figure 1.2 The interior of the *Casa del Habano*, Melía Cohiba, on the Malecón, Havana City Province, where a Canadian tourist enjoys one of the island's prized smokes. The cigar being smoked cost US$22, about a month's wages for the average worker in Cuba (July 2010). Photograph by J. L. Scarpaci.

Figure 1.3 Dollar-store snack display cases where Cuban products compete with European ones, and where most Cubans since 1993 have become acquainted with foreign brands. Hotel Ancón, Trinidad, Cuba, 2008. Photograph by J. L. Scarpaci.

Canada, may wish to enhance their marketing mix (price, product, placement and promotion), refocus communications strategies and reposition products and services. As an empirical benchmark on consumer behavior, the work will form the basis for international marketers who wish to target the South Florida, Cuba and Spanish-speaking Caribbean and Central American markets. It will also serve as a 'snapshot' about consumer knowledge (Figure 1.3) after more than half a century of central planning.

Our book makes plain that Cubans on the island are not mere twins of their South Florida cousins. They have assembled an impressive amount of information about brands, hold strong opinions about their likes and dislikes and wish they had the consumer purchasing power to acquire some of those products and services. They deserve that right.

2 A History of Cuban Retailing, 1902–2011

This chapter sketches some of the principal features of Cuban retailing over the past century or so. From a fragmented and disrupted distribution system at the end of the Spanish-American-Cuban War (1868–1878, 1895–1898), the island's retail sector entered the twentieth century dominated by Spanish immigrants and small Cuban entrepreneurs. By the time of the revolutionary fervor of the 1950s, the island's major cities reflected the retailing hierarchy common to most U.S. and Canadian cities because of the prevalence of chain department stores that offered variety and low-cost products. It was in the smaller towns and countryside where mom-and-pop operations, systems of barter and U.S. sugar company stores prevailed. In 1959 and into the early years of the following decade, the evolution of a market-based retail sector was eliminated, as nationalizations became the norm and even petty commerce was taken over by the socialist government, driven into the shadows of the 'black market,' or else eliminated. The vicissitudes of Cuba's retailing reflect that its political economy and marketing ran the full gamut of possible options within a relatively short span. At the chapter's end, we aim to answer three questions:

1. To what extent could Cuba today (2012) be considered a consumer society?
2. How has the socialist system prevented Cuba from becoming a consumer society?
3. To what extent has consumer behavior shifted from passive socialist consumers to consumers who take cues from a limited retail market?

This historical overview offers insight into these and related questions about patterns of consumption on the island.

THE SPANISH IMPRINT

Mercantile relations and a feudal economy trace their origins to Columbus's voyage to the island in 1492 and the subsequent development of the seven *villas* (military outposts) around the island. Between 1500 and 1515, explorer and island governor Diego de Velázquez led a brigade of 300 men across the island. Their search for mineral wealth yielded few high-value finds. Nonetheless, between 1512 and 1519, the *villas* of Santiago, Baracoa, Puerto Príncipe (Camagüey), Bayamo, Trinidad, Sancti Spiritus and Havana had been established. Most of the indigenous population—Guanajatabeyes, Siboneyes and Tainos—were killed off or died by the middle of the sixteenth century (Scarpaci et al. 2002, 7–11). Unlike Aztec and Mayan Mesoamerica or Incan Andes, no pre-Colombian production, trade or agricultural system existed in the Antilles upon which colonial trade could be grafted.

The original island capital of Santiago de Cuba proved no more successful than the second capital (Havana) in ensuring proper norms of trade where regulated through Spanish customs houses. As a thinly settled island, the island's strategic location on the Florida Straits, between Florida, Mexico and the Bahaman Channel, ensured good access to maritime commerce and, to the chagrin of Spanish authorities, contraband and pirating. Illicit trade with Dutch, British and French ships provided limited exchange with other European colonists who sailed the waters of the Caribbean Sea, Atlantic Ocean and Gulf of Mexico. In 1740, the king of Spain authorized the creation of the Havana Royal Trade Company (Real Compañia de Comercio de la Habana) to more carefully control trade between Madrid and its Cuban colony.

British control of Havana for 11 months in 1792 changed the nature of trade. Foreign trade was opened between England and Cuba directly in 1763, and three years later the island was trading freely with the newly independent American colonies along the Atlantic and Gulf of Mexico seaboards. New sugar technology was imported from the British colony of Jamaica, as were some 5,000 slaves for work on sugar plantations (Kapcia 2005, 27). This pattern of agricultural commodity production prevailed until the establishment of the Cuban Republic in 1902. It was characterized by highly fragmented trade and commerce, focused on particular crops (first coffee and tobacco, then sugar in the nineteenth century) that surfaced at specific harvesttimes and were funneled through certain ports. For the majority of the Cuban population, which was two-thirds rural in 1899, work, employment and peaks in retailing centered around payments rendered after harvesting. For example, sugar might have been planted once or twice in the areas surrounding particular sugar mills. Between that time and harvest, there was considerable under- and unemployment, and it is still referred to as the *tiempo muerto* (dead or low season). Erratic employment and retailing often centered around company stores, the latter consisting mainly of American sugar mill production.

U.S. sugar mills provided considerable retailing to workers on isolated, rural sugar mills scattered across the island. Like company towns in many parts of the world, the sugar mill sold virtually everything, including housing, retail merchandise and food. It held a near monopoly over the workers in Cuba. Staten describes this retail structure this way:

> The best (or worst) examples of this existed at the large American sugar mills with their segregated American and Cuban zones. The sugar mill was the dominant force in these areas providing virtually all the local employment and becoming a transmitter of American values. In addition to working as laborers and as low- to mid-level administrators, Cubans were hired as surveyors, accountants, clerks, teachers, engineers, technicians and physicians for the mill . . . Stores managed by the sugar mill sold almost exclusively American products. Cubans came to adopt the American consumer culture. (2003, 55)

Cuba's long-standing position as a Spanish colony and its reliance on tourism and agricultural-based exports (sugar, rum, tobacco) accounts for its deviation from the 'classic' pattern of identifying national marketing stages in the twentieth century. A prototype of stages of marketing among developed industrial economies often includes the following four eras. The production-oriented period in the U.S. and Europe spanned the first decades of the twentieth century and emphasized production efficiency. Techniques such as assembly-line design and component sequencing, the introduction of Taylorism developed at Henry Ford's automobile plants and related time-assembly factors were typical of the era (Woods and Roberts 2011). Henry Ford's classic adage that "customers could have any color of car that they wished as long as it was black" characterized the orientation on production alone.

A second era that lasted roughly until World War II was sales-oriented, and shifted the locus from the factory per se to advanced production and distribution techniques. Sales-oriented marketing aimed to sell surplus goods produced by manufacturers who might have miscalculated consumer demand.

In the postwar period the market-oriented stage emerged, when consumers increasingly made purchasing decisions according to the attributes of price, quality and convenience. A rising middle class with growing expendable income coupled with more retail outlets than the generation before them made this possible.

Starting around the late 1980s or 1990s and continuing until today is the value-based marketing era. The growth of massive discount retailers and e-commerce means that marketers should strive to give customers greater value than their competition. Comparative shopping/pricing coupled with a focus on marketing towards lifestyles characterize this marketing era (Levy and Grewal 2009).

How might these eras line up with Cuba? Clearly, there was a delay of at least a decade or two in the appearance of the first three eras on the island. As the discussion following will show, small merchants—many of them recent Spanish immigrants—prevailed during the first half of the last century. Sales-oriented marketing was evident in the late 1920s and early 1930s and prevailed until just after World War II. Cuba manifested all of the traits of the marketing-oriented era until the 1959 Revolution.

However, with the nationalizations and elimination of most private enterprise in the 1960s, the value- and lifestyle-based marketing eras have not materialized. A brief overview of marketing and retailing in Cuba, to which we now turn, sets the stage for understanding consumer behavior and marketing today.

MARKETING AND RETAILING IN THE NEW REPUBLIC

Retailing and wholesaling in the new republic (post-1902) followed many of the unspoken and legal guidelines that existed in the nineteenth century. A mostly white, Spanish, and now increasingly American, influence would leave its mark on Cuban retailing during the first half of the twentieth century. It is noteworthy that the rest of Spanish Latin America gained independence 80 years before Cuba. The island was beset by considerable challenges in trying to gain either economic or cultural autonomy. First, the independence wars during most of the latter half of the nineteenth century left the island considerably impoverished. Spanish government and entrepreneurs were reluctant to invest in infrastructure and other public works projects during the colonial struggle. The terms of the U.S.-imposed Platt Amendment, moreover, gave considerable advantage to the Americans who wrote the laws and occupied the island. Nationalist forces on the island were divided, which weakened any comprehensive, national or Cuban agenda. On top of that, "there was a sense of delusion among those who had fought or supported the war" (Kapcia 2005, 61).

Gott (2004) argues that the 'imperial retreat' of the Spanish in Cuba during the last century was unlike other European colonizers who returned to the continent after suffering losses. For example, in the 1960s, white settlers from Mozambique and Angola returned to their motherland, as did the French in Southeast Asia a decade before. Spain had long strived to whiten Cuban, pushing the proportion of white settlers over the 50 percent mark. And by the time the American occupation during the Platt Amendment (1898–1902) ended, Spain had achieved that. In the early twentieth century, the traditional corners of Spain—Asturias, Galicia and the Canary Islands—continued as the primary senders of new immigrants to Cuba (as was Angel Castro, Fidel Castro's father). Occupying American forces under the direction of General Lionel Wood helped to further the 'whitening' process. The American Counsel General, Frank Steinhart, an officer from the previous war, drafted laws to curb Chinese and black immigration; the latter attempting to come from Puerto Rico. Gott (2004, 119) claims that at least 40 percent of the half-million Spaniards that arrived up to 1920 remained in Cuba and did not return to Spain.[1] Instead, they remained in all levels of commerce, particularly retailing, which is often attributed to the common Cuban expression still used today; when someone is considered a hard negotiator or extremely frugal, they might be called a *gallego*

(Galician) with a quick pat on one's elbow, signifying the person is somewhat of a cheapskate.

The Spanish imprint on Cuban retailing proved to be indelible in Cuba, even during a half century of socialism. Until the Revolution, the term *bodega*—a name popularly applied to grocery stores that sell items other than food—was widely used on the island. It was mainly associated with the Spanish immigrant community. These family-owned enterprises were known for their long hours of operation, often from sunrise until midnight. Bodegas became the targets of legislation such as the 1910 *Ley de Cierre*, or Closing Hours Law, which restricted hours of operation to just 10 hours. Similar laws were passed in the 1930s and 1940s because it was apparent that business transactions were being carried out in the rear of the store. Naranjo-Orovio describes the bodegas as part of Cuba retailing and daily living this way:

> *Bodega* workers were typically young immigrants from Spain who worked and lived in the stores. Makeshift beds were set up in the stores to accommodate the workers. The poor living and unsanitary conditions became the subject of many jokes and theatrical productions. The *bodega*, in slightly altered form, continues in Cuba today. It is where Cubans go to present their ration books (*libretas*) and pick up foodstuffs. (2003, 504)

Jews also found a small but significant role in Cuban retailing in the early twentieth century, particularly following the breakup of the Ottoman Empire and increasing steam and air travel between the United States and Cuba. Two distinct Jewish communities emerged in Cuba (Levine 1993). Bettinger-López (2000) shows that the differences were not just based on linguistic and cultural traditions either. Syrian and Turkish Sephardim arrived on the island as poor immigrants who intended to remain in their new homeland. They labored as street vendors and peddlers, "struggling to earn enough money to buy food, clothing, and other basic necessities for their families" (Bettinger-López 2000, 68). American Ashkenazim Jews, however, were motivated mainly by commercial interests and sought to establish export-import companies, retail stores and small factories.

At the end of World War I, the U.S. Department of Commerce, through its Bureau of Foreign and Domestic Commerce, had clearly taken President Woodrow's claim to heart: "The business of American foreign policy, is business itself." Part of the launch of the 'American century' meant a thorough inventory of marketing and advertising methods, as well as descriptive accounts of retail and wholesaling practices abroad. In the Americas, this meant detailed studies Bolivia, Mexico, Bolivia, Cuba and other countries, with the intent of showing American investors "just what advertising can do in helping to solve their foreign-sales problems" (Sanger 1919, 6). A general description of export opportunities to Cuba and ways to solve the foreign-sales 'problems' began this way:

> Cuba, one of the most densely populated and one of the richest of all the Latin American countries, lies only seven hours from Key West, Fla., with which it is connected by a daily ferry service carrying both passengers and freight. Semiweekly or even more frequent sailings from both New York and New Orleans make these important ports easy of access. Importing nearly everything it consumes and exporting nearly everything it produces, the island offers a tempting field for manufacturers of foodstuffs, textiles, machinery, musical instruments, chemicals, drugs, and other important products included in its pre-war per capita imports of $53.60 . . . It offers a particularly inviting field to those manufacturers whose goods can be attractively packed or aggressively advertised. (Sanger 1919, 6)

The accurate but debilitating description of the island's growing dependence on U.S. models of consumption would later provide fodder for the revolutionary student movement and the 26th of July Movement of the 1950s. In classic dependency development fashion (Cardoso and Faletto 1979), Cuba in the early Republican era was destined for uneven development because of, in Sanger's words, "importing nearly everything it consumes and exporting nearly everything it produces." The U.S. Commerce report further enticed prospective investors with this assessment:

> Cuba offers an ideal experimental field for the advertiser who is either in the market with his product or desirous of testing the power of advertising as applied to Latin American markets. (Sanger 1919, 6)

Not surprisingly, trade and consumer advertising assumed multiple formats across Cuba and by the end of World War I had clearly entered the sales-marketing era. It included export-trade journals, direct-by-mail advertising, newspapers, motion pictures, streetcar advertising, billboards, handbills and sample packages, advertising calendars and novelty items and window displays and in-store demonstrations (Sanger 1919, 3). Fast-forward a century and all that remains in the early 2010s are window displays and in-store demonstrations (Morales 2009).

American investors, advertisers, potential merchants and marketers were warned about the need to implement radical changes into their Cuban marketing plan because, in Havana at least, 95 percent of the population was described as Latin, either racially or through Latin influence. Spaniards purportedly operated three-quarters of retailing (though no explanation is given about how the 'Latinness' of the consumer differs from Anglo-Saxon tastes and preferences). U.S. merchants wanting to enter the Cuban market were warned about the slowness of transactions that typify "Latin . . . organization and customs" (Sanger 1919, 9). Marketers were cautioned that print advertisements in newspapers and magazines were not required to carry the explanatory term "advertisement" as was required by law in American publications.

Newspaper advertisements allegedly varied in graphic quality and marketing impact as well (Figures 2.1, 2.2 and 2.3). With just 400,000 *habaneros* in 1919, only two morning and two evening newspapers would have been expected based on the pattern in U.S. cities of comparable size. However, 13 daily newspapers circulated in the capital city alone, prompting one publisher to comment: "It is a poor month in Habana when at

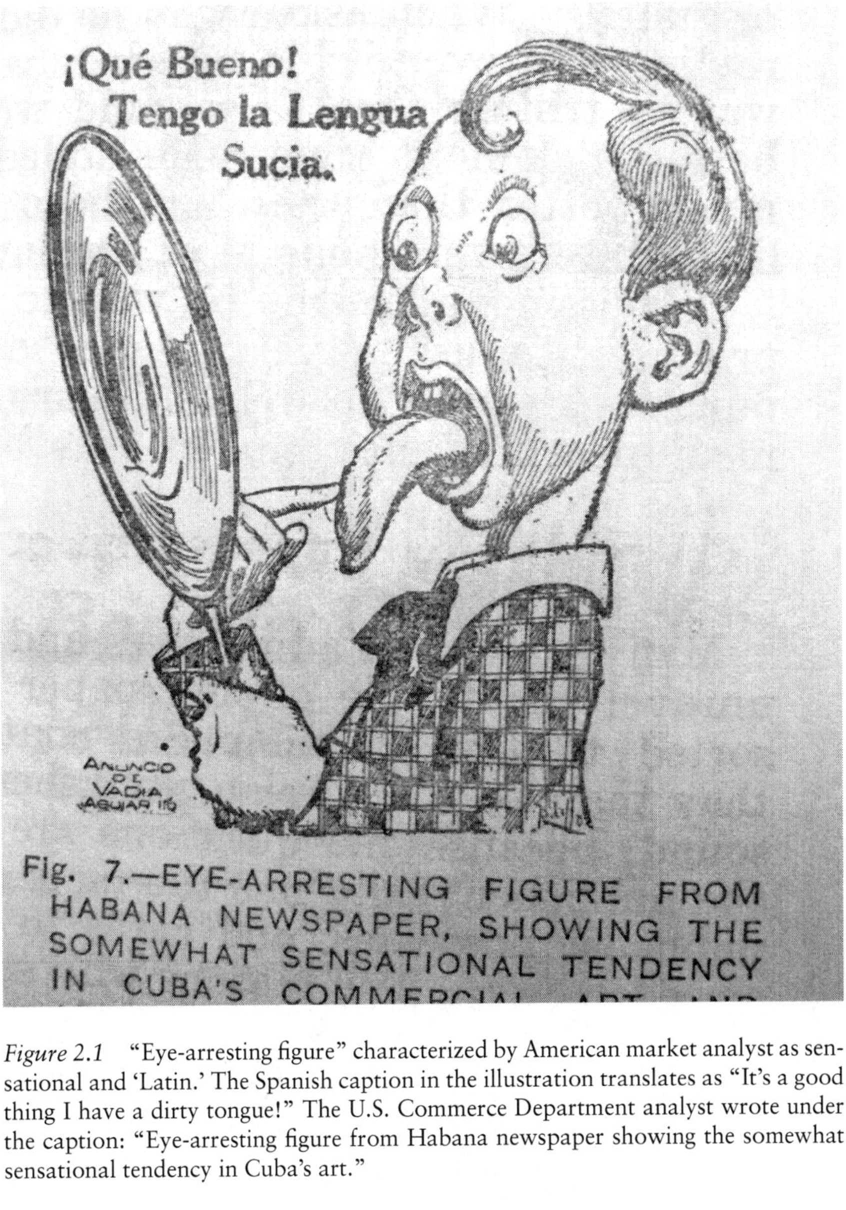

Figure 2.1 "Eye-arresting figure" characterized by American market analyst as sensational and 'Latin.' The Spanish caption in the illustration translates as "It's a good thing I have a dirty tongue!" The U.S. Commerce Department analyst wrote under the caption: "Eye-arresting figure from Habana newspaper showing the somewhat sensational tendency in Cuba's art."

FIG. 10.—A CIGAR ADVERTISEMENT IN A HABANA DAILY, CHARACTERISTIC OF A FAVORITE TYPE OF PICTORIAL TREATMENT AMONG THE BETTER CUBAN COMMERCIAL ARTISTS.

Figure 2.2 A favorably reviewed newspaper advertisement because of its quality pen-and-ink image. The cigar advertisement reads, "The three things a guajíro [Cuban cowboy or farmer] loves: his girl, his horse, and Flor de Tomás Gutiérrez tobacco."

least one paper isn't born and when another doesn't die" (Sanger 1919, 19). Today, just 400,000 copies of a single daily newspaper (*Granma*) are printed across the entire island (Tamayo 2010), though various weekly, special interest (youth and labor) and provincial newspapers do exist. Recent research examining Spanish-language media in both Latin America

Figure 2.3 An advertisement for the *Bazar Inglés* (English Bazaar) department store in Havana. The U.S. Commerce Department analyst characterized the ad like this: "A favorite type of illustration among Cuban retailers; used to direct attention to wearing apparel, shoes, furniture, perfumery, and other dissimilar articles." The first line of the Spanish copy in the ad translates as "The gnome discovers what's good," and the last line states, "ask for your catalogue."

and Spain identifies Cuba has having a very restricted realm of media that is heavily censored by the government (Artero 2009). Reporters without Borders (2011) corroborates that assessment in its report, which states that Cuba ranked 10 places from the bottom of 178 countries in its 2010 Press Freedom Index.

THE ARRIVAL OF DEPARTMENT STORES

By the middle of the Republican era (1902–1958) Cuba witnessed the introduction of large department stores of Spanish and Cuban ownership. Retailers such as Ultra, Bazar Inglés, La Filosofía, Flogar and Isla de Cuba opened stores in Havana as well as other major cities such as Santiago de Cuba and Camagüey. By the time of the Revolution, La Epoca, El Encanto, El Bazar and Fin de Siglo had captured one-quarter of the retail market. These chain stores invested heavily in standardized retailing operations and related wholesaling. Supermarkets and five-and-dime stores characterized this era of mass-produced consumer durables and perishable goods. Evidence of this in Cuba comes in 1924 when F. W. Woolworth opened stores in several provinces. In 1929, F. W. Woolworth published a 50-year anniversary volume tracing the store's humble beginning in Watertown, New York, to the development of 2,100 stores around the world. As the originator of the five-and-ten-cent store, Woolworth's stores prowess in retailing was transformative as they drew on the principles of mass merchandising and retailing to distribute low-priced household goods turned out by the Industrial Revolution. The retailer had established firms outside the U.S. in Canada, Great Britain, Germany and Cuba (Woolworth 1929, 22). The description of Cuba in the tome reads like this:

> In the shadow of historic Morro Castle, there are now eight Woolworth stores, four of these in Havana. The thousands of tourists who visit there are astonished at the high place which the Woolworth service has so quickly earned with the Cuban people.

In Cuba, Woolworth stores were called "Ten Cent," purportedly because it was difficult for Spanish speakers to pronounce the vowels and the *th* sound in 'Woolworth' and the *ts* sound at the end of 'cents.' Four stores operated in Havana, but none of them was literally in the shadow of Morro Castle. The main store was on Galiano and San Rafael in the municipality of Centro Habana. It was called the "Corner of Sin" (*La esquina del pecado*) because young men would go there to flirt with the female employees. Another was located in Calzada de Monte in the municipality of Cerro. Old Havana's pedestrian mall, Obispo Street, housed the third Ten Cent and the 'new' Havana of the modern Vedado section of the city was home to the fourth store (at the corner of 23rd and 10th).

Woolworth's "Ten Cent" franchise in Cuba was famous for its low prices, cleanliness and efficiency. After the Triumph of the Revolution—when retailing began deteriorating and falling under state control—the Ten Cent stores were able to retain some of these attributes, but they too deteriorated and ultimately disappeared. In the late 2000s, a state retail company—TRD—converted the former Ten Cent store on Galiano into a pricey (e.g., hard currency versus pesos) hardware store, and replaced the once striking glass display cases wrapping around the exterior with black, polished granite, hardly an inviting exterior for low-end retail. Havanans, with their quick wit and street humor (*choteo*), have started calling the store a "the funeral home on Galiano" (Coyula 2011).

If Havana has long been the center of the island's political, economic and cultural lives, then in the retail sector the 'grand' department stores of Centro Habana in the 1950s formed the heart of Cuban retailing in post–World War II Cuba. Between 1945 and 1959, this concentration of both high- and medium-cost stores was along Galiano and San Rafael Streets in Centro Habana. Raquel Mena was a young woman in the 1950s and recalls the retail environment this way: "At that time, everything you needed or wanted was located in the [Galiano and San Rafael street] shopping district, where there were really good stores . . . I remember that at that time, the smells in the streets [around the large department stores on Galiano and San Rafael] and around El Encanto [department store] in particular, the smell of perfume prevailed." Her contemporary, Sonia Varone, adds, "It wasn't only a place to go shopping, but it was a place to stroll around . . . When people used to say, 'Let's go shopping in Havana,' it was curious because everyone would dress up" (Fernández 1998; our translation).

Since the Revolution, that Centro Habana retail focus has disappeared. In fact, when *habaneros* talk of going downtown (*al centro*) today, it could be one of several places (Scarpaci et al. 2002). The Galiano and San Rafael retail activity took on the economic and social functions that an important regional shopping mall might assume in the contemporary era.

The first self-service supermarket entered Cuba through the chain retailer American Grocery in the late 1920s. In 1942, Sears Roebuck and Company opened its doors as well, followed in 1952 by the firm Minimax Supermarkets, which in just seven years managed to open 25 stores across the island. The notion of self-service retailing was the antithesis of the Spanish *bodega* model, where customers requested an item (fruit, vegetable, consumer durable) from the clerk, and the clerk would then show the customer the model. Even today in Spain, small shopkeepers operate this way and at farmer or open-air markets, merchants discourage shoppers from handling the merchandise in any fashion. However, this self-service aspect of retailing was taking hold in Cuba three decades before the Revolution.

CUBAN RETAILING AT THE DAWN OF THE REVOLUTION

To situate the habits of the Cuban consumer on the island today, it is necessary to trace some key aspects of Cuban retailing and consumption over the past 50 years. The socialist system of marketing, retailing and advertising has influenced the consumption of products and services in key ways. Transforming the island's economy for the socialist revolution meant expropriating foreign businesses and eliminating Cuban enterprises. In the cultural realm, it meant shifting the gaze from New York, Paris, London and Madrid to within the island, and to points east of Berlin (Kapcia 2005, 137). Despite this refocusing, the socialist consumer has not been completely isolated from global consumer tastes, values and trends. Although the island was virtually closed off to foreigners other than members of the socialist bloc (CAME) and the former USSR, thousands of Cubans traveled abroad on scientific, educational, cultural and military missions. Product placement in films from Europe, Latin America and even the United States played a key role in this process.

When Fidel Castro came to power in 1959, more than 60,000 retail stores were in operation. Retailing was characterized by three types of stores. One small group consisted of both large mixed and specialized stores run by national and foreign capital (mostly U.S.). These stores clustered in the larger cities, which meant mostly the provincial capital cities across the island (Pinar del Río, Havana, Matanzas, Santa Clara, Santi Spiritus, Camaguey and Santiago de Cuba). A second group included small businesses scattered across the country, but in the hands of immigrants—Spanish, other Europeans and Chinese—the latter coming to the island in the mid-nineteenth century to work on the railroads. A third group concentrated in the countryside and in small towns, a good part of them belonging to the owners of agricultural enterprises. These three groups provided the products and brands for the population at that time.

Cuban consumption in 1959 was comparable to a few industrial capitalist nations of that era. Table 2.1 indicates the ratios of selected consumer durable products—in this case, telecommunication wares—across a sample of nations. Significantly, Cuba ranked first place for television ownership (54.1 television sets per 1,000 residents), and in second place for radios (just behind Uruguay); it even had a greater proportion than Belgium, Switzerland, Japan and Italy.

Cuba was so well endowed with television sets within Latin America that even second-place Venezuela had achieved only half of Cuban levels. The surrogate measures of material consumption in Table 2.1 provide a point of reference for assessing the consumption of more basic and primary goods such as clothing, shoes and food. We do not ignore income, life expectancy, cause-specific mortality and age-specific mortality rates that varied by residential location, income, race and class in prerevolutionary Cuba. However, consumer durable consumption remained particularly high in 1959.

Consumption levels changed abruptly when the Castro government assumed power. The 1960 Consumer Protection Law (*Ley de Protección al Consumidor*) mandated sanctions for any infractions of retail laws. For instance, the law required that wholesale and retail food distributors track the movement of food products and other goods that were deemed as 'essential.' Law 890 issued on October 13, 1960, quickly followed and nationalized all Cuban firms, which included 46 food wholesalers and the largest retail stores selling manufactured products (Table 2.2).

Table 2.1 Comparison of Selected Consumer Durable Goods (Televisions and Radios) in Cuba, Latin America and Selected Industrial Nations, 1959

Country	Pop. ('000s)*	TV sets (000s)**	TV sets x per mil	Radios ('000s)***	Radios per mil.
Argentina	20,407	400	19.6	3,350	164.5
Bolivia	3,360	—	—	200	59.5
Brazil	67,704	850	12.6	4,000	59.1
Colombia	13,824	150	10.9	800	57.9
Costa Rica	1,076	—	—	75	69.7
Chile	7,316	—	—	700	95.7
Cuba	**6,745**	**365**	**54.1**	**1,000**	**148.3**
Dom. Rep.	2,900	16	5.5	98	33.8
Ecuador	4,065	—	—	120	29.5
El Salvador	2,386	16	6.7	40	17.2
Honduras	1,726	—	—	32	18.5
México	33,924	600	17.7	2,800	82.6
Nicaragua	1,373	6	4.4	35	25.5
Panamá	1,033	8	7.7	130	125.9
Paraguay	1,687	—	—	105	62.2
Peru	10,524	28	2.7	600	57
Uruguay	2,796	15	5.4	700	250.4
Venezuela	7,122	200	28.1	750	105.3
Belgium	9,104	392	43.1	—	—
France	45,240	1,368	60.2	10,793	238.6
Italy	49,356	1,573	31.9	6,014	121.8
Spain	30,049	140	4.7	2,500	83.9
Switzerland	5,259	79	15	1,388	263.9
Japan	92,430	3,299	35.7	14,610	159.6

Source: (*) United Nations, Demographic Yearbook, 1964, pp. 120–28.
(**) United Nations, Statistical Yearbook, 1960, p 611.
(***) United Nations, Statistical Yearbook, 1960, pp. 608–09.

Table 2.2 Largest Retail Stores Selling Manufactured Products in Cuba that were Nationalized in 1960

Almacenes Ultra S.A.
Cía. Distribuidora de Medias S.A. (Roseland stores)
Gabriel, Sixto y Cía S. A. (Fin de siglo stores)
La Filosofía S.A. (Inc.)
La Isla de Cuba, S.A. (Inc.)
López y Río S. en C. (owners of Bazar Inglés)
Los Precios Fijos
Menéndez Hermanos (owners of Ls Nueva Isla)
Solís Entrialgo S.A. (owners of El Encanto)
Tiendas de ropa y Sedería La Opera S.A.
Tiendas Flogar S.A. (Inc.)

These companies were nationalized without compensation by the terms of the Business Office Law (Ley a la Oficina Nacional) issued by the National Agrarian Reform Institute (Instituto Nacional de Reforma Agraria, also known as INRA). The law was created to operate all stores and warehouses handling fruits and vegetables. Subsequently, on October 24, 1960, the first minister and president of the Republic issued a resolution that nationalized, among others, seven foreign-owned retail chains: General Distributors S.A.; Minimax Supermercados S.A.; Supermercados Ekloh S.A.; F. W. Woolworth Co.; Sears, Roebuck Co.; Kodak Cubana Ltd.; and Simmons International Ltd. By the end of that same year, state ownership had become the predominant form of business control. To handle these businesses, Law 933 created the Ministry of Internal Commerce (MINCIN, or Ministerio de Comercio Interior) in February 1961. MINCIN's mission was to manage and implement state policy that regulated all aspects of retailing. By late June 1962, more than 6,500 street vendors lost their rights to sell a wide array of articles and petty services. That same month more than 4,600 small shops and stores selling clothing, shoes, cloth and hardware items also came under state control. Retail nationalization culminated in 1968 with the following highlights:

- A rationing system imposed in March 1962 introduced the food ration book (*libreta*). Tickets and coupons are used to redeem certain industrial and manufactured items that are distributed by the Committees for the Defense of the Revolution (CDR).[2] The following year a food-ration booklet for food and a booklet for manufactured items become the dominant distribution modes for retail items that were previously provided by the private sector.
- State firms devoted to retail trade include food products, clothing, shoes, furniture and jewelry, all subject to regulation by MINCIN.
- Eyeglass and pharmaceutical manufacturing are transferred to the Ministry of Public Health.
- In 1965, 37 regional retail companies in different provinces outside Havana City are transferred to local management, whereas MINCIN operates eight that existed in the capital.

Not surprisingly, restructuring and nationalizing retailing had dire consequences for retailing, wholesaling and logistical operations. First, supplies of merchandise decreased considerably. Second, these new state creations gradually lost their ability to control their operations in ways that private holdings had operated; supplies, capital investments, advertising and distributions had to be coordinated with other newly created government companies, and with personnel who had little experience in these fields. Many public workers received positions for political patronage instead of particular skills in logistics, accounting, capital management, marketing, inventory control or human resources. Bottlenecks in managing supplies and distribution networks kept goods and services from reaching consumers in ways that had been outlined normatively. Third, for a variety of reasons, many Cubans who worked in firms that became nationalized lost their jobs, refused to work for the newly created state entity or decided to emigrate. Many assumed that leaving Cuba would be a short-term process, until the Revolution collapsed or the U.S. invaded. Others left the island merely to be reunited with their family. Fourth, merchandise levels dropped so suddenly that many state agencies never reopened or else remained shuttered for long periods. In the process, many workers entered the agricultural workforce and never returned to retailing, wholesaling or manufacturing with state companies. Lastly, and this problem is evident to even casual observers today, building, factory and office maintenance deteriorated so greatly that in many cases it became impossible to return them to their previous functions.

Taken together, these forces contributed to a pauperization of retailing across the island, and it became both a joke and symbol of poor-quality goods and services. The socialist narrative of state domination of the economy became an important tool in promoting the agenda of the Revolution and eliminating any residual of a bourgeois or consumer society. Activities previously referred to as commerce (*comericio*) or retailing (*actividad*

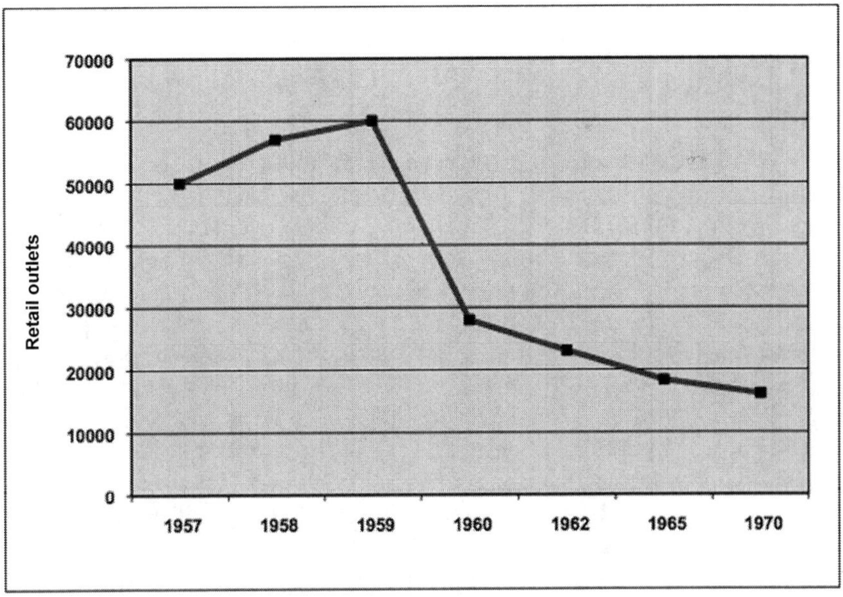

Figure 2.4 Retail outlets in Cuba, 1957–1970.
Data source: "Apuntes para la historia del comercio interior en cuba, MINCIN, 1986." (Ministry of Interior Commerce memo). Calculated by the authors.

minorista) were called *despacho* (office or workplace) activities in local parlance. Seemingly overnight, customers and consumers (*clientes*) were now referred to as users (*usuarios*). So radical was the transformation of retailing, with its reliance on state distribution of food and limited durable goods, that a good deal of knowledge about retailing traditions and culture was lost across Cuba. As the population ages and those who remember the elements of market-oriented retailing die off or else emigrate, there has been a need to try to recapture some of that knowledge or else retrain workers who have some knowledge about customer service and other retail practices. This has been particularly notable in the hard-currency (non-peso) sector in tourism.

During the two years leading up to the Revolution, the number of retail establishments increased by 20 percent to about 60,000 retail outlets nationwide. A decade later, seven out of 10 retail stores had been shuttered (Figure 2.4).

The 1970s marked a time when the government tried to reorganize some of the chaos in retailing and came up with new formulas to do so. One strategy was MINCIN's Law 1236 in September 1971, which transferred more than 16,000 retail stores and their 75,000 workers to local People's Power (Poder Popular) across the country. MINCIN, in turn, took charge of managing the agricultural quota system (*acopio*), food and restaurant services and various kinds of social and industrial services.

INSTITUTIONALIZING CONSUMER BEHAVIOR RESEARCH IN CUBA

MINCIN developed the most thorough database on Cuban consumer behavior of any entity in the world. In the course of its institutional existence, it relied on a consumer panel for moment-specific and longitudinal research that consisted of more than 20,000 families. During the course of its existence, MINCIN conducted 4,000 research investigations over a broad range of household consumer topics such as expenditures, pricing, substitution effects, brand preference, packaging and related topics. Findings derived from this body of research provided metrics to determine what items to offer in the basic consumer basket of goods and services; decisions that impacted the industrial-production side as well as retailing, product placement in stores and related marketing practices. However, the unraveling of the Cuban economy in the early 1990s, triggered in part by the disappearance of favorable terms of trade between the Soviet Union and its trading bloc, hit the island's economy hard. Negative trade balances grew; the Special Period in a Time of Peace forced even greater austerity measures and MINCIN was eliminated. With the retreat from the consumer behavior research field, a huge gap developed in understanding and monitoring purchase and consumption habits of Cuban consumers.

TEPID MARKET REFORMS

Another start-and-stop market approach in the 1980s was evident in the agricultural sector. Some farmers participated in a contractual relationship with the state, in which they pledged to produce certain yields that would go to the state at a specific price, in exchange for seed, fertilizer and related inputs, or a combination of the three. This farmer–state production agreement is called the *acopio*. In April 1980, Decree 66 emitted by the Council of Ministers created the Free Farmer Market (Mercado Libre Campesino), which, for the Cuban government at that time, proved to be a radical departure from the state-controlled production and distribution practices of the three previous decades. Essentially, the decree authorized primary (farmers and ranchers) and secondary (food processing, canning) producers of food products to sell 'surplus' (after fulfilling the state *acopio* and distribution obligations) goods in specified farmers' markets. This supply-and-demand approach, however, was short-lived; in 1982, the government took a big step backward and eliminated those markets.

Despite the vicissitudes in the consumer market, ordinary Cubans were learning about what the rest of the world was consuming. By the 1980s, for instance, it was common for Cubans to watch an American film or dubbed television series nightly, despite the adverse political climate that prevailed between Washington, D.C., and Havana. By the time the Special Period in a Time of Peace opened the tourist lanes from abroad in the early 1990s, Cubans saw the number of foreigners increase from around 100,000 to over two million in just a decade. Tourists displayed brand names, logos, magazines, sporting equipment and other foreign consumer products.

Betancourt (1992) studied the relationship of retailing and wholesaling exchanges in the 1980s by using data from the Cuban government. His assessment indicates that Cuban wholesalers were selling about half of their goods to the retailing sector; a high figure compared to other economies where a greater portion usually goes to business wholesalers (B2B versus B2C). Another striking pattern of the 1980s in Cuba was the relatively high level of retailing in the food and beverage sector:

> The most striking pattern that emerges is the high and increasing percentage of sales made up by food stores, i.e., from 48.2 percent in 1982 to 52.5 percent in 1988. The corresponding percentage in the U.S. was about 25 percent in 1987. (Betancourt 1992, 10)

This pattern indicates that as production challenges rose in Cuba during the 1980s, consumer durables (furniture, clothing, appliances) had become less available to consumers, leaving the food and beverage sector as one of the few outlets for out-of-pocket and discretionary expenditures. At the same time, the quality and quantity of food provided by the *libreta* (ration book) was declining as well (Martínez Fernández et al. 2003). Between

1980 and 1985, the number of retail establishments fell from 28,719 to 28,593 whereas food and drinking establishments grew by 26 percent to 28,323 over the same period (Betancourt 1992, 13). As we discuss in Chapter 4, half of the top 10 Cuban brands are beverages.

In the midst of the experimentation of the 1980s and 1990s arose new retail and distribution outlets as the state continued to tinker with retailing options for the masses. These changes stemmed from a broader process called the "Correction of Errors" (*rectificación de errores*) because of the Communist Party's Third Congress pronouncements in 1986. The Congress decided that Cuba should stop imitating other socialist countries. Among the many changes unleashed was a return to Che Guevara's values—once Minister of Industry from 1961 to 1964—whose criticisms against the bureaucracy and its weaknesses had promoted volunteer work brigades to perfect a more enlightened attitude about work. Fidel Castro had supported these efforts even before the Congress meeting and started the challenging task of delinking Cuba's socialist revolution from the ill-fated Soviet "model," only to usher in the Special Period in a Time of Peace in Cuba after the USSR collapsed (Scarpaci et al. 2002, 145–146).

In wholesaling and retailing, the Correction of Errors meant that food and manufactured items were being distributed through a new format of markets (often open-air or with tables inside in a building in what appear to be a flea-market-type arrangement), farmers' markets, fish markets, a state-owned chain called *Supermercado Centro* and two smaller chains called *Amistad* (friendship) and *Cañonazo* (cannon blast). By the end of 1985, sales figures generated by this new retailing totaled 932 million pesos (about US$34 million), of which about 60 percent was from foods and the balance from consumer durables.

With hindsight, it would appear that these changes in retailing and distribution slowed the downward spiral of retailing and supply-chain management across the island. The measures helped to invigorate a business culture and professional practice (marketing, accounting, finance, management) while improving the previously tarnished image that many Cubans had about retailing. Like the fate of MINCIN, however, the collapse of the socialist trading bloc and generous subsidies from the USSR (swapping one ton of oil for one ton of sugar) ended this form of retailing. It was a foreshadowing of the tragic Special Period and a draconian decline in the quantity, quality and availability of myriad consumer products and services.

THE SPECIAL PERIOD AND THE TRANSFORMATION OF CUBAN RETAILING: 1990S TO 2011

The first years of the Special Period in a Time of Peace—a phrase coined by Fidel Castro in August 1990—was a response to failed economic policies on the island as well as a disruption of the socialist camp. Its name (*período especial en tiempos de paz*) reflected the militaristic and organizational proclivity that the socialist leadership had employed since 1959 to rally Cubans around a cause to fend off a total collapse of the socialist experiment. Not since the early years of the Revolution—the guerilla struggle against Batista in the Sierra Maestra and the defeat of the Bay of Pigs invasion of April 1961—had the Castro regime faced such a powerful challenge. The labeling of the crisis reflected the serious disruptions and shortfalls in imports of key machinery, materials, oil and cash from the Soviet Union and the former socialist nations of Eastern Europe. A national emergency had gripped the island's economy, and internal consumption would get priority over imported goods:

> During the economic crisis of the 1990s, Cuba neglected investment in favor of consumption. This priority is readily observable in the low share of capital goods' imports relative to consumption goods. The insufficient levels of investment will redoubt in low growth rates in the future and the inability to pull the economy out of the low-growth trap in which it currently operates. (Pérez López 2002, 521)

To be clear, though, this was no treat for the average consumer; it merely meant that the Cuban government could not afford to import items in hard currency. Cuba was practically paralyzed. Food scarcity became so acute in 1993 that thousands of people developed a condition of temporary blindness called polyneuritis. Although it was remedied with an infusion of vitamins made available to the masses, it seriously underscored a precarious state distribution and production system that was robbing millions of Cubans from a basic need. The Special Period seemed to be a dead-end street as the government was forced to invest limited resources on 'emergency' projects like the blindness problem mentioned in the preceding, as well as water purification, waste removal, keeping the lights on and other basic functions of governance. Although the appellation "period" would suggest a few years or so, Canadian economist and longtime Cubanologist Arch Ritter (2010, 229) wryly observes that it:

> has lasted almost two decades. Many outside observers have imagined that Cuba would in time follow Eastern Europe and the former Soviet Union in making a transition toward a more market-oriented economic system and perhaps a Western style of pluralistic democracy. This has not happened. The modest economic changes of the early 1990s have not led to sustained reform . . . it has appeared that gerontocratic paralysis might endure well into the 2010s . . . When a process of transition does arrive, it will likely be unexpected, confused, and erratic, and it will probably not fit the patterns of Eastern Europe, China, or Vietnam.

Several policy shifts by the government took place at the outset of this period. The economy opened up to joint-venture businesses and international tourism. In 1993, possessing dollars was decriminalized by the authorities and the masses were granted access to hard-currency stores, which previously had been referred to as 'diplo-stores' (*diplotiendas*) because only Cubans with legal access to hard currency (diplomats, mainly) could buy goods there. This new, hard-currency retailing sector restructured retailing and allowed Cubans to learn about modern products and services and shop—or at least window-shop (*vitriniando*)—in ways not seen since 1959. It also provided a chance for the business professions to reemploy their skills and for Cubans to study marketing management, accounting, finance and related fields to accommodate these limited market overtures.

The sending of remittances to the island, mainly from the United States, supported the surge of dollar-based retailing in the 1990s. Small self-employment professions were licensed and by the mid-1990s had reached 200,000 workers (*cuentapropistas*) (Peters and Scarpaci 1998). Taxi drivers, cobblers, artists, mechanics, plumbers, masons, the renting of rooms and 12-setting home restaurants became popular trades. Except for the home restaurants (*paladares*), which could hire only family members, all trades were single-employee operations, which became cumbersome. Cubans, ever wise about consumer and labor laws, devised ways to circumvent the restrictions. For example, a tire repairer (mostly for bicycles) could not use an air compressor because it required a separate license. In addition, no mechanical work on the bicycle could be done legally because that too would require a license. In many instances, other adults in the same household or a neighbor would secure a license in a parallel field to provide the services. As Orwellian as these tales sound, it gave a small percentage of the labor force (never exceeding 2 percent until 2010 or so) a taste of entrepreneurship, and allowed consumers to shop around for the best products and services. Advertising was expensive and certainly prohibited in radio, television and print. A small sign mounted perpendicular to the front of house, for example, would be subject to a fee (for the privilege of advertising). As a result, WOM became the main form of advertising and marketing.

Concurrent with these changes was the creation of hard-currency companies and services. At first, the dollar was used, but in the early 2000s it was dropped for the euro. Around that time the island introduced a sort of local, hard-currency legal tender called CUC, which could only be used on the island and originally was exchanged in money-exchange houses on par with the U.S. dollar. When the euro was adopted, dollar holders who wished to use them were subject to an 80-cents-on-the-dollar exchange rate; 10 percent of the loss to the dollar holder was a 'fine' for using dollars, and another 10 percent was (arbitrarily) applied as a service fee. Despite these labyrinth regulations, as well as an overall rise in prices in both pesos and hard-currency rates, some semblance of a market retail economy had commenced. It was largely expensive for Cubans, who worked in, say, tourism, where they could obtain CUCs as tips, and it was mostly prohibitive for those who had no one off the island to send remittances as they toiled in a peso-only economy.

Whereas the introduction of hard-currency enterprises in 1993 onward had deepened income segregation, it helped pull the Cuban economy out of its economic tailspin. These new firms, some Cuban and others joint ventures, at least became incorporated with managerial guidelines about business operations. Like firms elsewhere, the primary goal was to turn as much profit as possible by responding to particular market needs. Many of these new firms belonged to a larger holding company, which had fairly flexible and transparent articles of incorporation. Each holding company, in turn, fell under the domain of a Cuban ministry, or even directly under the Cuban State Council (the highest level of government, comparable to the U.S. president's inner cabinet, but with sweeping powers). Directors of those new corporations could only compete for funds from the holding companies and respective ministries under which they were incorporated. To be clear, it is markedly different from the way a truly private firm would try to raise capital from investors or by selling stock. Turning profits was the principal way that these companies would garner favor from the central government. Table 2.3 shows the major holding companies that were created in the retailing and tourism sectors.

Most of the companies belonged to the State Council. The major retail chains are CIMEX, CUBALSE (both pertaining to the State Council), and TRD-Caribe (belonging to the Revolutionary Armed Forces). Principal tourism-sector companies include Cubanacán, Gran Caribe (Ministry of Tourism) and Gaviota (Revolutionary Armed Forces).

Joint ventures (*empresas mixtas*) played an important role in transferring business acumen to Cuban workers. One unprecedented practice in the 1990s was the development of *perfeccionamiento empresarial*, loosely translated as 'business improvement,' which was promoted mainly by the companies managed by the Revolutionary Armed Forces (FF.AA, or *Fuerzas Armadas Revolucionarias*). Proponents of *perfeccionamiento empresarial* often formed high-level management teams who had received formal training in marketing management. In essence, the practice "guaranteed loyalty, avoided corruption, and maintained strict control over information" (Gimeno Chocarro 2003). An overwhelming number of foreign brands also burst into these new dollar stores like a tidal wave, as did a new set of national brands across product and service categories such as food products, clothing, shoes, electronic equipment, household appliances, personal hygiene and other categories. This flood of new brands aimed to satisfy latent demand in the tourist sector (gift shops, small shopping malls in or near hotels) and gradually shifted over to hard-currency stores frequented almost exclusively by locals.

New retail chains that operated in hard currency appeared across the island to satisfy the new demand for these products and services, and to tap into the circulation of hard currency that joint-venture operations, international tourism and remittances had swept into Cuba (Figure 2.5). These stores slowly spread from west to east, from Pinar del Río to Baracoa. Between 1993 and 2006, the number of retail stores doubled, but still amounted to only one-sixth of 1959 levels. In the first six years of the Revolution, Cuba's retail units decreased by 53 percent, largely the result of eliminating private property and businesses. When tepid market reforms came about in 1993, only about 4,200 stores were in operation. Fourteen years later, 5,000 new retail stores had opened.

In 2005, retail revenues reached $1.34 billion CUC,[3] among which the CIMEX Corporation had captured 43.7 percent of the market, followed by TRD Caribe and Cubalse with 21.9 percent and 18.8 percent of the market, respectively. Non-hotel restaurant sales generated $287 million CUC,

Table 2.3 Major Companies, Joint Ventures and Holding Companies Operating in Hard Currency in Tourism and Retailing (most were created after 1993)

MINTUR (Tourism Ministry)	cubanacan	Caracol	Palmares
		TIENDAS UNIVERSO (*)	Rumbos (*)
	Horizontes (*)		Islazul
	GRAN CARIBE		
CONSEJO DE ESTADO	HABAGUANEX	Hoteles Habaguanex	
MINCULT (Culture Ministry)		ARTEX	
MINAL (Food Ministry)	CORALSA CORPORACION ALIMENTARIA S.A	LOS PORTALES S.A.	
		CERVECERIA BUCANERO S.A.	
		Coracan	

Continued

Table 2.2 Continued

State Entity	Holding company	Retail company	Food & hotel sector
CONSEJO DE ESTADO **(State Council)**	CIMEX	Panamericana TIENDAS PANAMERICANAS	El Rápido
		havanatur	
		PHOTO SERVICE	
MINFAR (Armed Forces)	GAESA	TRD Caribe	
			gaviota tours
CONSEJO DE ESTADO **(State Council)**	(*) CUBALSE	TIENDAS MERIDIANO (*)	
		DITA (*)	
CONSEJO DE ESTADO	PAlco	PALCO CENTRO COMERCIAL	PALCOHABANA
		RIO ZAZA	
		BRAVO Cárnicos Hispano-Cubanos	
		PAPAS&Co.	
		CORALAC S.A.	
MINCIN **Interior Commerce Ministry (retailing)**	SUCHEL	SUCHEL CAMACHO S.A.	

Source: Constructed by the authors based on company sources and various Cuban institutions.

(*) Company no longer exists but played an important role in opening up the economy in 1993. This set the stage for the dollarization of the Cuban ecoomy and the transformation of retailing over the following 17 years.

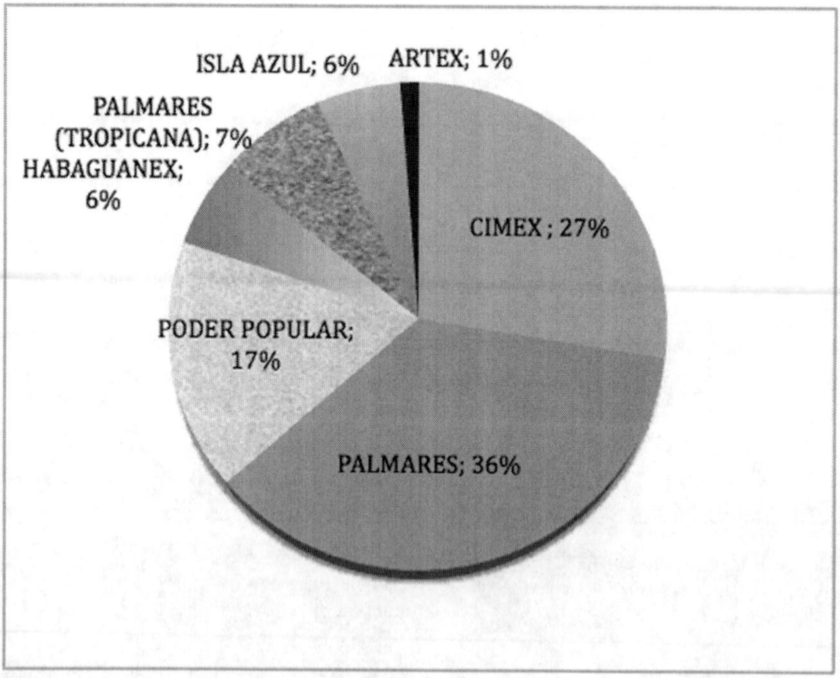

Figure 2.5 Non-hotel food establishment revenue distribution by state company, 2009. Calculated by the authors.

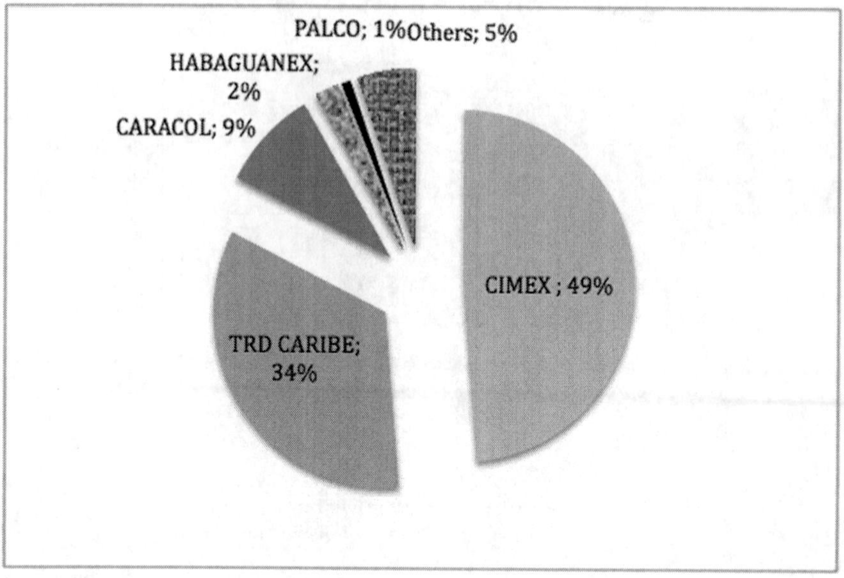

Figure 2.6 Distribution of retail revenues by major state stores, 2009. Calculated by the authors

with Palmares in first place with 43.5 percent of the market, followed by a distant CIMEX and Cubalse (Figure 2.6). The Poder Popular group was the fourth largest non-hotel restaurant entity, whose affiliated companies are Palco, Sylvain, La Flora and other state entities. A smaller portion of revenues from the restaurant sector was generated from taxes and fees from self-employed workers' home restaurants.

THE SOCIOLOGY OF TIME AND *HACER COLA* FOR CUBAN CONSUMERS

Waiting is a ubiquitous experience that transcends both space and time. Edna O'Brien (1995, 177) comments on its universality when she writes:

> Everyone I know is waiting . . . and almost everyone I know would like to rebut it, since it is slightly demeaning, reeks of helplessness, and show[s]we are not fully in command of ourselves. However, not everyone experiences waiting in the same fashion, because waiting is stratified. (cited in Auyero 2011, p. 7)

Socially patterned and reflecting power differentials, Schwartz contends that waiting mirrors social systems: "Typical relationships between the individuals' position within a social system . . . [reveal that] the more powerful and important a person is, the more others' access to him must be regulated" (Schwartz 1974, 847). In Cuba, this means the ordinary Cubans waiting for appointments with key decision-makers (*dirigentes*) will pass through a labyrinth of offices, appointments and schedules to resolve problems. But our concern is with the temporal obstacles that the masses confront in everyday living (*la vida cotidiana*).

Waiting, then, is also a form of powerlessness. Various scholars have conceptualized the role of waiting and its sociological significance. Fox Piven and Cloward (1971,100) used the term the "weary people" to describe the lines of the poor in the U.S. welfare states evident in the Great Depression of the 1930s and the Great Society of the 1960s. Foucault (1979) argued that making people wait was a deliberate "governing technique" so that the masses recognized state authority. Bourdieu (2000, 28) contends that waiting is one of manifold ways for people to experience the effects of state power, and for the state apparatus to impose it: "Making people wait . . . delaying without destroying hope . . . adjourning without totally disappointing," combine to strengthen domination. Auyero's (2011, 6) insightful essay about the poor in Buenos Aires waiting for public assistance argues, "waiting experiences persuade the destitute of the need to be patient, thus conveying the implicit state request to be compliant clients."

Cuban humor (*choteo*) addresses the curse of waiting and is a coping mechanism to mitigate tension caused by inefficiency, underproduction, bureaucratic bottlenecks and a limited retailing network. Waiting in line (*hacer cola*) is a popular topic of conversation on the island, and in popular humor. One joke,[4] admittedly on the *noir* side, goes like this: A Cuban guy says to his friend: "Boy am I tired of always waiting in line: a line for meals, another line for medicine, and one for household items! You know what? I'm gonna get rid of Fidel and then it'll be good riddance with all these lines!" Three months later, the same guy runs into his friend and asks: "So, how did it go with you getting rid of the commander in chief?" To which his buddy replies, "Oh man! Really bad! To get rid of Fidel, you gotta wait in line!"

To be sure, waiting in line is not the sole domain of any particular political economy. Waiting is also a by-product of underproduction and scarcity. Another joke about food scarcity goes like this (but only makes sense in translation knowing that the Spanish word papa is the word for both potato and the pope): "What do the Agrarian Reform and the Vatican have in common? In 50 years, they've only produced four potatoes!"[5] What these and countless other tongue-in-cheek remarks indicate is that access to basic goods and services in Cuba today entails a cost, one that goes beyond the financial and emotional; it is, significantly, a temporal cost as well. Indeed, the poor around the world, in both centrally planned and free-market economies, frequently must wait in line. Capitalist market failures during the Great Depression and the OPEC gasoline price shocks of 1973 in the United States were illustrative. So too were consumer lines in the last decade of the former USSR, or the near food shortages during the rule of Mao Tse-tung.

For decades, the line forming outside a store in Cuba has been a common feature of the landscape. Because of the importance of the extended family, it is common for grandparents and grandchildren, aunts, uncles and siblings to pool resources, and having time to wait in line is a coping mechanism in contemporary Cuba. On any given morning, one can see lines forming in front of a state-owned bakery, the ration-book-controlled bodega, a money-exchange house (called CADECA or *casa de cambio*) or in front of a dollar store. These lines are thick with retired elderly and the housewives who join them after the children have gone to school. Powerlessness among those waiting is not just evident by the act of forming a line, but can also be exacerbated by clerks working inside the store.

We authors have witnessed this across the island. For example, a store may be scheduled to open at a given hour. Cubans patiently seek shade outside the store and wait for the opening time. A few minutes after the scheduled opening time, a customer will tap lightly on the glass window of the door and gesture to the wristwatch (real or not) on the hand, signaling that the store needs to be opened. Inside the store, however, clerks may ignore the window tapping, point to another clock in the store or on their person that shows a different time or come to the door and give an excuse about why there will be a delay in opening the shop. A few of the Cubans waiting patiently outside will sigh; some will leave, but most will accept the delay and, begrudgingly, continue waiting.

One of the first thing one of us noted (JLS) when first coming to the island in 1991 was that upon entering a store (peso or dollar) and approaching a counter, the following scene was typical. If five clerks were working in the store, behind a counter or perhaps walking through the aisles, it would be common to see one on the telephone (conversing socially), one might be applying makeup, painting fingernails or fixing his or her hair, two would be deeply involved in a conversation and not even notice that a customer had entered the store and the fifth, perhaps, might approach or ask in a few minutes whether they could be of assistance. Whether these two examples result from the power differential between state employees and customers or because the clerks had no sense of ownership (the store can lose money without personal costs to the workers or owners; no sales commissions are given to clerks), are beyond the scope of this chapter. The point remains that Cuban consumers have been disciplined by the silent weight of time, and have few choices in changing the reality of retailing on the island today.

CONCLUSIONS

To what extent could Cuba today (2011) be considered a consumer society? How has the socialist system prevented Cuba from becoming a consumer society? To what extent has consumer behavior shifted from passive socialist consumers to consumers who take cues from signals in a limited retail market? This historical overview offers insight into these and related questions about patterns of consumption on the island. The direction Cuba was headed in the first half of the twentieth century indicated that the marketing eras—production, sales, marketing and value—had developed with the lag time of a decade or two behind North Atlantic market economies. The 1959 Revolution marked an about-face in this sequence and the value era was interrupted. Between the early 1960s and early 1990s or so, the state had managed to provide a modicum of basic foods, clothing, housing, education and health-care services, in keeping with its socialist principles. However, the disappearance of preferable terms of trade with the former USSR and its trading bloc forced the Cuban economy to open up to foreign

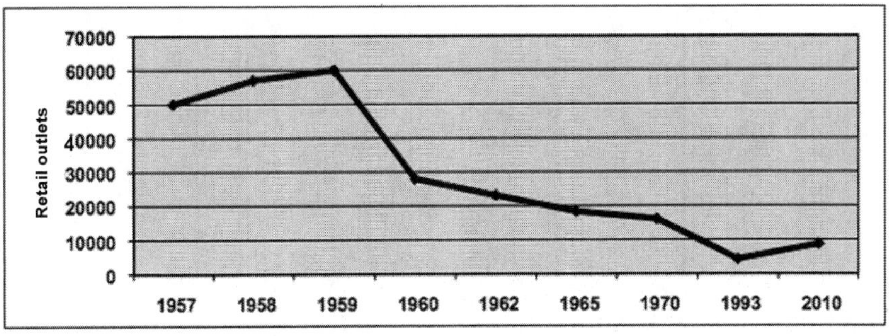

Figure 2.7 Number of retail outlets in Cuba, 1957–2010. Calculated by the authors.

investment and currencies. In the nearly two decades since these reforms, consumption and consumer behavior are gradually reflecting the kinds of market operations and decision-making found elsewhere. In over half a century, more than 90 percent of the island's 1959 retail outlets had disappeared, though that trend seems to have bottomed out (Figure 2.7).

This chapter has shown that advertising and marketing in the early twentieth century were important forces in allowing companies to differentiate themselves in a crowded marketplace. The Spanish imprint of small-shop retailing became more diversified with the twentieth-century advent of the modern department or variety store. Spanish, Cuban and U.S. stores secured a place in the markets of Havana, Santiago de Cuba and other large cities. The human capital that developed in the retail and advertising sectors of the Cuban economy during the first half of the last century has all but disappeared. In short order, though, the island appears to be recovering those skills and behaviors. Today, after five decades of little modern marketing communications at work, consumers find themselves relying exclusively on personal product experience, WOM and in-store display and information gathering, which the following chapter examines in more detail.

3 Cuban Consumers and Brand Awareness

INTRODUCTION

In this chapter, we address contemporary consumer behavior regarding brands—national and imported ones—a topic that, until now, has only been analyzed in very general terms over the past five decades. We begin with a brief discussion of brand awareness and brand preference and review a much-researched model called the consumer-based brand equity (CBBE) and consider its application to Cuba in the near future. As the 2010 BP oil disaster in the Gulf of Mexico reveals, brand perceptions can change quickly, even after a decade of rebranding and marketing communication strategies. The main body of the chapter presents findings of a survey of 780 consumers conducted in 2006—the first national brand awareness and preference survey ever released to the general public—and assesses findings about both international and national brands. The findings set the stage for exploring the way in which Cubans express aspects of Cubanness (*cubanidad*) in their perception of national brands, a topic for the following chapter.

CONTEMPORARY CUBAN CONSUMERS AND BRANDS

At roughly the 50-year mark since consumer consumption changed radically, we set out to develop exploratory research questions to better understand consumer behavior and brand awareness in Cuba. We devised a list of 32 widely recognized product and service categories that reflect Cuban consumption at the retail level. Significantly, there were no previous studies conducted on this topic in Cuba, prodding us to search out potential behavior patterns in market economies and other nations that, like Cuba, have started moving away from a centrally planned economy. This latter set of nations is small and includes Vietnam, China and a few of the Eastern European nations in the 1990s. We draw on the consumer behavior literatures from those cases when appropriate. Accordingly, our findings possess considerable strategic value as they surpassed all expectations about the depth of consumer knowledge on the island because of the absence of conventional advertising channels. As discussed in Chapter 2, it has been over 50 years since a for-profit consumer product or service has been advertised on television, and Cuba was one of the first Latin American nations to carry television broadcasts (Artero 2009).

We begin by explaining what we mean by brand awareness and preference before turning to the Cuban context. *Brand awareness* is the extent to which consumers can either remember or recognize a brand. When a consumer reflects on brands in a product category, those brand names that come to mind constitute brand awareness. They are normally recalled using a category cue (i.e., clothing, electronics, automobiles). If someone is presented with a list of brand names, logos or pictures of packages, those that can be identified constitute brand awareness. *Brand preference* means that consumers are likely to extract greater utility with readily recalled brands than those brands that are not recalled. Preference for a particular niche brand or product category may be high in a particular market segment, but register relatively low in the broader market.

The classic example of full brand awareness in market economies is when the brand itself (as a proper noun) becomes synonymous with the object or service (noun) it represents. Thus, Kleenex and Hoover are used interchangeably for paper tissues and vacuum cleaners, respectively, in part because they were pioneers in the field, but also because years of consumer preference and steady market performance have embedded them firmly in the sphere of everyday consumption. Cuba is, of course, different in this regard. However, we define brand awareness as the knowledge the consumer has about a product, service or brand.

At its simplest level, brand awareness can be determined by asking people about whether or not they have heard of a brand that is presented in the form of a question or a list of brand names. This is referred to as *assisted recall*. A related method that is quite valued by marketers is unassisted recall. In this context, consumers volunteer the names of products and services within a given category. An open-ended question in the unassisted recall format might be: "Tell me all the web browsers with which you are familiar." The consumer would then begin to rattle off his or her list: "Internet Explorer, Safari, Firefox, Netscape . . . etc." The stimulus is usually verbal as opposed to visual. It can be gleaned by a prompt as simple as "What brands do you remember in this product category?" Firms greatly value unassisted recall prompts more than assisted recall ones because the former indicate a deeper awareness of the brand in the mind of the consumer.

Feelings about particular brands result from a broad set of experiences accumulated over time. They might be forged based on actually using the product or service, knowing others who have or being familiar with an associative behavior surrounding the product or service. As is well known, brands are not just names that separate products and services from each other. Rather, they constitute a synthesis of experiences and visual cues that include the name, trademark, symbols, logos, designs, schemata, jingles and taglines as well.

Brands also allow their makers to create associations and expectations in the mind of the consumer, who sets out to prioritize and satisfy certain wants and needs. Visual cues are particularly effective in framing how brands are promoted among consumers. This distinction most often takes the form of logos, color schema, the style of font, symbols and other elements that convey implicit values, ideas and even personalities. Given these qualitative and external extensions of brands, it is not surprising that a particular brand can be worth more than the physical value of the product itself. How brands are handled in the media is a crucial component for marketing; when things go awry, sometimes even the best public relations department may not be able to recapture lost value. For instance, British Petroleum (BP) set about to rebrand itself in the 1990s after the purchase of several U.S. and other foreign companies. Drawing on its two-letter abbreviation, the firm set out to reposition itself in the consumer marketplace as a comprchensive energy company, not just confined to hydrocarbons. British Petroleum began presenting itself as 'Beyond Petroleum,' and recast its rather stogy BP blue and white shield in the logo with a light green and yellow sunburst flower and text scheme (Figure 3.1). Green, of course, has long been part of a wide range of B2B and B2C branding makeovers that portend ecological stewardship (e.g., "greening").

In the aftermath of the raging oil spill starting on the Deepwater Horizon offshore drilling platform on April 20, 2010, in the Gulf of Mexico—40 miles from shore—it would appear at this writing quite difficult for BP to regain the pre-spill brand recognition and value it held in the minds of many consumers. Brands are, therefore, constantly changing and subject to a variety of factors that marketing and advertising cannot always orchestrate.

Two basic approaches exist in estimating brand value. One way is to assess the financial value and the other is based on the meaning that a brand has in the minds of consumers. Four dimensions frame how brand

Figure 3.1 Old (bottom) and new BP logos.

value is measured: *brand awareness*, *perceived quality*, *brand associations* and *brand loyalty*.

Awareness affects the perceptions and tastes of products and services. That is, people like being familiar with items they consume and are usually conditioned to perceive positive attitudes about things with which they are familiar. *Brand associations* are those interrelationships that connect the brand with the consumer, including product attributes (pleasant to look at, touch, smell or see), users' imaginations, brand personality, symbols and organizations affiliated with a brand. Consumer knowledge of brands gives firms a sense of their market penetration and provides metrics about product placement and positioning, especially regarding their competitors. Evaluating market position and penetration becomes central in designing and executing advertising campaigns. Even firms that are not yet in a particular product or service category will benefit from brand awareness knowledge because it will provide clues about where they might seek to position themselves in prospective fields, and with as little risk as possible.

HOW SOCIETIES THINK ABOUT BRANDS

One weakness of conventional psychological theories of branding is that they fail to generate the brand symbolism that adds brand value based on how consumers in certain societies envision themselves. Although many brands are sustained through reputation effects—particularly in specific service-drive and technology categories—cultural symbolism is proving a powerful force in getting consumers to relate to brands based on cultural features unique to their societies (Holt 2005, 273).

Motivation researchers such as Pierre Martineau, Joe Newman, Sidney Levy and Ernst Dichter brought brand symbolism into consumer research nearly 60 years ago. Nonetheless, marketing brand theories have captured brand symbolism and subsumed it under the main psychological models without teasing out its unique attributes. Douglas Holt has attempted to develop a type of branding theory to account for how brands establish identity value by using symbolism. Specifically, this symbolism is tied to key attributes of national or ethnic culture that directly or indirectly embrace a national myth, value or folklore, thereby creating a kind of synergism between advertising and a particular product or service. Holt (2004, 2005) argues that static, individual-level constructs in marketing must tap into cultural and social constructions that come from unique historical settings.

Conventional branding theory, at least in U.S. marketing education and practice, draws on what Kevin Lane Keller has labeled the CBBE model. Numerous accolades have been bestowed upon Keller: his paper on CBBE (1993) earned him the Maynard Award, followed by the Marketing Science Institute's offer for him to write the touchstone volume about brands

(2002). This was followed by the *Journal of Consumer Research*'s offer for him to author a paper on branding (2003a). Thus, there is little doubt that his elucidation of the CBBE model remains the most comprehensive treatment of branding in American marketing practice and academics (Keller 1993, 1998, 2002, 2003a, 2003b). The CBBE model, moreover, expands upon earlier work by David Aaker (1991, 1996), whose synthetic branding constructs are designed to apply to many dimensions of branding, including brand symbolism. CBBE has formed a key component within the brand equity measurement arena, and Keller's model is similar to the Equity Engine approach that conceptualizes the brand as a mix of the emotional and the rational. This blend of emotional and rational is, in turn, measured according to performance characteristics and imagery. For example, a customer's relationship with a brand can be graphed along customers' attitudes on an engagement pyramid. This level of engagement, then, can be graphed according to customers' bias toward either an emotionally or rationally dominant relationship. So influential is Keller's CBBE model that Procter & Gamble—the world's largest consumer product firm—anchors its proprietary system of brand tracking on Keller's CBBE pyramid. These levels are salience, performance and brand imagery, judgments and feelings and resonance (Franzen and Moriarty 2009, chap. 17).

Holt (2004, 2005) argues that the CBBE model fails to treat brand symbolism as a qualitatively unique feature of a brand. Instead, symbolism is folded into a general model as a kind of brand association. We concur with Holt, at least to the extent that it can help us understand Cuban consumer behavior, because in Cuba, the repetition element of advertising has been absent. Moreover, the CBBE model rests on three axioms that are believed to apply to brand symbolism. Table 3.1 summarizes those axioms, critiques their theoretical basis and then explains why they fail to account for brand value and symbolism in the case of Cuba.

The results obtained in the present study have applied and basic research value. Firms that currently export or produce brands or services that are sold in Cuban markets should find strategic value in them. Firms wishing to position themselves in the market in the future will also find value here when the political and business conditions favor their entering Cuba. At the theoretical level, our findings should help in understanding how crucial the reconceptualization of the CBBE model and the role cultural values and associations play is in understanding consumer behavior in such a unique setting.

BRAND AWARENESS AND PREFERENCES STUDY AMONG CUBAN CONSUMERS

Our survey findings and analysis provide a departure point for understanding Cuban consumer behavior, brand awareness and brand preferences over

Table 3.1 Axiomatic Assumptions of the Consumer-Based Brand-Equity (CBBE) Model and its Relevance to Cuban Consumer Values

Axiom	Cultural Theories of Branding Critiques	Relevance to Cuban Consumer Values
Brand symbolism is successful when it is strong, favorable and unique.	The "strong, favorable, and unique" properties are metrics, not components, of the model. Fails to specify how brands build these associations.	Axiom is premised on an individual-level model that is unable to explain any collective interpretation of brand symbolism. Scarcity of basic goods in Cuba makes it unlikely that individuals have established many—if any— close relationships with brands. Axiom and CBBE model rely on universal constructs such as quality, adventurous life style, and fun, which are culturally specific.
Brand symbolism consists of abstract association.	Keller and Aaker argue that this "brand DNA" or "brand essence" includes categories such as user imagery, quality perceptions, organization, symbolism, benefits, and personality. Cultural researchers contend that specific stories and images help consumers understand brand symbolism, vs. abstractions.	The reduction of measurable abstractions such as "fun", for instance, is likely used in CBBE because it can be traced by preferred methods that can be used in survey or laboratory experiments. It is unlikely that Cuban consumers could accurately reflect such abstract feelings given the prevalence of scarcity of basic goods like soap, coffee, cereal, and razor blades.
Brand associations exist as "knowledge structures" in the minds of individual consumers.	Assumes that thinking about a brand's association leads to a deeper or higher level of "knowledge structure." Cultural theorists argue that consumers find resonance with brands because they construct stories in which they find value. For instance, consumers hold comparable "knowledge structure" about Adidas, Reebok, and Puma as they do Nike. However, Nike narratives surrounding Michael Jordan or Spike Lee may resonate more in consumers minds because the stories are more powerful and credible than Nike's competitors.	CBBE is premised on repetition and modern communication channels to deliver brand message. Such channels are largely absent in Cuba, at least for the three-quarters of the population born after 1959.

a wide range of products and services. This research represents the first glimpse of the level of brand awareness under current conditions, which, to be clear, are heavily regulated and exceptional. The advent of massive international tourism promotion two decades ago, the decriminalization of the dollar in 1993, the rise of remittances sent to the island and the slight opening of small businesses have sparked an unheralded level of new products and services. The spread of state retail chains provides a venue to display thousands of brands—mainly available with only hard currency—in front of the island's residences. To what extent do these brands resonate with consumers? Put another way, we ask: "What position do these myriad brands occupy in the minds of Cubans?"

Several key points about the island's consumers should be taken into account before interpreting these survey findings. First, nearly three-fourths of the islanders were born after 1959, a threshold when foreign imports of consumer goods drastically fell off; they would over the next few years narrow to a trickle—especially U.S. goods—and what little imports existed had come from Europe, Canada, Mexico and, of course, the Soviet bloc. Well-known retail districts such as the department stores of Centro Habana in the capital city, or retail chains such as Woolworth's and Sears, would cease operation by the early 1960s (Scarpaci et al. 2002, chap. 3). Therefore, the standard placement venues of consumer items nearly vanished.

Second, the Cuban Revolution dissolved much private property and nearly all private businesses. In its absence, the state became the sole supplier of goods and services. As would be expected, decisions about what, where and how to sell rested in the political workings of the Cuban socialist leadership and higher echelons of state ministries; the government today still assumes it knows what is best to allocate, at what frequency and at what price.

A third aspect of Cuban consumers and markets is that post-1959 Cuban retailing would ultimately be provided by a single organization: the state. Decisions about price points and how to distribute and promote products under this kind of political economy have always been mysterious; something Cuban *choteo* has been quick to promulgate. Fourth, and this point we have underscored previously, promoting products and services is done without the conventional tools of advertising and general publicity. The only clues about product or service availability and, possibly, their quality, come from WOM or the length of a line in a public store. In a society of low consumer consumption, these are the signals that Cuban consumers use to determine what is available for legal purchase. These four factors, therefore, frame the context in which consumer brand awareness develops in Cuba.

Survey findings will show that even Cuban brands are held in high esteem among consumers. Havana Club (rum), Cubitas (coffee), Varadero (rum) and Mulata (rum) are a few of the national products that most consumers recall and hold in high regard. Not surprisingly, international brands too have made their mark on the consumers' psyche. These are the same brands recognized in other corners of the world, but decidedly not in the same rank order: Coca-Cola, Heineken, Nestlé, Adidas and Nike, among others, cling in their minds (e.g., Bacardí).

RESEARCH OBJECTIVES AND DESIGN

The purpose of the survey is to understand the level of brand awareness among national and international brands by means of a purposeful sample of Cubans stratified by age, gender and region. Their brand knowledge was applied to diverse groups of mostly products, and a few services, to determine the degree of awareness based on a simple ordinal scale.

Before 1993, the term consumer (*consumidor*) and user (*usurario*) were used interchangeably, although the term 'consumer' carried connotations of bourgeois behavior. In the first three decades of the Revolution, 'consumer' carried this negative baggage and was used rarely in official state discourse. In general, the term is used in reference to buyers in overseas market, or occasionally to international tourists on the island. Rarely is the term used to refer to Cubans. Instead, the word client (*cliente*) is constructed, which apparently carries less ideological connotation than the 'consumer' label. For example, one significant state-run business publication in Cuba is *Opciones* (Options). Its subtitle is *The Economic and Financial Weekly Paper of Cuba*. In many ways, it is the official economic publication of record in that it aims to provide information to the Cuban business community, which consists of Cubans who hold administrative positions in state firms, and the international business community (at least those who read Spanish; no English online version of *Opciones* is available). Our search on the home page (www.opciones.cu) for articles relating to 'consumers' revealed just eight hits: seven of them referred to consumers in the context of overseas sales and prices of rice, tobacco, sugar or nickel and cobalt. One article referred to consumers in the U.S. and another mentioned them describing a product convention held at the renowned Hotel Nacional in Havana. The only article[1] to use the term *consumer* in the conventional way marketers would enlist it was in an article in 2006 that was describing 'end users' in both B2B and B2C settings. To describe 'end user,' the Spanish phrase *consumidor final* is assembled, which does not address the act of freely purchasing a product or service such as it does in a market context. Alas, we are entering new conceptual and ideological territory in this study.

Having discussed this semantic differentiation, the Special Period also appears to have provided space for more conventional marketing terms than in the earlier years of the Revolution. An official department of 'consumer affairs' has operated to handle the conventional type of consumer complaints regarding product failure or quality issues, service matters detected in state stores and the normal array of matters that consumers in countries across the world would be concerned about.

We used face-to-face interviews of Cubans over the age of 18 using semi-structured open and closed questions. Project leaders at the large state firm CIMEX trained employees on survey protocol at various retail establishments, state-run restaurants and government-owned fast-food outlets operated by CIMEX. All of these retail outlets operated in hard currency. Each trained surveyor in a retail store interviewed between three and five informants who were in the store either browsing or purchasing. The survey team followed predetermined age and gender quotas to ensure as many consumer attributes as possible. Because this was a convenience sample and there were no previous studies about Cuban consumer behavior and retailing, ours remains an exploratory study. Our goal is to use the survey findings to generate a series of hypotheses that might be corroborated in subsequent studies.

The survey was oriented to capture consumer information mainly in Havana City Province because although it holds just one-fifth of the national population, nearly 40 percent of all hard-currency purchases take place there. We also included retail stores in eight other provincial capitals (Table 3.2). In the case of Matanzas, we included the towns of Varadero and Cárdenas because of the large amount of Cuban tourist workers who circulate in the region and the concentration of dollar stores in those towns. Moreover, the purchasing power of many workers is quite high among those who work in hotel and tourist-related services, who have access to hard currency in the form of gratuities. Most of the beaches and hotels in that province are within a two-hour drive of Havana. The national sample size reached 780 interviews across nine provinces (out of 14 and the special municipality of the Isla de Juventud, formerly the Isla de Pinos) during the summer of 2006. Just over half (55 percent) were women and more

Table 3.2 Distribution of Informants by Province

Province	Number of Informants	Percentage
Pinar del Río	15	1.92
Havana	20	2.56
Matanzas	25	3.21
Villa Clara	20	2.56
Cienfuegos	15	1.92
Camagüey	30	3.84
Holguín	25	3.21
Santiago de Cuba	35	4.49
Havana City	595	76.28
Total	780	99.99%

Source: Morales and Hernández (2006). Differences are due to rounding.

than one-third (36 percent) were between 18 and 29 years of age, whereas another 41 percent were between 30 and 49 years old. The majority (59 percent) were blue-collar workers, 15 percent were full-time students, 9 percent were 'housewives' who did not work outside the home and the rest were retirees. About one-third (32 percent) had a high school (e.g., 12th grade education) degree (education is mandatory until the ninth grade) and another 28 percent held college degrees.

CONSUMER BEHAVIOR FINDINGS

Brand power was the key driver about whether or not to buy a product or service under current retail conditions. Four of 10 (41 percent) informants considered that the brand was the principal reason for choosing a product or service; the breakdown was that the brand "always" (21 percent) or "almost always" (20 percent) was the main selection criterion. Another third (32 percent) felt that the brand "sometimes" was influential, and the balance (26 percent) claimed that brands "never" or "almost never" factored into their decision-making. This latter group (26 percent) of brand-independent shoppers stated that quality (72 percent), price (66 percent), likes (37 percent) and need (35 percent) drove their purchase decision; informants were able to identify all of the factors that influenced their decision, hence the multiple responses.

Quality turned out to be the most important aspect of brand selection. In a cash-poor nation, where incomes rarely exceed US$20 monthly, nine of 10 respondents identified the quality criterion as the main purchasing driver. This was followed by price (46 percent), image (39 percent), durability (37 percent) design (21 percent) and being fashionable (18 percent). We then asked about the marketing channels that consumers used to inform their purchases. Previously purchasing an item (70 percent) and point-of-sale presence and promotion (64 percent) were the most important reasons and channels for identifying a product. In order of importance, the remaining factors were: WOM from family and friends (47 percent), magazines (39 percent), foreigners (26 percent; had told them about it or else had seen tourists using or wearing the product), television (19 percent; this refers to product placement in foreign movies that are shown on TV because Cuban television broadcasts do not use television commercials to promote consumer goods and services) and radio (11 percent).

The most challenging part was to differentiate brand awareness by country of origin. We simply asked informants to list all the foreign brands they could in one question (Table 3.3) and all Cuban brands in a related one (Table 3.4). A total of 711[2] unique brands could be identified, of which just over half (56 percent) were foreign.

Building on the questions about national and international brands, we set out to explore the "Cubanness" of the consumer's world in socialist Cuba. By this, we sought unassisted responses to the following statement:

Table 3.3 Top 25 Most Recognized Foreign Brands in Cuba 2006 and Global Ranking (for World Consumers, Shown in Parentheses)

Cubans' Brand Awareness Ranking (Global ranking shown in parentheses)	% Sample Identifying it via Unassisted recall	Product Category
1. Adidas (31)	58	Shoe
2. Nike (31)	39	Shoe
3. Reebok	30	Shoe
4. Sony (26)	22	Electronics
5. Fila	17	Shoe
6. Puma	11	Shoe
7. Phillips (48)	11	Electronics
8. Sanyo	10	Electronics
9. Coca Cola (1)	10	Soft Drinks
10. Panasonic	10	Electronics
11. LG	8	Electronics
12. Christian Dior	6	Perfume, Clothing
13. Nestlé (63)	6	Foods
14. Wilson	6	Sporting goods & clothing
15. Calvin Klein	5	Clothing, fashion accessories
16. L'Oreal (53)	5	Shampoo, cosmetics
17. Mango	5	Clothing
18. Tommy Hilfiger	5	Clothing
19. Daytron	4	Electronics
20. Lee	4	Clothing
21. Channel (61)	4	Clothing, fashion accessories
22. Samsung (20)	4	Electronics
23. New Balance	4	Shoes
24. LaCoste	4	Clothing
25. Giorgio Armani	3	Clothing, fashion accessories
26. Miscellaneous	2.9	Misc.

Source: Morales and Hernández (2006).

"The brands that remind you of Cuba are:____?" Given the island's long history with these products as well as the agrarian past in which sugarcane and coffee were key exports, it was not surprising to see that Havana Club (54 percent) and Cubita (coffee brand, 35 percent) were by far the

Table 3.4 Top 25 Most Recognized National Brands in Cuba

Brands	Percentage of Sample Identifying brand by Unassisted recall	Product Category
Havana Club	32	Sprits
Cubita	20	Coffee
Bucanero	17	Beer
Cristal	14	Beer
Popular	14	Cigarettes
Suchel	12	Perfume, soap
Thaba[1]	11	Book bag/backpack
Conchita	8	Canned goods
TuKola	8	Softdrink
Nácar	7	Soap
Coppelia	7	Ice cream
Ciego Montero	6	Bottled water
Cohiba	6	Cigar
Perla	6	Toothpaste
Alicia Alonso	6	Perfume
Bonabel	6	Perfume, Body soap
Batey	5	Laundry soap
Hatuey	5	Beer
Varadero	5	Spirits
Sedal	5	Shampoo
Criollos	5	Cigarettes
Sport	5	Body soap, perfume
H. Upman	4	Cigarettes
Habanos	4	Cigars[2]
Batos	4	Sport equipment
Miscellaneous	3.9	Misc.

[1]At least one state company conducts marketing studies by region based on consumer preferences and styles. Thaba, a backpack and book bag manufacturer, provides 200 styles of products and can cater them to a particular school, factory or other institution/organization. Sales peak in summer right before students head back to schools. Their B2B clients are other state agencies and they claim "That way, commercial chain stores can select their models. The balance of production satisfied particular client requests" (*De esa manera las propias cadenas comerciales pueden elegir los modelos. El resto de las producciones se realizan para satisfacer pedidos específicos de los clientes*). Source http://www.opciones.cu/leer.asp?idnuevo=1513, accessed November 3, 2010.

[2]*Habanos* is not a cigar brand per se, but is a registered trademark and product category brand that refers to Cuban cigars based on their origin. In this regard, it is unique within the list. We explore *habanos* in Chapter 5.

Source: Morales and Hernández (2006).

most popular items in this "Cubanness" category. Further down the list appeared Cohiba (14 percent), Habanos, Popular and Cristal (each at 10 percent); Bucanero (9 percent); and Thaba (8 percent). Except for the backpack brand (Thaba), Cubans, like many foreigners, identify tobacco, rum and coffee as synonymous with island attributes (Gold and Heller 2002; Scarpaci and Portela 2009).

BRAND AWARENESS AND RANKING OF BOTH NATIONAL AND FOREIGN PRODUCTS AND SERVICES

This research operationalized brand awareness as those brands that were independently identified by informants and the ordinal ranking (e.g., first mentioned, second mentioned, etc.) of such unassisted recall. Table 3.5 shows the product and categories and the number of informants able to recognize at least one brand (Cuban or foreign). In all, informants recalled close to 2,400 brand names.

The following table provides a breakdown of brand awareness and preferences. As noted earlier in the chapter, by *brand awareness* we refer to those brand names that the informants expressed through unassisted recall. We then asked respondents to identity their top preferences from the lists that they had just provided. Note that the percentages listed in the brand awareness columns represent the relative proportion of respondents in that category who identified that particular brand, and is not based on the overall number of informants in the survey (n = 780). Like the percentages appearing in the 'brand preference' column are the proportion of category respondents who indicated a particular preference. Only the top preferences are listed (Table 3.6).

DISCUSSION

Cuban consumer recall of national and international products and services reveals several noteworthy traits. U.S. influence and the spread of English as the lingua franca of global commerce have entered consumers' minds despite the elimination of mass communications advertising. English-language brand names (Photoservice, Hollywood, Tropical Island) and U.S. firms (even though Sears has not operated on the island in 50 years or McDonald's has never opened a restaurant there) attest to that finding. Despite the trade embargo and because of international production sites, U.S. products find their way to Cuban consumers via third-country exporters (e.g., Close Up toothpaste, Coca-Cola, Colgate, Del Monte foods, Marlboro cigarettes, Nike sporting apparel, Palmolive soap, Pepsi, Wilson sporting products and others).

Foreign brand awareness is broadening and will likely continue to expand, especially in product and service categories that lack local competition. For

Table 3.5 Number of Informants Having Unassisted Recall of at Least One Brand by Product & Service Category[1] (n = 780)

Beverages, alcohol
· Rum (749)
· Beer (771)
Beverages, non-alcohol
· Bottled spring water (719)
· Soft drinks (762)
· Powdered soft drinks (758)
· Juices (732)
Household supplies
Laundry-bar soap (682)
Laundry detergent (685)
Fashion & style
· Apparel (654)
· Shoes (676)
· Perfume and cologne (712)
· Wristwatches (694)
Beauty products
· Body soap (767)
· Toothpaste (738)
· Shampoo (603)
Tobacco Products
· Cigarettes (715)
· Cigars (654)
Snacks, deserts and confections
· Ice cream (743)
Packaged foods
· Jams and marmalades (606)
· Coffee (671)
Household Furnishings & Appliances
· Refrigerators (735)
· Washing machines (643)
· Fans (700)
· Blenders (529)
Consumer Electronics
· Electronic equipment (sound systems and televisions) (767)
· Sound systems (specifically) (693)
· Cell phones (399)
Automotive, vehicles
· Automobiles (747)
· Motorcycles and scooters (659)
Services
· Retail stores (government-owned) (743)
· Quick-service Restaurants (government owned and foreign franchises) (732)
· Taxi Services (632)
· Photographic Services (595)

[1]We enlist Effie Worldwide product categories but use the single rubric 'services' because there were so few service brands recalled in this survey. http://www.effie.org/na_competition/categories

Source: Morales and Hernández (2006).

Table 3.6 Brand Awareness and Preference for the 32 Product and Service Subcategories

Category	Brand Awareness Ranking					Brand Preference	
	1st	2nd	3rd	4th	5th/6th/7th/8th/9th/10th	1st	2nd/3rd
Body soap (n=767)	Lux (73%)	Sport (52%)	Bonabel (42%)	Palmolive (34%)	Nácar (27%)	Lux (32%)	
Laundry soap (n=682)	Candado (91%)	Batey (33%)	Oso (18%)	Rina (9%)		Candado (51%)	
Laundry Detergent (n=685)	Omo (71%)	Paloma (47%)	Diss (41%)	Radiante (24%)	Hogar (19%)	Omo (46%)	Paloma (12%)
Tooth paste (n=738)	Pepsodent (61%)	Perla (57%)	Colgate (55%)	Close Up (36%)	Natural Dent (23%)	Colgate (38%)	Pepsodent (25%)
Shampoo (n=603)	Sedal (75%)	Natural (34%)	L'Oreal (31%)	Four Seasons (30%)	Garnier (21%)	Sedal (32%)	Pantene (10%)
Spirits (n=749)	Havana Club (92%)	Mulata (23%)	Paticruzao (18%)	Varadero (16%)	Guayabita del Pinar (14%); Bacardi (13%)	Havana Club (42%)	
Beer (n=719)	Cristal (89%)	Bucanero (88%)	Heineken (46%)	Hatuey (35%)	Mayabe (28%)/ Bavaria (27%)	Bucanero (29%)	Cristal (15%)/ Heineken (12%)
Bottled Spring Water (n=719)	Ciego Montero (90%)	Las Lomas (15%)	Los Portales (12%)	La Cotorra (8%)		Ciego Montero (42%)	
Soft drinks (n=762)	TuKola (61%)	Coca Cola (57%)	Najita (53%)	Cachito (51%)	Pepsi Cola (34%)/ Tropicola (32%)	Coca Cola (20%)	Cachito (14%)/ TuKola (13%)

Continued

Table 3.6 Continued

Category	Brand Awareness Ranking					Brand Preference	
	1st	2nd	3rd	4th	5th/6th/7th/ 8th/9th/10th	1st	2nd/3rd
Powdered soft drinks (758)	Piñata (77%)	Toki (73%)	Caricias (43%)	Butti (31%)	Drinki (13%)	Piñata (38%)	Toki (34%)
Juices (n=732)	Tropical Island (75%)	Taoro (32%)	Conchita (9%)			Tropical Island (43%)	
Canned goods (n=606)	Conchita (55%)	Doña Delicias (40%)	Del Monte (17%)			Conchita (20%)	
Ice Cream (n=743)	Coppelia (73%)	Nestlé (60%)	Varadero (39%)	Alondra (29%)		Alondra (29%)	Nestlé (27%)
Coffee (n=671)	Cubita (89%)	Serrano (44%)	Hola (31%)	Pilón (20%)	Turquino (14%)	Cubita (35%)	
Cigarettes (n=715)	Popular (77%)	Hollywood (63%)	H'Upman (33%)	Criollos (30%)	Monterrey (19%)/ Vegas 19%/ Marlboro 17%	Popular (40%)	
Apparel (n=654)	Adidas (59%)	Nike (36%)	Reebok (24%)	Fila (20%)	Puma (17%)/ Levi's (17%), Mango (17%), Lee (15%), Calvin Klein (14%)	Adidas (19%)	
Shoes (n=676)	Adidas (73%)	Nike (51%)	Reebok (48%)	Fila (29%)	Puma (17%)/ Vía Uno (14%)/ Amadeo (13%)	Adidas (28%)	

Perfume (n=712)	Alicia Alonso (73%)	Mariposa (26%)	Carolina Herrera (14%)	Chanel (14%)	Coral Negro (13%)/ Christian Dior (12%)	Alicia Alonso (7%)	
Wristwatches (n=694)	Seiko (70%)	Orient (66%)	Rolex (41%)	Casio (35%)	Citizen (33%)	Seiko (27%)	Orient (20%)/ Rolex (17%)
TVs (n=767)	Panda (69%)	LG (61%)	Sony (54%)	Philips (40%)	Panasonic (36%)/ Sanyo (25%)	Sony (31%)	Panda (19%)
Refrigerators (n=735)	LG (77%)	Samsung (30%)	Daewoo (26%)	General Electric (20%)		LG (40%)	
Washing Machines (n=643)	LG (75%)	Daytron (38%)	Vince (36%)			LG (41%)	
Fans (n=700)	Daytron (37%)	Sanyo (34%)				Sanyo (18%)	
Blenders (n=529)	Daytron (59%)	LG (29%)	Osterizer (28%)			Osterizer (20%)	
Sound Systems (n=693)	Sony (81%)	Panasonic (55%)	Philips (40%)	LG (40%)	Sanyo (39%)/ Aiwa (19%)	Sony (45%)	
Automobiles (n=747)	Lada (68%)	Mercedes Benz (55%)	Chevrolet (41%)	Audi (38%)	Moskvich (31%)/ Toyota (29%)/ VW (26%)	Mercedes Benz (25%)	

Continued

Table 3.6 Continued

Motorcycles (n=659)	MZ (65%)	Suzuki (42%)	Honda (42%)	Jawa (33%)	Yamaha (30%)	MZ (14%)	
Cell phones (n=399)	Motorola (73%)	Nokia (68%)	Siemens (24%)			Nokia (27%)	Motorola (26%)
State retail chain stores (n=732)	TRD (80%)	Panamericanas (52%)	Caracol (50%)	Cubalse (36%)	Meridiano (18%)/ Cimex (17%)/ Universo (10%)/ Artez (7%)/ Habaguanex (6%), Sears (4%)	TRD (43%)	Panamericana (17%)/ Caracol (16%)
Restaurants, bakeries & cafeterias (n=732)	El Rápido (56%)	DiTú (39)	Doña Yuya (31%)	Palmares (28%)	Sylvain (14%)/ Rumbos (12%)/ Pain de Paris (10%)/ Dimar (7%)/ McDonald's (4%)/ Isla Azul (3%)	El Rápido (20%)	
Taxi Service (n=630)	Panataxi (86%)	OK (57%)	Coco Taxi (17%)	Cubataxi (10%)	Fénix (8%)/ Panatrans (8%)/ 55-5555 (6%), Havanataxi (5%)/ Havanautos (4%)	Panataxi (61%)	
Photographic Services (n=595)	Photoservice (94%)	Trimagen (34)%				Photo-service (34%)	

[1]Actually, many Cubans think of Cimex as a chain brand but it is the parent company of many retail stores including Tiendas Panamericanas, FotoService, Omni Video, CUPET (gas stations) and others. Consumers will see the Cimex logo in many of the above establishments, but they do not use the logo or band as their own retail outlet.

Source: Morales and Hernández (2006).

instance, in 2006 only 80,000 Cubans had cell phones at the time of the survey. However, more than half of the respondents could identify a cell phone brand name. By early 2011, the number of cell phone users on the island had risen to over one million (Morales and Scarpaci 2011b). The 12-fold increase in cell phone usage in five years marks both a significant dollarization of the consumer economy (because monthly usage fees must be paid in hard currency and not pesos) and considerable brand dissemination for electronic manufacturers such as Nokia, Samsung, LG and Motorola, among others. Survey findings about international electronic brands also reveal that LG and Samsung, barely a presence on the global scene 20 years ago, have surpassed the traditional global consumer appliance makers such as General Electric, Phillips and Frigidaire. This underscores the shifting industrial base of the emerging economies.

Cuban consumers have apparently brought a level of pragmatism to the classic consumer dilemma of preference versus brand recognition. Put another way, the cost of maintenance may be an important factor in separating awareness from preference. In some consumer categories (like cars), it is unlikely that any of the informants ever rode in a Mercedes-Benz though high-level government officials use them, as do members of the international business community. Nonetheless, Mercedes-Benz remained the preferred brand in its category. In lower-end consumer products such as watches, Rolex was recognized and ranked in third place, but was not the preferred one. Instead, Seiko took first place.

Not all globally recognized luxurious brands lead the recalled or preferred slots. In perfume, for instance, Alicia Alonso outranked other global brands such as Carolina Herrera or Chanel by a wide margin. As the following chapter shows, Alicia Alonso perfume resonated deeply among consumer focus groups with potential iconic brand value because the perfume reflects strongly held myths and values about what "Cubanness" means (see Scarpaci and Portela 2009, chap. 1).

These findings make a great deal of sense in the Cuban context. This is because there is a high level of formal instruction across the island (as there was in the pre-1959 era). High schooling levels correlate with high levels of aspiration, not just in the sphere of consumption, but also in personal, familial and social spheres too (Weinreb 2009). Nonetheless, the purchasing power of islanders is very low and it is unable to satisfy such high levels of aspiration. Cubans recognize the quality of certain brands and aspire to consume many of them but become frustrated because they do not have the money to buy them.

The Cuban case is very atypical from other socialist, emerging economies. Unlike China and Vietnam where small, medium and large private firms exist, Cubans do not have salaries that allow them to delve deeply and often in the consumer goods and services markets. Online applications such as PriceGrabber.com and related sites are not available for Cubans. Instead, product information comes from WOM or in-store demonstration and window-shopping comparison. Moreover, markets in what are ostensibly Communist countries (Vietnam and China) enlist massive communication outlets to promote goods and services and, in turn, ratchet up demand. Government pronouncements about what is a necessary or unnecessary consumer good or service, or what is appropriate consumer behavior, are much less common there than in Cuba (Venard and Hanafi 2008).

For most of the time since 1993, Cuba's B2C market has been framed by many different types of currencies (Cuban pesos, the CUC, the euro and other hard currencies) and many types of stores and outlets that accept different currencies.[3] Cuban stores, private agricultural markets and private self-employed workers work only in Cuban pesos where, unlike the state rationing system, the forces of supply and demand regulate price. It is noteworthy that the island's entire rationing system, which provides food and basic goods to 11 million people, also operates in the national currency. More upscale Cuban stores as well as joint-venture firms charge only in CUCs. In the island's B2B sector, firms exchange among themselves in both CUCs and Cuban pesos. Lastly, some self-employed workers also charge in CUCs or other hard currencies, whereas the underground economy negotiates all of these currencies. It should be noted that nearly every Cuban worker receives a salary in Cuban pesos. Only about 5 percent of the labor force receives a monthly bonus stipend of 10 CUC; they work for joint-venture firms or specialized state companies like Habaguanex (devoted to restoring Old Havana). This means that 80–85 percent of the source for the island's circulation of hard currency comes from abroad in the form of remittances, a topic we discuss in detail in Chapter 6.

CONCLUSIONS

Brand awareness is the first step in a brand knowledge and visibility. It is the product of various firm activities, including systematic advertising through the conventional (modern) channels of advertising. This study shows a surprisingly high level of brand awareness among Cuban consumers. We say 'surprising' because it exceeded our original expectations (Morales and Scarpaci 2010a). Brands evoke a strong social connation and strength across the island in a market that has lacked advertising for half a century. In Cuba, the consumer serves as the principal intermediary between the brand communicator, on the one hand, and a set of involuntary actions, on the other hand. These actions include discussing brand quality and performance with friends, family and in-store personnel. Cubans base a good deal of their brand preference on information gleaned from significant reference groups or else their own experiences with national and international brands and services. In other words, this viral marketing is 'authentic' in that it is not driven by paid marketers or preconceived ideas other than packaging information or in-store promotion by sales personnel.

We believe that promising work originally laid out by McDonald et al. (2000) in their comparative study of Vietnam with China and Eastern Europe would be germane to the Cuban case once large-scale chain supermarkets enter the island. The McDonald team found that Vietnamese shoppers often but buy little and attributed that behavior to "a combination of novelty seeking, a preference for fixed pricing and the desire for foreign brands. The high level of shopping frequency and low number of purchases resulted from a genuine enjoyment of shopping, a lack of planning and status seeking, not infrastructure or economic factors suggested by past researchers" (McDonald et al. 2000, 53). Years of pent-up demand for consumer goods could drive that shop often, buy little behavior, in which case store setting and ambience could be determining factors in keeping Cubans in retail establishments.

The findings here indicate that the CBBE model may not be the most effective method for advertisers and marketers to employ for capturing consumers' attention in a less regulated market setting. Cubans may be leery of newfound jingles and logos unleashed during a future market economy. WOM and brand value will likely continue to shape brand preference, at least until purchasing power rises and new icons about brand prestige influence consumer behavior.

This chapter also shows that despite limited purchasing power in hard currency, brand power exerts the greatest influence in the minds of Cuban consumers; 41 percent of informants claim that the brand's reputation in the most important variable in selecting a given product or service. We had expected price and/or availability to override brand value given the erosion of the national economy and the austerity measures that islanders have endured. These point-of-sale settings add value to this unique island where 'advertising without marketing' in the conventional sense prevails. In-store promotion fills a huge gap that would otherwise be filled by radio, TV, print and Internet advertising. In this regard, the role played by stores, firm knowledge about the product, sales personnel training and merchandising is noteworthy. Surprisingly, Cuban consumers possess a vast knowledge about both the accessible national products as well as international brands.

4 Iconic Brand Potential among Leading Cuban Products

INTRODUCTION

Branding approaches in understanding consumer goods and services span a variety of theoretical and methodological realms. Regardless of the paths taken to understand consumer behavior, they largely rely on modern mass communication channels to influence, persuade and cajole consumers into thinking about a product or service. A central tenet of those approaches is to repeat the message sufficiently so that a brand stands out amongst the 'clutter' that most consumers face on a daily basis. References to competitors, clever taglines, celebrity endorsements and the use of animals and children have long proven to be successful ways to position products and services in the minds of the consumer (Franzen and Moriarty 2009, 16–20).

The combined powers of globalization and marketing appear to be reaching all corners of the world (Belk et al. 1996), although the outcomes are highly uneven, particularly in Latin America (Scarpaci 2005). Shifts to market economies in Eastern Europe in 1989 presaged changes felt elsewhere in Vietnam, China and Cuba. Culture undoubtedly plays a role in how consumers in the less affluent world interpret messages about consumption, brands and market goods and services. Skeptics argue that the twinning of globalization and marketing will inevitably homogenize consumer culture (Belk 1995; Featherstone 1990). Still others contend that the power of globalization and marketing cannot drastically alter local patterns of brand preferences (Alger 1992; Featherstone 1991; Friedman 1994; Joy and Wallendorf 1996).

The brand awareness and consumer knowledge base discussed in Chapter 3 allows us to take stock of the following key points. First, Cubans have moved well beyond the government's long-standing (and arbitrary) classification of 'essential' versus 'nonessential' goods and services. The creation of the *libreta* and subsidizing basic goods is emblematic of that approach (Table 4.1). Second, the decriminalization of the dollar in 1993 opened up many self-employment opportunities, allowing the previously illegal acts of *maceteros* (hoarders, or literally those who hid dollars in flower pots [*macetas*]) to become unnecessary. Third, the Revolution's emphasis

Table 4.1 Marcoeconomic Policies and Consumption and in Cuba, 1959–2011

Period	Policies and Consumption-based Outcomes
1959–1961	Gradual privatization of foreign corporate holdings such as Esso, Hilton, Pan Am, and other multinationals. Agrarian reform measures limit the size of farmlands and break-up sugar and tobacco lands into smaller private or state holdings. Enactment of housing and property laws granting low or no rent on low-income workers. State controls housing market, especially property 'forfeited' by émigrés. Small and medium-sized firms gradually nationalized.
1962	U.S. trade embargo imposed. Soviet Union and Eastern European members of CMEA (Council of Mutual Economic Assistance) begin replacing American consumer goods on Cuban shelves. Cuba swaps 1,400 political prisoners (Cuban-Americans) who were captured at Bay of Pigs Invasion, for baby food and pharmaceuticals. The ration book (*libreta de abastecimiento*) is introduced, providing subsidized food, tobacco and rum, and personal hygiene products for households. Some consumer durable goods such as fuel (charcoal, kerosene) and light bulbs are also included.
1968	The 'Revolutionary Offensive' of 1968 entails the complete seizure of Cuba's smallest businesses: hot-dog carts, repair shops, vegetable stands, snack shops, and the like were driven underground or out of business.
Mid-1980s	The unraveling of the Soviet and CMEA economies impact foreign trade and consumption. While one ton of Cuban sugar was originally exchanged for one ton of oil, gradually these favorable terms are phased out. In the mid-1980s, some market liberalizations allow craftsmen and artists to sell their wares but this comes to a halt in 1987 with the introduction of the 'Correcting of Mistakes' policies that snuff out timid privatizations.
1989	Collapse of the Berlin Wall symbolizes a setback for communism; rationing tightens in Cuba
1991	CMEA is dissolved. Trade deficits mount in Cuba. Rationing of consumer goods and services deepens
1993	Fidel Castro announces the 'Special Period in a Time of Peace' (or 'Special Period'; Período Especial en el tiempo de paz) that includes, among other consumer-related policies, the decriminalization of the U.S. dollar. Now, Cubans with dollars can purchase consumer goods in 'dollar' or 'diplo' stores. Also, over 100 private-sector jobs (*trabajo por cuenta propia*) are legalized, requiring prospective licenses and fees to behind at the beginning of the month for household restaurants, cobblers, air compressor operators, mechanics, and other trades. Private agriculturalists and farm cooperatives given incentives to sell surplus goods in legal markets. Joint ventures are also encouraged and by 1996 exceed 400.

Continued

Table 4.1 Continued

1993 to present	Foreign remittances from the Cuban diaspora gradually increase as hard currency can now be used to purchase goods in non-peso stores. By 2000, remittances account for the single-largest source of hard currency, surpassing tourism. Increasingly, trained professionals abandon state jobs to work in tourism, joint-venture operations, or self-employment.
1994	The Cuban Convertible Currency (CUC) is implemented as a way to capture other hard currencies. CUCs can be purchased in national pesos, Euros, sterling pounds, and even dollars, but can only be used on the island. It becomes one of the highest (over-valued) valued currencies in the world because its exchange rate is set internally without corresponding gold reserves or Central Bank guarantees.
1995	Self-employment peaks at around 152,000 workers (still less than 2% of labor force). Sudden crackdowns ensure by state authorities for 'illicit enrichment' (*enriquecimiento ilícito*)
Early 2000s	Diplomatic and economic relations with Venezuela lead to discounted fuel imports from Caracas, a key pillar in the Cuban economy, for keeping electrical grid in operation. Cuban professionals, especially health-care workers and physicians, opt for foreign service in Venezuela as part of Fidel Castro and Hugo Chávez's bilateral relations to strengthen socialism. By 2010, more than 20,000 Cubans are working in Venezuela, and their ability to bring in consumer goods at discounted or no tariffs become important in many Cuban households. Remittances from Cuban workers in Venezuela, though much smaller than Cuban-American aid, increases. Joint ventures decline to just over 200.
2002	About half of the 152 sugar mills across the island are shut down for inefficiency. Government policies further encourage private agricultural producers to sell surplus crops in local agricultural markets (*agromercados*). Displaced sugar workers learn basic computer software skills at rural technical schools, work in mills that became industrial museum, or seek employment in private agriculture or tourism.
2004	Then U.S. President George W. Bush passes executive orders that limit the nature of cultural (or people-to-people) travel by U.S. citizens to the island. Impacts on tourist sector are considerable, resulting in a downturn of hard currency receipts.
2004	Fidel Castro adopts the Euro as the preferred foreign currency. Cubans using dollars are charged a 10% penalty and a 10% processing fee in an attempt to discourage use of 'green backs' (*fulas*).
2006	Power is transferred to Raúl Castro who promises a more 'orthodox line' of socialism in directing economy. Power outages, austerity measures and food scarcity increase as consumers search out goods in services in peso, CUC, and black markets to satisfy consumption needs.

Continued

Table 4.1 Continued

2007	Raúl Castro allows Cubans to stay in tourist hotels and allows the purchase of DVD player and computers.
2008	Cell phones are now legal and widely sold to the general public.
2010	Raúl Castro announces layoffs of some 500,000 state workers in September so the government can arrest mounting deficits, which was described as "the biggest shift toward private enterprise since the 1960s." Workers are encouraged to pursue work in the self-employment realm, where a relaxing of current lays should ease the infusion of these public workers. Ration-book provisions diminish further and there is official discussion in the state newspaper, *Granma*, about eliminating the *libreta*.
2011	Cuban Communist Party announces at the VI Party Conference in April the legalization of the sale of homes and apartments as well as an expanded automobile market. However, no specifics had been announced as of this writing (6/2011).

Calculated by the authors.

on material versus nonmaterial rewards has eroded considerably since the demise of the former USSR. Today, Cubans across all social strata must survive and make ends meet while living in what has become a seemingly endless and downward spiral of living conditions (Espinosa-Chepe 2010; Henken 2005; Weinreb 2009; Blue 2004). Fourth, the rise of tourism from just a few hundred thousand in the early 1990s to over two million in the early 2000s exposes Cubans to a panoply of brands that had previously been out of view. These include an array of international logos such as Lacoste, Rolex, Adidas, Nike, Reebok, Apple and Ray-Ban, among others. Lastly, Cubans have long been exposed to product placement through U.S. and other foreign films shown in theaters, TV and in rented VHS tapes and DVDs. Although a raging 'cold war' between the U.S. and Cuba has now passed the half-century mark, the Cuban people have long been able to separate the U.S. government from its citizens and culture.

This chapter builds on the previous one by focusing on national brands by examining to what extend iconic brand potential exists in the form of consumer associations of *cubanidad* with the leading Cuban products. Given the incompatibility of the CBBE model in the Cuban case, we approach this question of Cuban identity by examining the potential of iconic brands and their attachment to national myths, values and folklore. We enlist data gathered during field research conducted in Cuba in July 2010 that consisted of running 10 focus groups composed of 84 participants that explored brand awareness. A central goal of the field research was to explore the potential of taking popular national (e.g., Cuban) brands and assessing their ability to become iconic brands, a topic to which we turn in the following section.

ICONIC BRANDING

Iconic branding is a subset of a broader approach to advertising and marketing that can be subsumed under the heading of 'cultural branding.' Perhaps the most popular tenet of this strand of marketing is 'nation branding,' a topic that has received much attention in recent years (Dinnie 2008; Szondi 2007). Most of the conventional consumer behavior research, however, emphasizes repetition and persuasion to position products and services in the minds of consumers (B2C) and businesses (B2B) (Berkowitz 1997). Category benefits presented through conventional branding strategies make people feel certain ways that, in turn, provide metrics so that marketers and brand managers can identify product value (Bogdan and Biklnin 1998). This kind of branding assumes that most repetition or communication is good provided it is retold often enough. Most contemporary branding activities also emphasize lifestyle; that is, one does not just sell a product or service. Rather, a particular way of living that reinforces consumer identity and personality must be reflected also. Examples include Bud Light's focus on comedy, beer-drinking antics and relaxation, or Nike's use of celebrity endorsement (and Reebok's refusal to do so). In all instances, the products have clear messages about what value their products can add to consumers' lives.

Holt (2004) and others, however, argue that really successful brands—iconic brands—achieve phenomenal success by bundling their messages with elements of national myths that are widely held and shared by the target

Table 4.2 Summary of Iconic Features among Coca Cola, Corona and Snapple in the United States

Coca Cola	Corona	Snapple
GIs receive free Coke in WW2; product associated with defeat of Nazis and liberty	Spring breakers in Mexico return to college towns want to drink Corona; product placement in college bars in late 1970s	Unconventional marketers enter natural tea field in 1980s and early 1990s
In 1960s, the demise of the 'corporate man' and the rise of the 'peace movement' takes hold as depicted in Coke ads by non-traditional businessmen	Mid 1990s ads show beach scene with 'nothing happening' and becomes the 'reverse positioning' of Corona	Snapple employee reads from consumers; appeals to common folks interested in natural products that are depicted in Snapple ads by non-traditional businessmen
1980s ads emphasize multicultural diversity	1990s–2001 Corona continues with sublime aquamarine scenes	Mid 1990s Snapple loses focus on its unique proposition; sales decline

Calculated by the authors.

audience. The richness and diversity of national myths is, that like brands, they can be communicated through storytelling, which can translate into specific messages tailored for segments of the consumer market (Szondi 2007, 13). Unlike the search for lifestyle affinity, cultural branders suggest that successful brands develop because of a synergism that their product or service resonates with widely shared myths, folklore and cultural symbols (Holts 1995). Marketing campaigns carried out by Coca-Cola, Corona and Snapple illustrate how these national myths can be grafted on marketing campaigns in the United States (Table 4.2).

Iconic myths in the United States include, but are not limited to, portrayals of the American frontier (e.g., Marlboro man), rugged individualism and the 'melting pot.' The peace movement of the 1960s and 1970s and the civil rights movement offered venues for Coke to tap into this mythmaking, as did Snapple's attempt (though short-lived) in showing regular folks making a simple product that was good for the consumer (a strategy that also worked well for Ben and Jerry's ice cream). To place these in comparative context, we turn to a discussion of our constructions of national myths in Cuba.

CUBAN CULTURAL LORE AND VALUES

What might the cultural myths be for Cuban marketing? Figure 4.1 outlines our conceptual and operational model of constructing, operationalizing and measuring *cubanidad*. We begin with the possible components of an iconic construct definition based on our review of the literature on 'Cubanness' or *cubanidad*. The literature examined place- and cultural-specific identities

Table 4.3 Iconic Construct Categories for 'Cubanness' for Cuban Products and Services

ICONIC CONSTRUCTS OF "CUBANNESS" FOR CUBAN PRODUCTS & SERVICES	
Marianismo Machismo	Social meanings of gender
Underdog (David v. Goliath) Creativity & Resourcefulness	Creativity
Sugar & Tobacco Heritage	Sugar & Tobacco Heritage

Calculated by the authors.

Table 4.4 Chi-Square Analysis of Focus Groups

	Gender	Creativity	Ag Heritage
Popular (cigs)	6	0	3
Montecristo (cigar)	0	2	22
A.Alonso (perfume)	24	63	8
Bucanero (beer)	32	8	0
Havana Club	11	0	26
Cubita (coffee)	6	0	28
Chi-square 198.09, df 10, p=.0001			

Calculated by the authors.

stemming from an assessment of national myths and folklore. Our measurement specification stage led us to propose the following rudimentary iconic categories about Cuban culture lore and values: machismo-marianismo (including related socially constructed notions of gender such as *la quinceñera* and other rites of passage), creativity (e.g., problem solving, *resolviendo* and *solucionando* on a daily basis), the underdog (David and Goliath myth) and the roles of sugar- and tobacco-based products in the

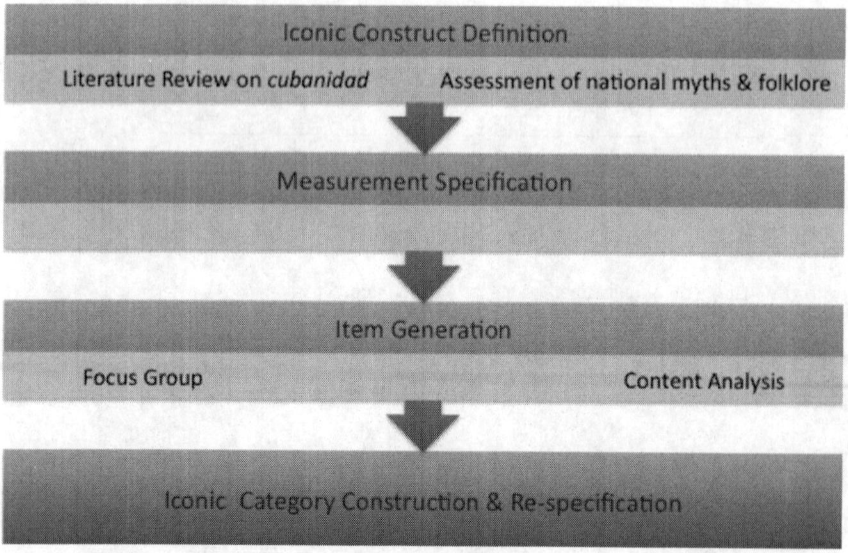

Figure 4.1 Iconic construct model for *cubanidad*.

island's agro-export economy (Table 4.3). Fieldwork allowed us to reassess our item generation through focus groups and content analysis for both latent and manifest content. Upon further analysis, iconic category construction and respecification led us to combine two similar categories (David versus Goliath and creativity) into a single grouping.

Machismo-marianismo

The social construction of gendered roles plays a powerful force in shaping narratives about the island's material and nonmaterial culture. From the iconic fiery and sultry *mulata de fuego* of historical times, to the fierce and cunning bravery of the twentieth-century bearded guerilla fighters, tales of male (*machismo*) and female (*marianismo*) comportment lace themselves through the island's literature, music and popular culture.

Machismo in Cuba and throughout Spanish-speaking Latin America and the Caribbean refers to the cult of masculine virility that celebrates sexual prowess and aggressiveness. Sierra Madero (2006, 73) argues that Cuban machismo's imprint in contemporary culture stems from its long(er) relationship with Spain, not gaining independence until 1898, some seven decades after most American colonies achieved sovereignty. For instance, the Cuban Constitution of 1902 inherited Article 432 from the Spanish Penal Code, which justifies a husband's killing of his wife and her lover should he find them in a compromising situation. The killer would only face exile in such acts of passion. Such highly specified gender roles in the early twentieth century were also critical of homosexual and effeminate behavior. The weekly magazines *La Semana* and *Carteles* did much to portray antithetical masculine and homosexual behavior as a national outrage. Aberrant male behavior that suggested a homosexual lifestyle was called *pepillismo* and *garzonismo*, which quickly became public objects of ridicule and moral weakness. To be labeled[1] as such in the early twentieth century conveyed a "pejorative semantic meaning and became the maximum insult against masculine honor and dignity" (Sierra Madero 2006, 82; our translation).

Contrasted with marianismo (see the following), machismo embodies highly stereotypical ideas about male gender roles. Essentially, its social value—at least for some men—in Cuba and elsewhere is to ensure the special privileges of men versus women in its sociological, cultural and ideological manifestations. Despite the Revolution's efforts to elevate the role of women, the leadership of the Cuban Communist Party has long been criticized for its lack of female leaders. González-Pagés (2003, 291) argues that:

> [s]ince at least the nineteenth century, machista concepts of masculinity have been applied to young boys from the time they are born. The male, instilled with a sense of machismo, feels it necessary to constantly demonstrate his virility. The phrase '*demusetra que eres un*

> *hombre*' (prove that you are a man) exemplifies this way of thinking. Women that attempt to redefine gender boundaries and perform tasks traditionally considered in the male domain are sometimes attacked as *marimachos* (tomboys).

Some might argue, for instance, that Fidel Castro—like many of the bearded revolutionaries that fought in the Sierra Maestra—manifested machista attributes. Although only married once (to Mirta Diaz-Balart in October 1948), he has sired at least nine offspring. In his revolutionary youth, he was nicknamed *el caballo*, perhaps because of his athleticism—he was named Cuba's high school 'Athlete of the Year' (Deutch 2008). He is perceived as someone who exhibited bravery and stamina while fighting against the corrupt regime of President Fulgencio Batista (1982–1958) in the Sierra Maestra mountains from 1957 to 1959, but perhaps also because of his stature (purportedly 6 feet, 3 inches tall) and virility.

Marianismo is, in many ways, the gendered antithesis of machismo, though the Cuban version departs greatly from this construct. Taken from the name of the Holy Virgin Mary (*la santísima virgen María*), this norm casts the woman as subservient to men. Seen as fragile, strong in moral character, beautiful and docile, this gendered role is common throughout most of Catholic Latin America. Contemporary Cuban women, however, would cringe at the notion of subservience. In fact, although women in Cuba gained the right to vote in 1934, it was decades after most of Europe and the United States granted suffrage, but before every other Latin American nation except Ecuador (1929), Chile (1931), Brazil (1932), Uruguay (1932) and Saint Lucia (1924; see Women's Suffrage 2010). The 1959 Revolution has generally enhanced the status of women across the island but it is fair to say that Cuban women were less disenfranchised than most women in the Americas before the Revolution.

The Special Period created a new literary space for female expression led by a group of younger women writers. Zoé Valdés (1959–) has become one of the most celebrated feminist and erotic writers. Her 1995 book, *La nada cotidiana*, depicted common folk—but especially women—rejecting the political rhetoric of the socialist leadership in light of the severe material shortages. Her protagonist seeks refuge through sexual encounters and affairs and serves as a check against—or at least a challenge to—a machista society. Subsequent short stories, novels and poems incorporate vernacular and slang, and include free-spirited women searching for many forms of liberation, filled with passion and love (Figueredo 2003, 373–74). This empowering form of sexual expression and femininity is very different from the passive, Roman Catholic infused role of submissive women, as in the Virgin Mary. Valdés's lyrical and poetic touch has resonated with women in and beyond the island.

CREATIVITY AND RESOURCEFULNESS

During the colonial period (1514–1898), Spain referred to the island as the Fidelísma Cuba (most faithful Cuba) because it remained her last colony in the Americas. The long tenure allowed the island to cultivate the fine arts as perceived by the peninsular elite in the cosmopolitan regions of Madrid, Barcelona and elsewhere in Spain. At the same time, the history of slavery infused Cuba with millions of slaves whose linguistic, agricultural, fine arts and musical contributions have made a lasting mark. Scholars often refer to this unusual mixture of ethnic and cultural ingredients as an *ajiaco*, or stew. As an island, it has been vulnerable to external geopolitical forces that have been able to limit the arrival of foreign products; the independence struggle from 1869 to 1898, the Cuban Missile Crisis of 1962 and the U.S. trade embargo underscore this strength.

Cuban schoolchildren learn of the many historic 'firsts' that distinguish their nation, though we note that many are subject to debate. In 1794, the first steam engine allegedly operated on the island. In 1837, the first rail service on the island was implemented, well before the mother country had one. Italian inventor Antonio Meucci designed and operated the first 'talking telegraph' in Havana in 1849, which was a precursor to the telephone (The U.S. Supreme Court recognized Meucci, and not Alexander Graham Bell—with whom he worked—as the inventor after Meucci's death). In 1881, Havana boasted the first public telephone system in Latin America followed in 1890 by an electric street lighting network (Segre et al. 1997, 34).

At the same time, however, the island has spawned a list of athletes, artists, musicians and politicians who have left their mark on world history. Cuban anthropologist Fernando Ortiz was one of the first to value the island's resourcefulness. As an ethnographer bent on intensive interviewing and oral history, Ortíz (1995) eschewed grand theory such as Gramsci's "pessimism of the intellect." In lieu of such broad-stroke interpretation, Ortíz posited "the optimism of the will," which used as its main object focus the life-affirming creativity with which Cuban popular sectors countered serious challenges to material shortfalls (Portell Vilá 1939; Ortíz 1995). Salgado (1999) traces this hybridity among the island's rich literary tradition that brought the neo-baroque genre of writing to Cuba. Writers such as José Lezama Lima (1910–1976), Alejo Carpentier (1904–1980) and Severo Sarduy (1936–1993) explored the way in which New World baroque cultural artifacts in the colonial era served as markers of discontinuity with Spain, and embraced a new 'hybrid' way of interpreting dance, literature and music in Cuba. In the contemporary era, those same writers and scores of athletes and musicians signify the presence of the 'talented Cuba' on several world stages. In everyday living (*la vida cotidiana*), resourcefulness as a cultural value has been driven by necessity; a deteriorating economy and the U.S. trade embargo force Cubans to reuse items. Thus, old eight-cylinder 'gas-guzzler' American cars from the 1950s and before rely on small-cylinder diesel motors and carburetors from Soviet Ladas and Moskvich cars. Electric motors taken from old Soviet and U.S. refrigerators now operate pulleys and lathes in carpentry, artisan, machine, tool-and-dye and bicycle repair shops. A poorly endowed Cuban consumer market leaves no room for discarding much of anything (Weinreb 2009).

THE UNDERDOG (DAVID V. GOLIATH)

Since at least the beginning of the 1868 Ten Years' War against Spain until today, Cuba has projected itself as the victim of seemingly insurmountable external forces. Beginning with Spanish colonial rule, Cuba has faced great adversity. The U.S. occupation of the island under the Platt Amendment (1898–1902), the Republican era (1902–1958, also known as the neocolonial period by the island's leadership) and the contemporary revolutionary era (1959–present) are the most recent historical periods of this national belief. Most political discourse on the island refers to the *imperio yanqui* (Yankee Empire).

Collective and individual actions, however, underscore the island's quest for surmounting these obstacles. José Martí, considered the 'apostle' and founding father of the Cuban independence movement, captured this sentiment in much of his writing while in exile in New York City and Tampa. His often quoted description of life in exile captures that sentiment: "I have lived inside the monster; I have seen its entrails—and my sling is that of David" (Martí 1895, cited in Wilkinson 2010). That Martí died in battle stands as a symbol of individual sacrifice for the homeland.

Other revolutionary figures—but from the twentieth century—echo this sentiment. Fidel Castro used the metaphor often as noted here in the 1980s:

> What is our flag? It is the flag of Martí . . . the flag that so many millions, hundreds of millions admire around the world, everywhere, even by those who are our adversaries, including those who do not share our views, because as they say to us: We do not think the same, but we admire you for what you are doing, because you are the country that stands up to the giant, the atomic giant, the nuclear Goliath . . . Cuba's struggle is that of David against Goliath. (Castro 1998, cited in Wilkinson 2010)

Dozens of guerilla and student fighters of the 1950s are eulogized across the island as martyrs because they gave their lives in the face of overwhelming odds so that Cuba might be free. The capturing of over 1,000 CIA-trained exile forces who tried to retake the island in the Bay of Pigs was a strategic military and symbolic victory for Fidel Castro and the Cuban Revolution; when Vietnam 'fell' to North Vietnam troops in 1975, it provided a universal David-and-Goliath parallel for Fidel Castro to use ever since then. The death of Che Guevara in Bolivia, an Argentine who fought with the Castro brothers, embodies this notion. His efforts to travel to the poorest regions of Africa and Latin America aimed to educate the masses about their oppression and teach them to rise up against the forces of international capitalism, hegemony and imperialism. For the past four decades, schoolchildren across the island chant daily their desire "to be like Che." Victories earned at the Pan American or Olympic games invite eloquent (and long) discourses by the island's leadership about how such a small nation could earn so many medals while competing against countries with tens, and even hundreds, of millions of residents.

SUGAR AND TOBACCO

Cuba is synonymous with both of these crops because they are intricately tied to the economy and history of the island (Moreno Fraginals 1964). Sugar ruled as Cuba's most important industry since the early nineteenth century, and held on to that position until the 1990s, when tourism surpassed its annual revenues. When Moreno Fraginals (1984) called the island a "sea of grass," he graphically captured the planting of sugarcane across Cuba's rolling plains and valleys. The island's black population, today a majority if its mixed-blood derivate is included, derives largely from the Spanish importation of African slaves to work the sugar plantations. Production in the early independence years (post-1902) reached 4.2 million tons in 1919, and generated unprecedented wealth. Sugar developed in large measure due to the early adoption of the railroad. U.S. and British capital financed the clearing of forests, the spread of the rail network and the opening of new markets overseas. The peak pre-Revolution harvest came in at 7.2 million tons in 1953. Indeed, throughout the twentieth century, the expression "Sugar is King" held meaning across an island the size of the state of Pennsylvania.

During the first decades of the Revolution, Cuba substituted the USSR and the Soviet bloc nations for the U.S. market. For a while, one ton of sugar was even exchanged for one ton of oil from the former Soviet nation. By the 1980s, however, such favorable terms of barter shifted as the forces of *glasnost* and *perestroika* began to dismantle the Mijail Gorbachov administration in Moscow. This shift in trade, coupled with lagging infrastructure maintenance in Cuba (rail lines, sugar mill processing plants, harvesting equipment), crippled sugar production. A bountiful harvest of 8.1 million tons of sugarcane in 1989 plummeted to 3.2 million tons in 1998 (Santamaría-García 2003). In 2002, more than half of the more than 150 mills were closed because it had become costlier to produce sugar in Cuba than to process it and sell it (Scarpaci et al. 2002). In 2009, less than two million tons were harvested. Shuttered mills have been turned into industrial museums or used as retraining centers for workers who relied on sugar for their livelihoods (Scarpaci and Portela 2009).

Sugar and its derivatives, however, have been important elements in the island's material and nonmaterial culture too. Many non-Cubans tend to find Cuban beverages and pastries sweeter than what they are used to. The development of the rum and molasses industries has spawned important export markets. Social and personal flattery in Cuban Spanish embrace derivatives of the word 'sweet' and includes variations of the Spanish world *dulce* in everyday, commercial and personal speech. The saying *A quién le amarga un dulce?* (Who does a sweet person make bitter?) carries special meaning in Cuba. The late Cuban singer Celia Cruz even developed a bit of a trademark by interspersing *azúcar, azúcar* in her melodies, a trait that remix rappers and reggaetón singers perpetuate in their music.

Perhaps the key by-product from sugar is the molasses that leads to Cuban rum, undoubtedly one of the most universally recognized world liquors. The fermented molasses is distilled and its liquid ferments are aged in oaken casks. Principal cocktails consumed on the island and abroad include the *Cuba libre* (cola and rum), *mojito* (sugar, lime, mint leaves, seltzer water, rum) and the daiquiri (lime juice, sugar, crushed ice and rum). Rum is to Cubans what vodka is to Russians, wine is to the French and beer is to Germans.

Like sugar, tobacco forms part of the world's imagination about the island's products and material culture, and is mired in a long history of monoculture and exports (Ortíz 1995). Cuban cigars became a mainstay in North American and European retail stores in the early twentieth century, and the so-called 'five-cent Cuban cigar' was a mainstay in U.S. and Canadian retailing. The island capitalizes on more than two centuries of tobacco growing, a craft brought to Cuba by Canary Island immigrants who settled in what is Pinar del Río Province in the western province of the island. Unlike sugar production, which relied heavily on African slaves, tobacco production was largely a 'white' man's form of agriculture. A unique combination of rich soil and a moderating climate helped to produce some of the world's finest cigar wrapper and leaf tobacco. Leading brands include Cohiba, Partagás, Romeo y Julieta, Montecristo, H. Upmann, Trinidad and others. Production of cigarettes has been enhanced in the past few decades with the support of Brazilian capital. Visitors to the island will remark often that for an island that promotes a world-class health-care system, cigarette smoking is pervasive though cigar smoking is decidedly less common.

To explore these ideas of cultural and iconic branding further, we turn to a discussion of the methods that form the empirical basis of this chapter.

METHODS

One of us (JLS) held 10 focus groups in Cuba between July 20 and July 28, 2010, for the purpose of gathering information on what Cuban consumers

Figure 4.2 Top 10 Cuban brands used in focus groups, 2010.

think about the leading Cuban brands that were identified by Morales (2009; Figure 4.2). Each focus group was conducted in Spanish and followed a protocol that was approved by an Institutional Review Board team at a U.S. university. A total of 84 participants, ranging in age from 18 to 72, participated in the sessions. They resided in five jurisdictions in the vicinities of the cities of Havana (Cerro, Lawton, Habana Vieja, Centro Habana, Plaza and Marianao) and three jurisdictions from the vicinity of Trinidad (Trinidad, Sancti Spiritus and Cienfuegos).

The principal investigator introduced himself as an independent researcher and professor of marketing who was interested in understanding Cubans' opinions about the most popular Cuban brands. Three guiding questions framed the audio-recorded sessions:

What do you like about the product?
What do you dislike about it?
Is there anything Cuban about this product?

Each session lasted 25 to 40 minutes. The principal investigator pledged anonymity to each participant. The sessions took place around kitchen tables in locals' homes. Participants were compensated $2 CUC, roughly the equivalent of 50 pesos (or 14 percent of the average monthly wage in Cuba), for sharing their opinions about the 10 most recognized Cuban products.

FINDINGS AND DISCUSSION

Transcribed and translated focus-group results produced nearly 24,000 words of text. A graphic representation of how frequently those words were used appears in a 'word cloud' where the size of the font is in proportion to how often the word was used (Goldenkoff 2004). Not surprisingly, the words like *really*, *Cuban*, *quality*, *brand* and *good* were used most often, given the nature of the question (and the propensity of informants to often speak as spokespersons for 'everyone' in their responses; see Figure 4.3).

A Chi-square value of 198.09, with 10 degrees of freedom (df), generated a p-value of 0001 (Table 4.4), allowing us to reject the null hypotheses that all categories were equally capturing iconic meaning. Data were calculated using a 6 x 3 matrix consisting of Popular, Montecristo, Alicia Alonso, Bucanero, Havana Club and Cubita as products, and marianismo/machismo for construct A, creativity/underdog for construct B and agricultural heritage legacy as construct C (see Table 4.3; see also Preacher 2001).

The keyword tabulations are partially summarized in the following, but with the important caveat that we exclude the discussion of price as a negative aspect (Table 4.5). Almost all informants complained about high prices. Limited purchasing power makes regular consumption of these goods an infrequent occurrence even though—as we shall see—some are consumed more often than others. In short, we take it as a 'given' that price is a major dislike about the top 10 Cuban brands.

Cuban consumers are outspoken about their product likes and dislikes. A half-century ban on advertising most products on television, print media and on radio (except for a single broadcast aimed largely at tourists) has not deterred Cubans' usage of consumer-related terms such as *price*, *quality*, *supply*, *demand*, *affordability*, *brand* and *expensive*. In the socialist settings of Eastern Europe and the former USSR, scarcity and product

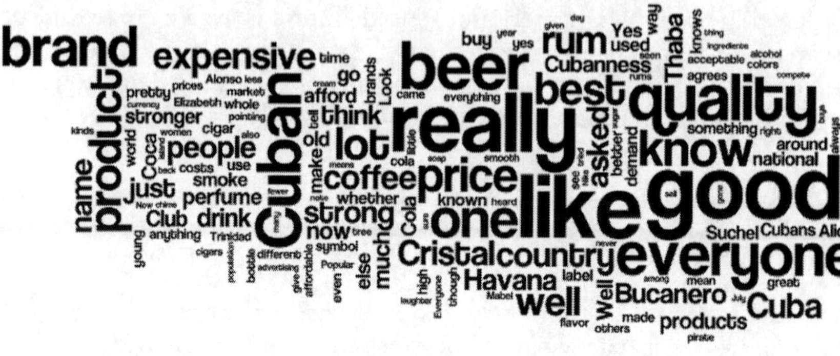

Figure 4.3 'Word cloud' representation of recorded focus-group interviews after transcription and translation. The font size of the words reflects how often the word was used. Graph calculated by algorithm at www.wordle.com on September 7, 2010.

Table 4.5 Key Aspects from Focus-Group Comments about Leading Cuban Brands

Positive Attributes	Negative Aspects	Iconic Potential
SUCHEL (soaps, shampoos, moisturizing creams)		
good quality product good cleaning agents pure ingrediants; no harsh additives	none	none
POPULAR (cigarettes)		
good, strong & affordable	increasingly expensive	Cuban flag colors on pack
TUKOLA (cola-flavored soft drink)		
Widely preferred over Coke A 'real' Cuban cola More sugar than cola taste	none	Cuban flag colors on can
CRISTAL		
a popular and tasty 'light' beer 'preferred beer' good with food	product tampering issues	national tree on label green can like lush island
BUCANERO (beer)		
strong beer good without food good Hatuey replacement competition for Cristal	none	pirates, indep. spirit, rebels ships on design sea part of Cuban history
MONTECRISTO (cigar) known worldwide synonymous with 'habanos'	no one had ever smoked one	reflects Cuban heritage
ALICIA ALONSO (perfume)		
most praised of all products good design attractive packaging	nothing	symbol of Cuban culture classy lady smart & feminine transcendental figure tropical fragrance
THABA (backpack manufacturer)		
widely used less expensive than foreign	poor quality fabric/ stitching competition from Cuba Tropical	widespread [not associated with education even though millions use them]
HAVANA CLUB (rum)		
universally recognized built on Bacardi' branding	other less-known brands just as good	name, Giraldia, recognized from adverstising

Continued

Table 4.5 Continued

Positive Attributes	Negative Aspects	Iconic Potential
recognized from advertising tourists like it (so it must be good)		"El Ron de Cuba" (e.g., calenders, caps, vests)
<u>**CUBITA**</u> (coffee)		
good quality name; map; traditional crop	bitter, scarce, not as good as Turquino, Serrano & other brands prohibitively expensive	

Note: The Giraldía is a symbol that is associated with Havana because it depicts the wife of Spanish explorer Ponce de León who set out for Florida from Havana, but never returned. The iron ornament adorns the top of a building in the city."The Rum of Cuba"

Calculated by the authors.

quality were often major consumer concerns regarding everyday goods (Stitziel 2005). In Cuba, though, informants have little apprehension about expressing their tastes and preferences for leading tobacco, alcohol and perfume brands that, theoretically, the socialist leadership would consider as objects of conspicuous consumption, vice, idle time (*ocio*) or nonessential consumer goods (Quirk 1993, 644; Frank 2006). Political and social analysts on the Left continue to dichotomize life in Cuba as self-sacrificing and noble, and characterize Cuban Americans as mired in mindless consumerism. However, our findings suggest otherwise. Note the following posting from the New Left blog about contemporary Cuba:

> Exiled Cuban 'dissidents' . . . [are] doing their best to lose themselves in conspicuous consumption and neo-conservatism, as far from the average Latin American citizen as practicable. (Ransom 2008)

That sentiment holds true for Cubans on the island, with the important caveat that their dreams of 'conspicuous' consumption are just that: aspirations.

Consumer desires to acquire affordable coffee, reasonably priced rum and quality personal hygiene products appear to fit reasonably within many consumer wants in the new millennium. A potential contradiction in this consumption scheme, however, is Raúl Castro's September 2010 announcement that new jobs in the small but promising self-employment sector may prove to be a Pandora's box. Since the decriminalization of the dollar in 1993, a two-tier class system has emerged. Those earning pesos from the state sector usually struggle to satisfy even basic material needs. Allowing more workers to labor in hard-currency or even peso-generated self-employment could widen the gap between the 'haves' and 'have-nots.'

In local parlance, it addresses the double-moral syndrome (*doble moral*). On the one hand, workers contribute to satisfying basic goals such as universal health care and education, public safety and the construction of a new and better society. Altruism drives such aspiration. On the other hand, individual sacrifices for personal consumption can potentially weaken the collective mission. Critics of capitalism have long denounced the individual-collective tension of the *doble moral*. As one scholar of Cuban consumption posits:

> Some Cubans worry that even the small measures already taken will create class tensions and increase resentment between those earning state salaries and those with access to dollars, given the new opportunities for conspicuous consumption. Raul Castro is clearly hoping that greater buying power will distract from any friction. (Weissert 2008)

Cuban consumers are unique because their broad range of brand knowledge has developed without countless media repetition. Of the cornerstones of marketing—placement, price and promotion—in-store demonstration and WOM advertising remain paramount in Cuba (Morales 2009). Moreover, Cubans express strong opinions about popular national brands. Like consumers worldwide, the role of reference groups (friends, families, seeing tourists use products) is important in shaping brand preferences.

Popular national products remain resource based—sugar, coffee, tobacco, rum—but there is also a place in the unassisted recall corners of the Cuban consumer's mind for consumer durables such as Suchel products (in this case, Bonabel moisturizing cream and Fres soap). To examine to

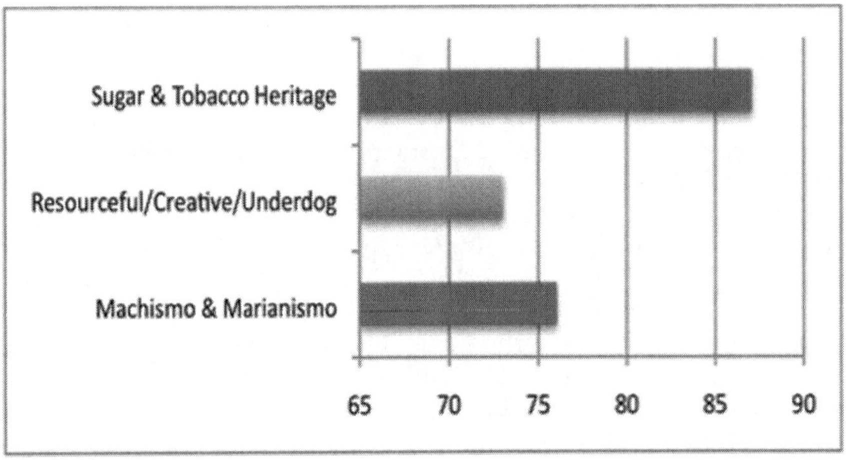

Figure 4.4 Frequency of mentions of iconic constructs for leading Cuban consumer goods, 2010 (n = 237).

what extent the contents (words) of the focus groups represented aspects of the national myths we outlined earlier, we tabulated all the focus groups according to references to the three myths (Figure 4.4).

The 237 references to a Cuban iconic value reveal four main findings. First, the 'sugar and tobacco' legacy registered more comments (87) than the second-place (marianismo-marianismo, 76) or third-place (creativity, 73) categories. This is not surprising in that half of the leading products (cola, coffee, tobacco and alcohol products) derive from these products in some measure.

Second, the Thaba backpack and Suchel soap and moisturizers failed to reveal any myth affiliations. Our suspicion was that the backpack might stand as a symbol of the Revolution's commitment to universal and free education, and thus reflects the 'creativity' dimension. We also thought that perhaps the soap products would tap into a sub-myth that Cubans wash often and that this local product might stand as a stalwart symbol of purity and cleanliness, and therefore reflect the marianismo myth.

A third finding is that focus-group members clearly differentiate between the 'light' Cristal versus the 'strong' Bucanero beers, even though just 0.4 percent alcohol content differentiated the two beers. However, in each focus group, several participants pointed to the green (lighter-looking) Cristal can and would read the label *suave* (smooth) aloud, as well as reading the *fuerte* (strong) word on the darker (heavier-looking) Bucanero can. Modifiers of Cristal's lightness included "easy to drink" (*fácil de tomar*), "goes well with food" (*va bien con la comida*), "the women prefer it" (*las mujeres la prefieren*) and "for relaxing" (*es para relajarse*). The heavier Bucanero pulled in the opposite direction: "good for parties" (buena para las fiestas), "it's more for men" (más bien para los hombres), "it's good for dancing" (*buena para bailar*) and even "it gets you drunk quicker" (*te emboracha más rápido*); all characterizations of extroverted machista behaviors.

Lastly, the product revealing the most national myth content was Alicia Alonso perfume, even though very few informants had used the fragrance. It registered strongly on the 'creativity' (64) and marianismo (24) myths.

Responses to the question, "Is there anything Cuban about this product?" produced uneven but interesting responses that build on the iconic branding potential (Figure 4.5). We had expected the less-expensive items as well as those with historical iconographic symbols embedded into them to score highly in this exercise. Brands with "Cuba" or "Havana," for instance, would certainly lend themselves to this association. Nonetheless, it was Alicia Alonso perfume that outscored the second-place product (Bucanero beer, with a salty-dog pirate and older vintage ship in the sea on its label) by a two-to-one margin.

Consumers tended to emphasize three reasons for the Cubanness of this living legend's marketing force. First, Alicia Alonso, the *prima ballerina de Cuba* (First Lady of ballet) for decades, represents artistic talent and creativity (Figure 4.5). At 90 years old, she is a living legend in ways that Fidel

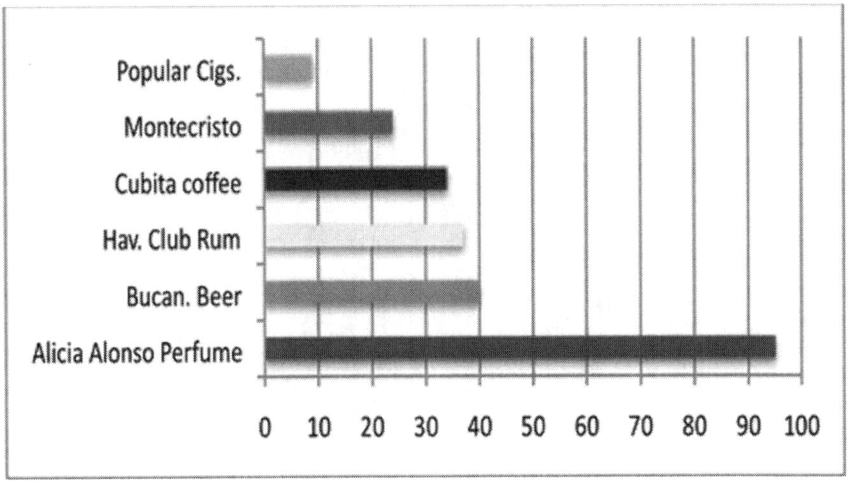

Figure 4.5 Frequency of iconic responses per leading Cuban consumer product, 2010.

Figure 4.6 Alicia Alonso. Prima ballerina of Cuba. Photograph courtesy Frank Alvarez.

Castro, Che Guevara and other revolutionary figures are not.[2] She exudes several national myths: overcoming adversity and using professional and feminine talent to bridge ideological gaps. Cuban national and regional ballet performances have reached all corners of the world, despite considerable opposition in some places to the Cuban Communist government. Cuban sensuality, it could be argued, is embodied in the product and the woman herself, at least in her youth (Figure 4.6). Like all perfumes and cologne, a sensory pleasure helps users detach from a mundane world.

Second, both the person and the product exude elegance and femininity. This national myth takes advantage of strong beliefs about the roles of men (machismo) and women (marianismo). To be sure, Cuban women's roles are much less passive and submissive than those found in parts of Central America, the Caribbean or South America. Whether through dance, art or music, Cubans value this sensuality.

Third, Alicia Alonso (the woman) represents how a resident of a small island can have an impact worldwide, or at least the potential to do so. This is also evident in Cuba's quest to excel in sport, spread the Revolution and serve as a cultural goodwill ambassador wherever it can. Such a strong national perception taps into the myth that the island can produce heroes, not in the context of the David-and-Goliath Cold War tensions between the *imperio yanqui* and the *isla*, but between someone who lived before and after the Revolution, and who excelled during both eras.

What is it about her background that taps into these national values? Working in classical dance in a country known for rumba, cha-cha-cha, son, salsa, reggaetón and related musical and dance forms, she and her husband, Fernando Alonso, perfected much of their early art form in New York City. Under the guidance of Richard Pleasant and Lucia Chase, Alicia Alonso performed dance with the Ballet Theater, which was founded in 1939. Her exposure to the Russian dance teachers and her tutelage under Enrico Zanfretta and Alexandra Fedorova deepened her knowledge of both classical and modern dance (Hechevarría 1998). While studying and performing with the School of American Ballet, she worked with George Balanchine, Anatole Vilzak and Anatole Oboukhoff. Nevertheless, it was her unprecedented interpretation of *Giselle* that cast her as the prima ballerina in the field of romantic ballet, as well as her accomplishments in contemporary and neoclassical ballets.

Cubans respond to the success of her career, which overcame physical and political obstacles. In her early 20s, she grappled with hypersensitivity to light, a problem that would plague her throughout her life and from which she would never fully recover. Even though she was successful in New York, she frequently returned to Cuba where, later, her dance company was renamed the Ballet de Cuba. *Dance Magazine* gave her their prestigious award in 1958, which was followed by the illustrious Pri Pavlova prize in 1966. Before the 1959 Revolution, she had done outreach with dance troupes in Puerto Rico, Mexico and elsewhere in Latin America (Simón 1996). In 1960, she returned to her homeland to direct the Ballet Nacional de Cuba. In this context, she has undergone both considerable praise and criticism; on the one hand, returning to her homeland was seen as an act of patriotism and representative of a desire to develop an art dear to her heart. On the other hand, some have criticized her for being tacitly complicit in not speaking out forcefully on civil and human rights transgressions by the Castro government, including the imprisonment of homosexuals, many of whom work in the performing arts (Lumsden 1996), and their 'reeducation' in the 1960s and 1970s (Terry 1981).

To what extent is there potential to develop iconic products within and outside Cuba that are conceptualized along the lines of cultural branding? The focus-group findings indicate the greatest potential rests in Alicia Alonso products and, to a lesser extent, Havana Club. Several informants identified the latter as 'the' rum of Cuba (as it states on the label) and only a few stated that they did not like it, or that substitute rums were widely available for less cost. Rum, of course, derives from the spring well of sugar as a powerful national myth. However, the closure of nearly half of the island's mills in the past decade, coupled with a saturated market of Caribbean rum, could make it difficult for this product to secure a position as an iconic brand. Moreover, Havana Club taps only into our "Sugar and Tobacco" myth category, whereas Alicia Alonso crosses and unites several myth categories.

Many cross-myth elements were expressed like this, one by a 33-year-old woman from Sancti Spiritus who said, "She, just like the product itself, represents the best of Cuba . . . what the typical Cuban woman aspires to in her own life: Success and elegance. And that matters as much here [in Cuba] as it does outside the island."[3] In this regard, Alicia Alonso is cultural icon, feminist and heroine. Her perfume is enhanced in many ways in consumers' minds that Havana Club is not; no transcendental figure is associated with Havana Club. Bacardí Rum is not sold on the island because the family went into exile (even though they supported Fidel Castro when he was a young rebel; see Gjelten 2008). From a marketing perspective, Alicia Alonso products are high-value-added goods that, on the export market, at least, could signify a chance to tap into the 'forbidden fruit' of Cuba, much like the allure the forbidden Cuban cigar holds in the minds of many non-Cubans. In short, Alicia Alonso holds the potential to become a national iconic brand provided consumer purchasing power allows for greater access to the product than the current economic setting allows. Internationally, the perfume could become an iconic brand if the image of a white, classical dancer could ever displace the image of the fiery mulatta as a national symbol and myth of the island of Cuba.

CONCLUSIONS

These findings hold promise for brand advertising in the near future when market forces and a broader array of consumer goods are both advertised and widely sold across the island. Such brand novelty will reflect the level to which Cuban consumers acquire experience about particular brands, both national and international ones (Alba and Hutchinson 1987). Because the island's consumers have familiarity with domestic and international brands, promotions (TV, radio, print, Internet, in-store) for these may be perceived as less appealing than the promotion of novel brands. Work by Nye et al. (2008) shows that differences in consumer knowledge will likely produce distinct processing goals for consumers exposed to ads sponsored by familiar brands, versus those who interpret and search for novel brands. The branding literature shows that consumers assess novel stimuli (in the case of free-market Cuba, this amounts to almost any advertising) in order to gain knowledge of the brand (Sujan 1985). Thus, future advertisements for unfamiliar brands (which will be many) may seem more novel and interesting to Cubans, but may also demand greater processing than in the pre-ad era, which has reigned for half a century. Alternatively, Cubans will probably engage in simpler processing and rely on more confirmation-based processing when exposed to marketing for familiar brands, such as the top 10 brands presented in this chapter.

This scenario will not likely happen until immediate needs for very basic consumer goods are satisfied; the pent-up demand for goods will be great. Companies introducing brands in Cuba may profit from comparative advertising, particularly when they are contrasted with those products that have a stronger or leading market positions. In the context of our work, this means Alicia Alonso will square off against Chanel, Havana Club will go head-to-head with Bacardí, Nike will encroach on Thaba and the many product lines of Budweiser (lime, dark, wheat) will have to deal with Cristal and Bucanero. Iyer (1988) argues that contrasting new brands with well-known ones may be interpreted by consumers as original; it may garner more notice and be seen as more revealing. This will exert new influences on Cuban tastes and preferences, and holds promise for exporting these Cuban brands. All of the top 10 island brands satisfy the basic criteria used in the brand naming industry: they are simple, easy to remember, hard to mispronounce, do not infringe on other trademarks and do not have negative connotations in English or other languages (Morris 2004, 7).

Our findings also build on Yadong and Peng's (1999) seminal work on competition and learning in emerging economies. One of their conclusions relevant to our work is the observation that a "country-specific experience is more important to performance in the early stage than in the late phase of overseas operations. This requires that multinational enterprises (MNEs) attach particular importance to experience during the early stages" (1999, 289). In the Cuban case, this may mean drawing on expertise in the large diaspora community, especially the heavy concentration in South Florida.

Because our sample comes from an island controlled by an authoritarian government, we have observed consumer behavior in unique, almost 'laboratory-like' conditions, assessing brand equity effects in the absence of conventional advertising. This allows us to revisit theories that prevailed in the 1980s that posited how advertising imposed an effects hierarchy that commenced when exposure to advertising culminated with a purchase. Brand managers in particular favored consumer purchase of the product to evaluate successful advertising campaigns (Franzen and Moriarty 2009). Later, the Awareness-Interest-Desire-Action (AIDA) model argued that the final *A* could result in nonpurchasing behavior; this includes seeking out more product information, visiting corporate websites or reviewing blog postings—all were desirable outcome measures (Grewal and Levy 2010). The Cuban case aligns with Ehrenberg (1997) and Castleberry and Ehrenberg (1990) in that users of a brand have a broader network of associations than nonusers. The potential for iconic branding within and beyond the island is considerable, and our cultural constructs will need to be further tested and refined in subsequent research.

5 Franchising as a Brand-Globalizing Process

The Case of *Casa del Habano*

Cuba has long been recognized as a stellar producer and exporter of premium cigars. The famous five-cent Cuban cigar was a mainstay of U.S. retailing in the early twentieth century. Even though Cuban cigars (and all other products/services) have been outlawed in the U.S. since President Kennedy's Proclamation 3447 (Embargo on All Trade with Cuba) in February 1962, the rest of the world pays dearly for these tobacco products. When the Cuban economy opened up greatly during the Special Period of the 1990s, then President Fidel Castro summarized the role of Cuban cigars in the nation's branding: "The cigar has made our country famous. It has given prestige to our country. Cuba is known among other things for the quality of its cigars" (Shanken 1994). The Cuban state-operated chain, *Casa del Habano*[1] (literally, the Havana Cigar House), is the mostly widely recognized Cuban franchise operating at a global scale. This is a joint-venture partnership between Spain and the Cuban government. Significantly, it is the largest franchise operated globally by the Cuban government.[2]

This chapter explains how the Cuban government promotes the core competencies of the *Casa del Habano*. Although it has only existed since 1990, by 2009 it was operating in more than 150 countries. Its first store in Cancún, Mexico, was a hastily assembled venture designed to sell Cuban cigars quickly to international tourists to capture hard currency for the ailing Cuban treasury. Since then, brand managers have emphasized a broader concept of service delivery to enhance brand equity among all things Cuban. This includes not only the promotion of the well-known top-shelf cigars (Cohiba, Montecristo, Romeo y Julieta, Hoyo de Monterrey), but also a wider price range of Cuban cigars, Cuban rums and coffees to accompany cigar smoking, and a well-trained staff to answer questions posed by the inquisitive novice smoker or the most sophisticated cigar connoisseur.

Casa lounges evoke the ultimate experience in cigar smoking: a relaxed setting, Cuban music, attractive personnel and other accoutrements conducive to the art of smoking. These lounges are rife with the elements of 'nation branding' that include venerable Cuban icons such as photographs of musicians in the Buena Vista Social Club, revolutionary Che Guevara, musician Benny Moré and U.S. writer and longtime Cuban resident Ernest

Hemingway. Cigar paraphernalia and related accoutrements include cigar cutters, ashtrays and stylish humidors crafted from precious tropical woods that display Cuban landscapes and symbols.[3] Casa hosts special VIP dinners throughout the franchise to herald the richness of authentic [4] Cuban-leaf cigars and to create both leisure and investment interest in the island. This chapter shows that the marketing strength of this successful franchise serves as a brand extension for other Cuban products and services. Whether selling watches in dollar stores in Havana or attracting foreign customers, Cuban branding strategies emphasize the role of in-store service and demonstration. This is a recurrent theme in Cuban business culture, about which little has been written. We situate the Cuban case within a brief historical account of franchising.

HISTORICAL OVERVIEW OF FRANCHISING

Firms have long studied successful ways to expose their brands to new markets. Successful brand development and expansion is one way to satisfy the needs of new customers as well as to increase brand value. One of the most successful ways of doing this is undoubtedly through franchising, which is an efficient and tested tool of brand management and company growth because it uses the benefits of comparative advantages to break down old paradigms about a product or service and establish new ones. Opening up marketing channels allows firms to position their brands in certain markets to reach the desired end user. Done across borders, franchising can be a powerful globalizing vehicle for brand managers. Paswan's (2004) study in an emerging market setting found that the relationship between accuracy of brand country of origin (COO) knowledge and COO image is key in a franchising context. Consumers' accuracy of brand COO knowledge is positively related to COO image. Inaccurate brand COO knowledge produces a confusing and somewhat negative image about COO. In the Cuban context, this means aligning the island's iconic images with the franchise's features.

In the late twentieth century and start of the present one, franchising had established itself squarely as part of the business model of many firms. Long gone are the days when Ray Kroc started specifying the philosophy and specifications of his McDonald's franchises, which today amount to some 31,000 establishments worldwide and employ 1.5 million workers (McDonald's 2010). Franchise retailers today understand the importance of product and service standardization. As a foreshadowing perhaps to what American retailing would look like, franchising retail sales accounted for 35 percent of all sales in the United States in 2000, 40 percent in 2010 and should reach 50 percent in short order. In turn, some 1,500 franchisors have developed 750,000 franchise businesses nationwide (AZFranchises 2010). Australian franchises generate some 14 percent of the national GDP and employ more than half a million workers. Brazil has seen explosive growth, too. The six years following 1995 saw franchise sales in Brazil increase from US$9 billion to US$21 billion, which prompted the national legislature to enact a franchise law (Law 8955) that is similar to other frameworks around the world. The law defines franchises as a:

> system whereby a franchisor licenses to the franchisee the right to use the trademark or patent, along with the right to distribute products or services on an exclusive or semi-exclusive basis and, possibly, also the right to use technology related to the establishment and management of a business or operating system developed or used by the franchisor, in exchange for direct or indirect compensation, without, however, being characterized as an employment relationship. (Amaral 2010)

Spain, a principal joint-venture partner in Cuba, is well known for its many small family businesses, but even there, franchising amounts to 8 percent of all retail sales. Licensing and franchising, mechanisms of globalization, are a clear example of the power of brands. Reliable data show that there are few countries that do not have at least one franchised establishment; even the North Korean capital provides the "Golden Arches" for visitors. It is unlikely, therefore, that franchising as a model of international business is likely to disappear. It offers a quick way for the host company (franchisor) to extend brands, trademarks, copyrights and other protected business assets to licensed arrangements (franchisees). Franchising has captured the imagination of business school professors, corporations and small solo-entrepreneurs as a viable method to capture market share.

The history of when franchising began has been dated to the time of the Crusades when Christian soldiers were given the authority to conquer and lay claim over territories, and to serve as representatives of European kingdoms. More recently, though, the mid-nineteenth-century operations of the Singer Sewing Company appear to denote the beginning of franchising during the Industrial Revolution. At that time, Singer used a franchise model to both expand sales and also to adapt to the customs and cultures in different regions of the world. Singer sewing stores operated as inroads not only for points-of-sale locations for Singer products, but it also allowed the firm to sell repair parts, sewing patterns and related items. Ford and General Motors followed in kind with local dealers to sell their cars, as did soda bottlers who aimed to reduce transportation costs by opening up regional bottling works (Dicken 2011). Hotels, car-repair shops, restaurants and other businesses repeated this franchising model. In most instances, many firms were able to expand their markets and bring their goods and services to faraway places.

In many ways, 1955 was a seminal year for franchising when the McDonald brothers and Ray Kroc (possibly the 'Father of Modern Franchising') creatively came up with the 'modern franchise.' Their model of selling hamburgers would become a template for other businesses across a wide array of sectors. This includes the transfer of technology, technical assistance and standardized production processes, just to name a few. As noted earlier, more than 30,000 restaurants have developed globally, and despite its linguistic and cultural variation (e.g., *Me encanta* campaigns directed towards Spanish consumers; respecting dietary customs in Hindu and Moslem nations) McDonald's has been both praised for business acumen while at the same criticized for eroding local food habits and culture (Appadurai 2004).

CONCEPT OF FRANCHISING

A variety of definitions can be found in the retailing and marketing literatures on the meaning of franchising. Cultural, economic, political and social factors within each nation shape and condition how the practice is defined and implemented. For our purposes, however, we will distill the essential ingredients for understanding the Cuban case under review. It is essentially a relationship between two economic organizations (public or private) that share a common goal. It may represent an advanced marketing tool for reciprocal international business, or it can serve as a tool for conquering new markets. In the Cuban case, as in other international marketing settings, franchising serves as a way to market brands, whether it entails fast food, tobacco, clothing or financial services. Franchising arrangements provide an overriding structure for brand promotion and development, but can also be tweaked to adjust for local conditions. Clear contractual guidelines outline the rights and responsibilities of all parties involved for a stipulated period of time. The etymology of the term captures these ideas; derived from the French word *francaise*, it means "free of all binding." Merriam-Webster's second entry for the term defines it thus: "the right or license granted to an individual or group to market a company's goods or services in a particular territory; also: a business granted such a right or license" (Merriam-Webster Online Dictionary 2010). The act of using a franchise—franchising—entails the following actors: franchisor (granting the act) and the franchisee (one who pays for a franchise).

CUBAN FRANCHISING: AN UNDERUTILIZED RESOURCE

The tobacco chain La Casa del Habano is the most successful national franchise operating overseas. This joint-venture firm is operated between the Cuban government and a British firm and is legally recognized as Habanos S.A. (S.A. stands for *sociedad anónima* or "incorporated"). Whereas most non-Cuban franchises operate globally under the conventional terms noted in the earlier part of this chapter, in Cuba foreign franchises function under "contracts of exclusivity" because of the dictates of the socialist government. These well-known brands with retail outlets in Cuba include Mango, United Colors of Benetton, Angie and Paul, Shark in the clothier sector, Pizza Nova in the food sector and Novotel and Meliá in the tourism sector, to name just a few.

The development of franchising by the Cuban government is woefully underdeveloped and remains a limiting factor in the growth of the island's economy. As we discussed at the outset of the chapter, franchising remains the most effective way to manage brands and export services and products of incomparable value. Its success has been proven in over 150 countries and on every continent. Nevertheless, it is unlikely in the short or medium term that the Cuban government will tap into franchising unless there is a radical political and economic shift that could remedy the weak and precarious economy. Reforms will be required in the Cuban state business sectors, joint ventures and the exports of products and services. Opportunities abound to exploit franchising, ranging from music, restaurants and leisure pursuits to hotel and travel services. For some, the much anticipated 'great opening'—a pronounced Cuban-style perestroika—has yet to take root on the island, and it has nothing to do with the Marxist-Leninist ideology that permeates the government. China, for instance, has more than 15,000 franchises. The Chinese success can be seen in the removal of some 300 million Chinese from abject poverty over the past three decades. A similar prospect awaits Cuba if only the political will existed. Two factors explain this situation.

One reason is that Cuba lacks any sort of international franchise organization that would help to promote, disseminate, organize and develop that business model. Decisions about trade and the economy remain vested with the central government. We believe this would be a first step in jump-starting an economy that has performed woefully these past 50 years. Franchising would afford hands-on training for the nascent business sector, permit the influx of much-needed foreign capital, create thousands of new jobs and accelerate and strengthen tourism and retailing. At the same time, it would revive businesses across the Cuban economy.

A second factor is that active franchise development in Cuba in the last five decades has been mostly confined to a single firm: the Casa del Habano. Founded only in 1990, it has been resoundingly successful. In 2011, 151 stores operated around the world and on every continent (except Antarctica). Two other Cuban franchises are also noteworthy, La Bodeguita del Medio and El Floridita, which operate in the restaurant sector; both names derive from popular tourist bars that Ernest Hemingway frequented and still operate in hard currency in Old Havana. These restaurant chains have not been as fully developed as the Casa del Habano chain because they lack a strong conceptual base for brand development as well as marketing strategies to fully exploit them inside and outside the island. Instead, their franchising has been the result of foreigners who have been keen on bringing them to their home countries rather than any coordinated business strategy on the part of the Cuban government.

DEVELOPING THE 'CASA DEL HABANO' FRANCHISE

Habanos S.A. has been able to promote a brand image and excellent service as a place to smoke Cuban cigars. It has been sensitive to the tastes of local cultures and consumers where it operates around the globe, and allows the franchisee to modify these cigar lounges to fit local conditions. The franchise also promotes cigar rollers such as José Cueto, who holds various Guinness records for rolling the largest cigars in the world. Cuban-leaf cigars create both leisure and investment interest in the island.

The success of the franchise depends on two key factors. The franchisor has been careful in mandating certain conditions throughout its retail stores. Businessmen and women have been carefully selected and trained about the nuances of cigar growing, processing, storing and smoking. Cigar lovers respond favorably to merchants who both share their passion for the product and who can share their expertise about a good that, perhaps because it has been banned in the largest consumer market in the world since 1961, or because it evokes an exotic and sensual allure globally, is conducive to creating a unique yet simple consumer experience.

Decriminalizing the dollar and other hard currencies in 1993 marked an important first step in showcasing the island's cigars to the international tourists who increasingly flocked to the island. Casa del Habano management bought into the notion that if a brand is going to base its image on the country of origin, then it had better have its own showcase at home. Because the local market lacks the purchasing power to acquire higher-end products, the firm targeted international tourists. It positioned itself within upper-end hotel retail galleries or along streets with lots of tourist foot traffic. Casa also promoted nontobacco products such as rum and coffee, beverages that are often consumed while smoking cigars.

Two types of retail stores emerged from this retail strategy. One was the same *Casa del Habano* and the other included specialized stores that sold cigars, rum, coffee and a variety of other products. Cigar paraphernalia such as cutters, humidors, ashtrays, lighters and other items contribute to the brand's uniqueness, not to mention the cachet among consumers who would return to their homelands with gifts of Cuban cigars and talk about the luxurious settings of this cigar parlor. Foreign media such as *Cigar Aficionado* carried interviews with Fidel Castro and the Cuban government, and *Casa del Habano* would promote annual dinners that would raffle off finely crafted humidors to the highest bidder; the humidors often carried the signature of Fidel Castro on the inside. In 1997, the Wim Winders production of the nearly US$23 million grossing film, *Buena Vista Social Club*, gave millions an up close view of life on the island (The Numbers 2011). It helped launch international careers for Cuban musicians Compay Segundo, Ibrahim Ferrer, Rubén González, Omara Portuondo and others. During that same decade and into the new millennium, photographs of

LA CASA DEL HABANO

Figure 5.1 *Casa del Habano* logo.

international celebrities smoking cigars, vacationing in Cuba or attending film festivals, including Arnold Schwarzenegger, Danny DeVito, Naomi Campbell, Robert Duvall, Robert De Niro and others, circulated in tabloids and other print media. In the U.S., cultural and educational travel

Table 5.1 Service Assessment and Customer Satisfaction Levels, *Casa del Habano*, 2004

Service Indicators	Very good (VG)	Good (G)	VG+G combined	Fair	Bad (B)	Very Bad	Total	Satisfaction levels, 1-5
Employees Attention & time devoted to customer	62.5%	27.2%	89.7%	6.5%	0.8%	0.3%	100%	4.56
Time it took to pay	66.2%	29.3%	95.5%	3.9%	0.5	0	100%	4.61
Customer treatment	71.2%	24.6%	95.8%	3.7%	0.5%	0	100%	4.66
Employees' demeanor & appearance	76.6%	22.8%	99.4	0.5%	0		99.9%	4.76
Technical knowledge of products	56.4%	35.7%	92.1%	7.2%	0.7%	0	100%	4.48
Comfortable setting for buying	69.7%	25.8%	95.5%	4.2%	0.3%	0	100%	4.65
Store cleanliness	82.2%	17.3%	99.5%	0.5%	0	0	100%	4.82
Overall evaluation of visit	73.2%	26.3%		0.5%	0	0	100%	4.73
Total	70.1%	26.1%	96.2%	3.4%	0.3%	0	99.9%	4.65

Note: Likert scale responses ranged from very poor (1) to very good (5). Differences in total percentages due to rounding.

rose from just a few thousand in the early 1990s to above 150,000 in 2004, making it the fifth largest nation sending tourists to Cuba. All these factors combined to create a huge buzz about all things Cuban, especially cigars.

A second type of retailing in Cuba developed to promote cigars, albeit in less luxurious settings than *Casa del Habano*. In this setting, Casa del Habano S.A. franchised small kiosks and stands within Cuban-run stores, gift shops and hotels to sell cigars in hard currency. Stores such as Caracol, Universo, Gran Caribe, Cubalse, Habaguanex, Palco and Grupo Gaviota extended the brand to tourists who frequented these establishments. One study of stores conducted in 2004 by Morales and Hernández found that well-designed window displays played a key role in promoting the *Casa's* logo (Figure 5.1) and, in turn, drove foot traffic and sales through those retail outlets.

Table 5.1 shows the weighted qualitative analysis by Universo services marketing features among selected outlets in Havana with a *Casa del Habano* store. It measures the application of a metric of standards on the design, staffing, supplying and operation of the cigar stores, coupled with sales data. The figure shows that Universo Partagás, 5th and 16th and Palco Club Habana performed the best. It is important to note that their locations are adjacent to a popular rice-and-beans and fried chicken restaurant, and the Havana Convention Center, respectively; these were important retail attributes of these high-volume cigar stores.

BENCHMARKING *CASA DEL HABANO* SERVICE MARKETING

Customer satisfaction, cigar quality and smoking accessories (cutters, lighters, matches, humidors, travel packs) shape consumer preferences in the Casa lounges. A pioneer study of 382 customers (all of them foreigners) in 2004 provides baseline service marketing measures in the early years of the franchise's expansion. On average, 19 out of 20 (96.2 percent) customers assessed the eight indicators in the survey as either 'very good' or 'good' (Table 5.2). *Casa del Habano* facilities received their highest evaluation for the cleanliness of the stores but their least stellar (though overall, quite high) service indicator was 'employees' technical knowledge of the product.' The *Casa del Habano* with highest sales figures (US$3 million at the Partagás store) was the only retail outlet located adjacent to the cigar factory, suggesting that customers enjoy seeing the cigar being made, asking rollers questions about the product and interacting with the production system. The customer service findings in Table 5.2 also suggest that the serious cigar smokers come to these stores armed with considerable knowledge about cigars and their accessories. Such information includes ring size, third-party reviews in cigar magazines, cigar-wrapper attributes and comparable prices of

Table 5.2 Customer Assessment of Havana *Casa del Habano* Service Features, 2004

Retail Chain	Casa del Habano Name	Evaluation/ observation	Reputation	Product Quality	Availability	Technical Help	Sales Personnel	Weighted Evaluation	Sales revenue 2003 $US
Universo	Partagás	G	E	E	VG	E	E	27/30	$3,046,700
Universo	Marina Hemingway	F	G	F	G	G	G	16/30	$366,400
Universo	Meliá Habana	E	G	E	VG	VG	VG	25/30	$500,800
Caralco	Palacio Artesenía	F	F	F	VG	VG	VG	18/30	$720,200
Caralco	Hotel Nacional	G	G	VG	VG	G	VG	21/30	$603,200
Cubalse	5th & 16th	E	VG	E	VG	VG	E	27/30	$1,200,000
Palco	Club Habana	E	VG	E	VG	VG	E	27/30	$825,000
Habaguanex	Conde Villa	F	F	F	G	G	F	13/30	$350,000

Source: Morales and Hernández (2004). Note: E=excellent, (5); VG=verygood (4); G=good (3); F=fair (2); P=poor (1).

similar products in third countries (Canada, EU nations, Mexico) and Cuban-seed products developed in the Dominican Republic, Honduras and Nicaragua (Shanken 1994).

The *Casa del Habano* also offers a comparative advantage over other outlets for Cuban cigars (both legal and illegal): authenticity. It is widely known that Cuban cigars—particularly the iconic Cohiba brand with its easy-to-replicate yellow-and-black paper cigar rings—are among the most widely counterfeited cigars in the world (Stubbs 2000). We authors have even been to hotels and resort cigar shops in upscale settings in Europe, Canada, Mexico and other parts of Latin America where we have seen counterfeited Cuban cigars being sold for hundreds of dollars a box. In the early 2000s, the Cuban cigar industry developed a hologram seal of authenticity that has gone a long way to thwart the selling of counterfeited and sealed boxes. Nevertheless, loose (single) cigars can be sold as the legitimate item to nonsavvy smokers, many of whom just want to purchase a few cigars for friends back home. The *Casa del Habano* guarantees that only authentic products are sold. Increasingly, consumer feedback on the quality of the franchise will enhance brand recognition and loyalty. One New York traveler in Playa del Carmen, Mexico, had this to say about his experience in a *Casa del Habano* shop in 2010.

> I stayed for a week at a resort in Akumal and made a day trip to Playa del Carmen. Unfortunately, I didn't have time to get to LCDH [La Casa del Habano] on that day, but emailed Alejandro [an LCDH employee] who was more than willing to deliver my order to me on the resort. He made a few excellent suggestions about cigars and could not have been more spot on with the ones he recommended. When I want to buy a Cuban cigar, and am willing to spend the money for it, I want to be certain that I'm buying the real thing and not one of the hundreds of counterfeits that street vendors (and resorts) are hawking. Case in point—the "same" cigars that were selling for $35 at my resort (which a fellow traveler bought only to find it was a knock-off) Alejandro had for almost half the price—and I was certain it was the real thing. If you are a cigar smoker, or are buying for one, don't even bother with the street vendors, hotels, or duty free shops. Go directly to La Casa del Habano (or email Alejandro) and spend your money there. (Trip Advisor 2010)

Independent customer feedback such as this will corroborate product quality over time.

The global distribution of Cuba's largest franchise reaches all corners of the world market (Figure 5.2). Generally, the 2011 spatial distribution of *Casa del Habano* franchises corresponds to 'pockets' of high-end consumers, and concentrates on the capital cities of these nations, or important secondary cities and tourist poles (Playa del Carmen and Cancún in Mexico). Western Europe dominates with 38 stores, with Germany leading the region with eight stores.

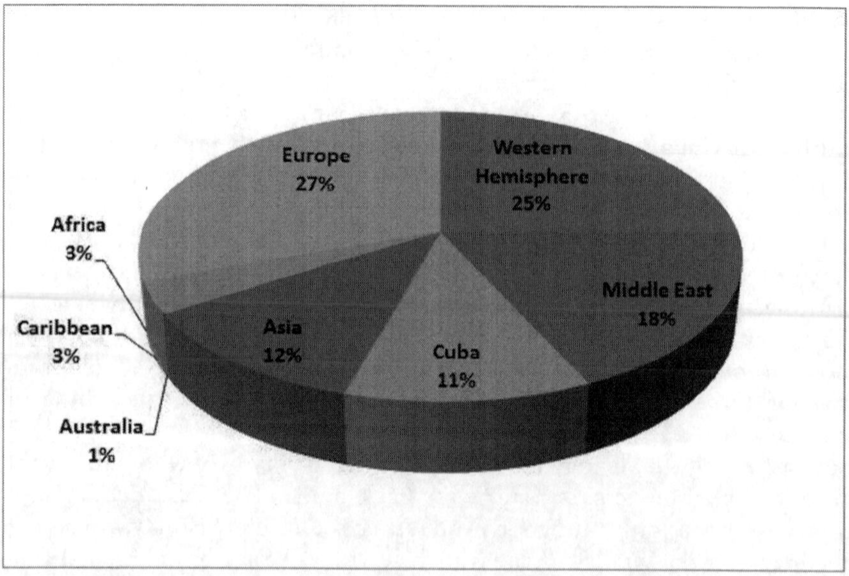

Figure 5.2 Number of Habanos S.A. franchises by region, 2010. Calculated by the authors.

Bulgaria has three stores, whereas the UK has only one in London. Europe is followed by the Western Hemisphere (excluding Cuba and Mexico) with 26, the Middle East with 24 and Cuba and Mexico with 13 stores each. This franchising strategy will be expanded with the recent acquisition by Imperial Tobacco of *Casa del Habano* as a joint-venture operation.

IMPERIAL TOBACCO

A new franchising model developed when the British consortium Imperial Tobacco decided to proactively anticipate conquering a large cigar market in the future: the United States of America. Cubatabaco, along with its joint venture Habanos S.A.—a corporation comprised in equal parts between the Cuban government and Altadis—is developing a strategy in light of economic reforms announced in Cuba in late 2010.

Habanos S.A. had captured 80 percent of the world market share in premium tobacco sales, excluding the United States (because Cuban cigars cannot be sold there). Sales figures for 2010 were $382 million (Figure 5.3). The company's 151 extravagant cigar lounges, La *Casa del Habano*, were joined by a new franchise, Cohíba Atmosphere Franchise, which opened six cigar lounges globally in 2010.

The success of *Casa del Habano* relies on three marketing strategies: brand structure, distribution scheme and franchise concepts.

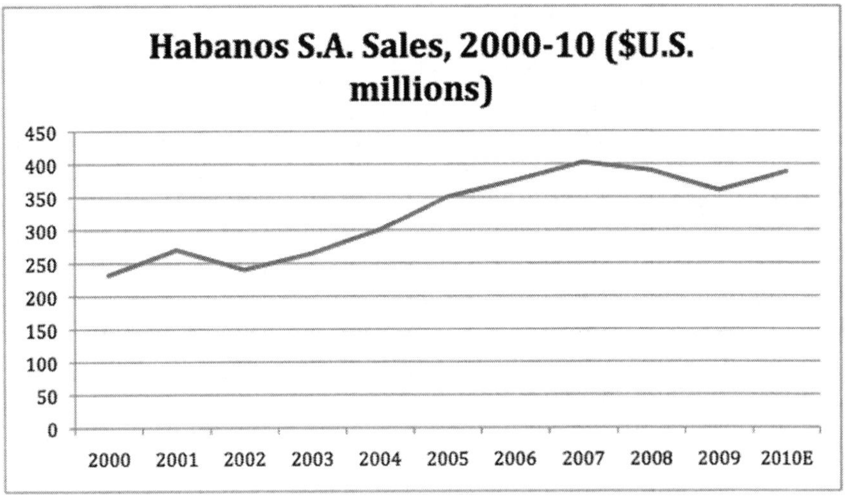

Figure 5.3 Habanos S.A. sales, 2000–2010.
Source: The Havana Consulting Group.

BRAND STRUCTURE

Brand structure permits the company to segment its markets and to position its brands. Every *Casa del Habano* employs the same brand structure. Two key elements guide the management and positioning strategies of each brand. Figure 5.4 presents the categories in which Cohiba cigars are situated. Product location across categories is expressed by the quality of the cigar's components: the aging of the tobacco leaves, the kind of packaging (box, tube type—glass, cardboard or cellophane) and humidor type (which consists of different materials). A second element depends on the type of vitola (length and diameter or ring size) for each cigar.

These brand features are not fixed, but rather fluctuate according to trends in the world market. New cigar categories and vitolas emerge according to the developing tastes of cigar smokers. The vertical axis in Figure 5.4 depicts the level of quality of the components and price for various brand structures. A cigar's classification can rise according to the quality of its ingredients. High-quality cigars, for instance, enlist more aged and cured tobacco leaf; the greater the aging, the more striking the wrapper luster appears in the Cohiba cigar packaging.

Each product category from the Siglo Series and higher brings a distinction and quality that surpasses the previous category and, accordingly, commands a higher price. Higher prices, in turn, limit access within each category by different segments of the cigar-smoking population. Beyond segmenting the marketing and positioning the brand, the classification process illustrated in Figure 5.4 enables marketers to narrow different market segments further. As cigar smokers gain more knowledge about taste and price, they are likely to switch categories and become more refined in their tastes and habits. Such patterning of consumer behavior permits Habanos S.A. to retain customer loyalty among clients who can translate their desires into cigar purchases and, gradually, ascend from one category to another. A long-standing and similar marketing strategy exists for capturing wine drinkers (Vaynerchuk 2010).

A similar process occurs along the x-axis of Figure 5.4. Some cigar brands have more vitolas than others. Montecristo, for instance, has a great number of vitolas and not all of them are currently on sale in the retail market. Decisions to release different lines of cigars depend on tastes and styles that are fashionable. For example, between 2007 and 2010, long and thin cigars had become less stylish, whereas short and thicker styles (*robustos*) had become more fashionable.

PRICE RANGES PER BOX ($USD)	CATEGORIES
$ 1,500.00	GRAN RESERVA
$ 1,200.00	RESERVA
$ 850.00	SPECIAL SERIES
$ 500.00	LIMITED EDITIONS
$ 230.00	SIGLO SERIES
$130.00	CLASSICS or STANDARD

Figure 5.4 Cigar brand structure.

Source: Data calculated by the authors based on fieldwork and interviews with managers and specialists at Habanos S.A. in Cuba and several franchises. Prices reflect market trends in May 2011.

Explanations for this change in cigar preferences may be that antismoking laws around the world mean less time for enjoying a smoke, which, in turn, gives robustos (and even shorter, more stout cigars, called nubs) an advantage over the longer, thinner cigars. Difficult economic times also limit the amount of leisure time (and disposable income) for enjoying a good smoke. Demand for long and thin cigars hinges on aspects of the macro-marketing environment. Cigar types that have become less popular can be withdrawn from the market and 'put to sleep' in specialized humidors. Out-of-style cigars are easily conserved up to 10 years until smokers' tastes change.

This brand structure allows each brand to retain its flavor, protect well-positioned standards and safeguard unique features. A quality-control network starts at the planting and harvesting stage, continues into the processing and rolling of the cigar and remains until the retailing phase.

The core competency of Habanos S.A. is making sure that this brand structure is carried out uniformly and across product categories. Communication strategies promote and protect all *habanos* as an original product with unique roots that allow clients anywhere in the world to identify any Cuban brand by its origin. To the cigar smoker, this means separating cigars made from Cuban seed (grown in the Dominican Republic, Honduras or Nicaragua, for example) from cigars made in Cuba.

BRAND DISTRIBUTION AND POSITIONING STRATEGIES

Several state-owned chain retail stores within Cuba sell Cuban cigars: Caracol S.A., Gaviota, CIMEX, Habaguanex S.A. and Grupo Palco. Each chain uses a network of sales outlets in each Cuban province, and each store is classified according to its particular features. A network of exclusive international

Figure 5.5 Habanos S.A. international distribution network.
Source: Designed by The Havana Consulting Group based on fieldwork and interviews with managers and specialists at Habanos S.A. and its website.

distributors is legally permitted to sell all brands of *habanos* within their respective sales area (Figure 5.5). The company also uses purchase-sale agreements for markets outside those assigned to exclusive distributors.

The company operates a well-defined marketing and distribution network (Figure 5.5). It supplies cigars to its distributors, who then distribute them to exclusive retailers and franchises in their sales districts. This latter group receives the products with a greater profit margin (the difference between the purchase and sales prices, less expenses and taxes).

LA CASA DEL HABANO

As noted earlier, Casa del Habano was the first Cuban franchise and is relatively new. It opened in Cancún, Mexico, as a single store in 1990 and was launched as a franchise in 1994. Selecting Cancún was strategically important because it is one of the primary tourist destinations for U.S. consumers. In addition, including all the brands of *habanos* under a single roof was paramount in positioning the Casa del Habano as a franchise and a brand. The Casa del Habano is a registered brand that serves as a large umbrella under which all Habanos S.A. cigars and their segments exist

Figure 5.6 La Casa del Habano brand structure.
Source: Designed by The Havana Consulting Group based on interviews with managers and specialists at Habanos S.A.

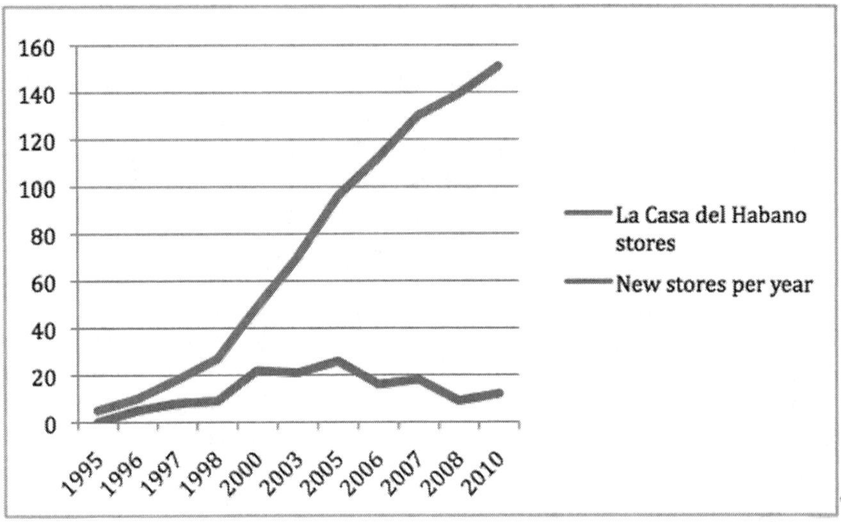

Figure 5.7 *La Casa del Habano* franchises, 1995–2010.
Source: Habanos S.A., calculated by The Havana Consulting Group.

At the apex of this well-defined pyramid are the Global Brands, where the emblematic Cohiba cigar is positioned, along with Montecristo, Romeo y Julieta, Partagás, Hoyos de Monterrey and H. Upmann. These cigars are arguably the icons of the cigar market.

Tier two contains the multi-local brands and includes Bolívar, Punch, Vegas Robaina, José Gerner, Quintero, Fonseca and others.

Niche brands occupy the third-tier spot and consist of Cuaba, Trinidad and San Cristóbal de La Habana.

Eighteen local brands form the bottom of the pyramid, of which the better-known cigars are Gloria Cubana, Guantanamera and Flor de Cano. In all, the pyramid houses 27 active brands; that is, brands that are still being produced and currently sold in various markets. In 2010, the company turned 15 years old and had opened 151 franchises (Figure 5.7).

THE NEW FRANCHISE: COHIBA ATMOSPHERE

This new cigar-lounge franchise is a permanent cigar showcase that goes beyond the cigar offerings of the Casa del Habano. Cohiba Atmosphere naturally surrounds the cigar aficionado with Cohiba brands. It is a marketing touch point for the Cohiba brand, arguably the most celebrated cigar in the world.

Cohiba Atmosphere uses six broad concepts to promote the attributes and values of the Cohiba brand and its many accessories. The seven concepts are maximum quality, promotion, pairing with food and wine, careful presentation, variety and mixtures in restaurants, corporate dinners (with global projection and/or global reach) and Habanos Sommelier Space, which in early 2011 was in demo and test mode.

Cohiba Atmosphere is a place where clients have access to all Cohiba products as well as cigar accessories. These accessories include books, magazines, clothing, museum pieces and other exclusive merchandise to create the concept of the "the Cigar Mecca" on a global scale. Unlike La Casa del Habano, the franchise is not a cigar retail store per se. Rather, it is a combination restaurant, private club and bar with a smoking area—all rolled into a single space. Each establishment is authorized and licensed by Habanos S.A. to use the Cohiba Atmosphere brand. Such authorization gives the locals access to a system of Cohiba Atmosphere services that are adapted to each country. The licensee pays an annual royalty to Habanos S.A. according to gross sales and as specified by a five-year contract. As of early 2011, Cohiba Atmosphere operated in Tokyo, Beijing, Hong Kong, Buenos Aires, Cancún and Prague.

THE UNITED STATES: THE NEXT CHALLENGE

Two unanswered questions loom over the horizon of Imperial Tobacco: the restructuring of the Cuban economy and the time when restrictions on travel by U.S. citizens are eliminated. These would appear to be key premises in the strategy to conquer the U.S. market.

The first point stems from an aggressive investment in tourism that the Cuban government is carrying out between 2010 and 2015. The goal is to increase by 50 percent the hotel capacity of 54,000 rooms in the island's key tourist poles. Investment will also be directed towards the construction of 16 golf courses and 11 marinas (Figure 5.8) for high-end tourism. Some 25,000 new rooms will be added to the nation's hotel capacity.

Habanos S.A. could increase the number of its La Casa del Habano franchises by at least 16 units throughout the island in just a few years. New golf courses and marinas would enhance their glamour appeal by having these attractive cigar franchises on their properties.

A second element is a preamble to a frontal attack by the company on the U.S. market the moment the trade embargo against Cuba is rescinded. Loosening travel restrictions for U.S. citizens could generate between $50 and $100 million of revenue for the company in just the first year. Perhaps as many as one million tourists will cross the Florida Straits in the first year of relaxed travel regulations. Over the first five years, there is good reason to believe this figure would only rise.

Both conditions are the basis for increasing access to the U.S. market. A wave of U.S. tourists across Cuba would allow Habanos S.A. to delight visitors with the 'forbidden fruit' (the Cuban cigar); an iconic symbol that

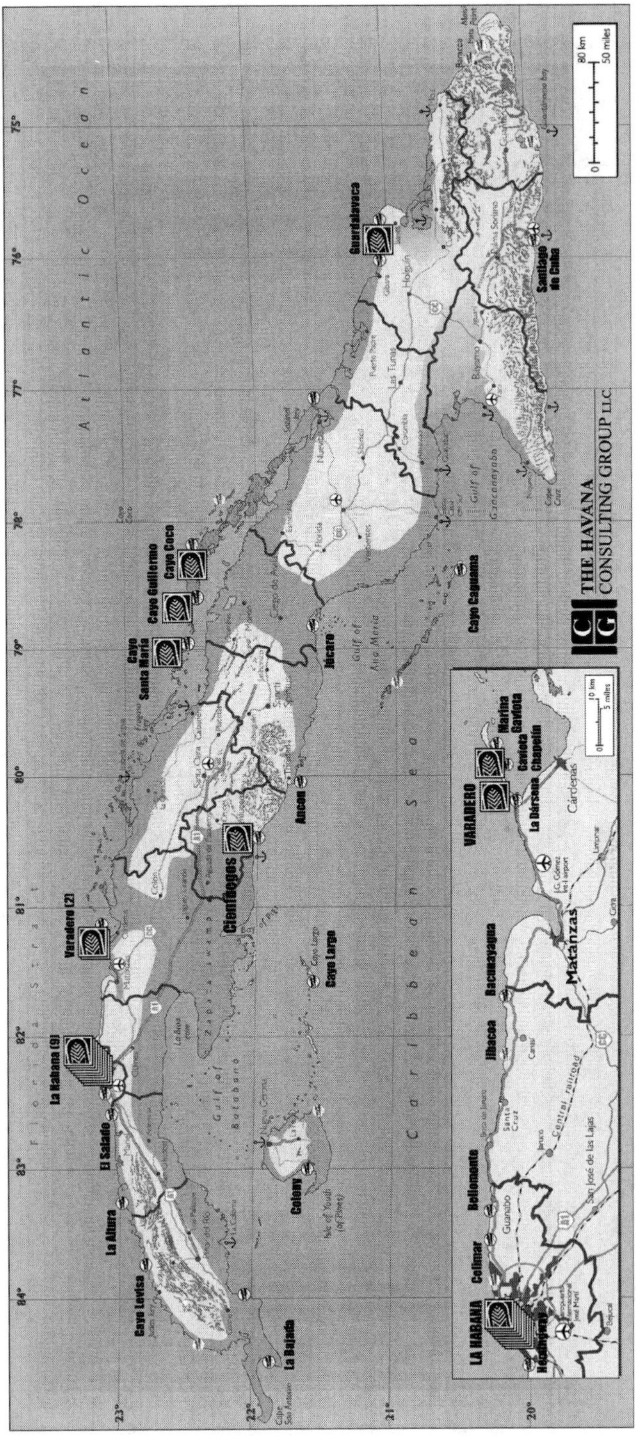

Figure 5.8 Distribution and features of Cuban marinas and *Casa del Habano*. Map courtesy of Armando Portela, The Havana Consulting Group.

Table 5.3 Conservative Demand Forecast for *Casa del Habano* in the United States and Puerto Rico within First Year of Lifting Trade Embargo

Categories	Top 'n' in USA	20% potential	Comments	Sources (Accessed between May 12-18, 2011)
Golf courses	100	20	Cigar smoking long associated with the sport	Golflink http://www.golflink.com/top-golf-courses/
Night clubs, bars & lounges	100	20	Special ventilated rooms make this a natural co-locational strategy	The Best in Bar Management http://www.nightclub.com/bar-management/the-top-100
Best restaurants	200	20	Special ventilated rooms make this a natural co-locational strategy	Zagat's Survey http://www.usatoday.com/travel/zagat-hotels.htm
Top 10 amusement parks	10	2	Special ventilated rooms make this a natural co-locational strategy	USA Travel Guide http://www.wrsol.com/usatravelguide/2009/05/10bestamusementparksinamerica/
Largest professional baseball parks with >30,000 seats	30	6	Special ventilated rooms make this a natural co-locational strategy	http://en.wikipedia.org/wiki/List_of_Major_League_Baseball_stadiums
National Football League Stadiums	16	3	Special ventilated rooms make this a natural co-locational strategy	Stadiums of Professional Football http://www.stadiumsofprofootball.com/nfc.htm
American Football League Stadiums	16	3	Special ventilated rooms make this a natural co-locational strategy	Stadiums of Professional Football http://www.stadiumsofprofootball.com/afc.htm
Top Cigar Smoking Cities 2011	3	6	Includes Miami, Las Vegas and Miami (assuming 2 per city independent of population size added below)	About Cigars http://cigars.about.com/od/cultureofcigars/a/cigarcities.htm

Continued

Table 5.3 Continued

New York-Northern New Jersey-Long Island, NY-NJ-PA	18	3	Roughly 18 million residents; Assumes 1 C.H. per million	U.S. Census http://www.census.gov/prod/cen2010/briefs/c2010br-01.pdf
Los Angeles-Long Beach-Santa Ana, CA	12	2	Roughly 12 million residents; Assumes 1. C.H. per million	U.S. Census http://www.census.gov/prod/cen2010/briefs/c2010br-01.pdf
Chicago-Joliet-Naperville, IL-IN-WI	9	2	Roughly 9 million residents; assumes 1 C.H. per million	U.S. Census http://www.census.gov/prod/cen2010/briefs/c2010br-01.pdf
Dallas-Fort Worth-Arlington, TX	5	1	Roughly 5 million residents, assumes 1 C.H. per million	U.S. Census http://www.census.gov/prod/cen2010/briefs/c2010br-01.pdf
Philadelphia-Camden-Wilmington, PA-NJ-DE-MD	5	1	Roughly 5.6 million residents; assumes 1. C.H. per million	U.S. Census http://www.census.gov/prod/cen2010/briefs/c2010br-01.pdf
Houston-Sugar Land-Baytown, TX	5	1	Roughly 4.7 million residents; assumes 1 C.H. per million	U.S. Census http://www.census.gov/prod/cen2010/briefs/c2010br-01.pdf
Washington-Arlington-Alexandria, DC-VA-MD-WV	5	1	Roughly 4.8 million residents; assumes 1 C.H. per million	U.S. Census http://www.census.gov/prod/cen2010/briefs/c2010br-01.pdf
Miami-Fort Lauderdale-Pompano Beach, FL	5	1	Roughly 5 million residents; assumes 1 C.H. per million in addition to its 'cigar smoking' propensity noted above	U.S. Census http://www.census.gov/prod/cen2010/briefs/c2010br-01.pdf
Atlanta-Sandy Springs-Marietta, GA	4	1	Roughly 4.2 million residents; assumes 1 C.H. per million	U.S. Census http://www.census.gov/prod/cen2010/briefs/c2010br-01.pdf

Continued

Table 5.3 Continued

Boston-Cambridge-Quincy, MA-NH	4	1	Roughly 4 million residents; assumes 1 C.H. per million	U.S. Census http://www.census.gov/prod/cen2010/briefs/c2010br-01.pdf
Totals	577 potential sites	94	Remarks: Likely openings within 1 year. Assumes a conservative adoption rate based on population size, type of establishment, sporting complexes, and reputation as a cigar=friendly city. See note below.	

Note: C.H. stands for *Casa del Habano*. Variables considered include population size, recreational and leisure establishments affiliated with cigar smoking, and city reputation as cigar-friendly setting. Estimates are deemed conservative as they do not take into account (1) cities with populations less than 1 million. Cities such as New York, Los Angeles, Chicago, Las Vegas, and Miami will likely have more than projected numbers noted above, (2) restaurant calculations based only on top 200, (3) excludes up-scale shopping centers or thematic shopping malls as well as unique locations such as waterfront retailing, horse race tracks, NASCAR, concert venues, ski-resorts, and other seasonal venues.
Source: Calculated by The Havana Consulting Group

has prevailed for half a century. If current (2011) prohibitions about not bringing anything back to the U.S. from Cuba prevail, there would be even more reason for U.S. cigar smokers to enjoy these Cuban cigar lounges while on the island. Promoting a "get-it-while-you-can" marketing strategy would serve Casa well.

How many Casa del Habano franchises might be built in the U.S. market in the first year following the end of the embargo? If the U.S. economy continues to improve, we estimate that about 100 franchises would open in the 50 states and Puerto Rico within the first year (Table 5.3), and as many as 250 within five years. These Casas, with sales of cigars, smoking paraphernalia (humidors, ashtrays, cigar cutters, magazines, merchandise) and cigar-smoking accoutrements (rum and alcohol, coffee and fine-dining offerings) could easily generate a $1 billion in the first year. Advertising would create a mélange of consumer images, such as Ruth's Chris Steak House or Smith and Wollensky's meets Buena Vista Social Club, Benny Moré, cha-cha-cha and Ernest Hemingway and Celia Cruz under a single roof. Adapting to local public-smoking laws could easily be remedied with ventilation systems. Habanos S.A. will likely rely on these sensual and symbolic associations with its coveted brands.

A Cuban cigar frenzy could break all preconceptions about how to savor a cigar. However, it might also prove challenging for Habanos S.A. to safeguard its obligations with the existing 151 franchisees. New York, Las Vegas, Los Angeles, Chicago, Boston and Miami could become a prime market for cigar lovers. Colocating Casa del Habano near professional football, baseball, hockey, basketball, theater and entertainment complexes would be a strategic colocational strategy. We envision limited editions of

Habanos S.A. cigar brands never before imagined will become the new, glamorous hotspots in these emblematic and spectacular cities. Super Bowl, FIFA World Cup, World Series, NASCAR and other special events would merit special limited editions (Morales and Scarpaci 2011a).

The problem with this scenario would be satisfying both old and new demand. Will production increase through new plantings in Cuba or by rolling more cigars? Are conditions apt for that? Alternatively, will the price of Cuban cigars simply rise to keep pace with demand? No doubt, this would be a rather pleasant challenge for Imperial Tobacco and its new franchise, Habanos S.A.

CONCLUSIONS

The ability of franchises to promote and open new markets is a time-tested retailing practice. Cuba's endowment of emblematic and iconic symbols includes, among other aspects of *cubanidad* identified in this book, the family of *habanos*. Despite the U.S. trade embargo that has been in effect since 1961, *Casa del Habano* has been able to open hundreds of stores outside the island. Casas contain a built-in brand structure that clusters tobacco quality with price. Much like the pricing of wine, cigar pricing and brand structure allow users to gradually evolve through more expensive products as tastes and disposable incomes rise. In just two decades, the franchise has coped with issues of counterfeit cigars by promoting its logo and using hologram-labeled boxes to prevent forgery and recycling of used boxes. Future growth in the U.S. market will likely adopt a colocational strategy aimed at U.S. cities, especially near sporting and entertainment complexes. Its success in a country just 90 miles north of the island may serve as a harbinger of future Cuban franchises.

6 Brand Development without Mass Communication Media

One of the most important marketing strategies is the planning that drives brand development. As this book thus far makes plain, the Cuban market is unique in several ways: lack of competition, state-only wholesaling, mostly state-only retailing and, most importantly, a lack of modern communication media for product placement and promotion. Despite those special features, there are certain brand-planning operations that are practically universal. These include planning for new brands, planning for established brands, contingency plans, strategic brand marketing and a hierarchical or pyramid strategy for branding (Lehmann and Winer 2002).

This chapter examines Cuban brand development without the use of mass communication media commonly found other countries. We begin by outlining some of the generic features of brand development. The bulk of the chapter examines the brand planning behind the most successful brands operating in Cuba today by companies such as Nestlé, Palmares S.A., CIMEX S.A., Havana Club Internacional and others. In reviewing these brands, we aim to highlight the unique yet shared aspects of brand planning in socialist Cuba.

THE ABCS OF BRAND PLANNING

All brands require some type of marketing research if they are to be successful, and the key to that success is a clear focus on brand planning. To be clear, brand planning is not isolated from other functions of the firm but instead is engrained in the running of factories, engineering firms, finance operations and human resources functions.

A few years ago, the joint-venture company Los Portales, the result of the Cuban firm Coralsa S.A. forming a joint venture with the Swiss giant Nestlé, began searching for a way to increase the sales of their carbonated beverages and bottled water. Their plan was to become the market leader within short order.

During the same time that Los Portales was repositioning itself in the beverage markets, a joint-venture tobacco company was considering a

Table 6.1 Selected Joint-Venture and State Companies Operating in Hard Currency in Cuba, 2011 (N.A. = not applicable)

Original Cuban Company	Foreign Investor or Parent Company	Investor country(ies) of origin	Joint venture name	Year of Joint venture name	Brand(s) names(s) in Cuba	Product or Service Category	Logo
Cubatobaco	Imperial Tobacco (Altadis, Seita (France-Spain))	England	Habanos. S.A.	1994	Cohíba, H. Upmann, Montecristo, and all Cuban cigars produced on the island	cigars	
CubaRon	Pernod Ricard	French	Havana Club Internacional	1993	Havana Club	sprits	
Cubatobaco	Souza Cruz	Brazil	BrasCuba	1994	Popular, Hollywood, H. Upmann, Partagás, Cohíba, Rothmans of Pall Mall	cigarettes	
Coralsa	Nestlé Waters	France	Los Portales	1995	Ciego Montero, Los Portales	Bottled water	
Coralsa	Proyectos Valencia en el Caribe	Spain	Bravo	1996	Bravo	Processed meats	
Coralsa	Nestlé	Switzerland	Coralac	1997	Nestlé	Ice cream	
Coralsa	Reuven International	Canada	Coracán	1995	Piñata	Powdered beverages	
Palmares	CIMEX	N.A.	Palmares	1994	Palmares, Ditu, Pan.Con, En familia, Dinos Pizza, Dimar	restaurants	
El Rápido	CIMEX	N.A.	El Rápido	1994	El Rápido	restaurants	

Source: Calculated by The Havana

Table 6.2 Cuban Ministry of Foreign Affairs Promotion of Foreign Investment

What advantages does our country offer foreign investment?
Besides security, which means having a stable political and social system with exceptional legal safeguards, Cuba offers:
• Natural resources. Mountainous landscapes in the eastern portion of the island and a shoreline greater than 5,700 kilometers and 4,000 tiny islands with virgin beaches that are apt for building any sort of infrastructure for tourism
• Mineral Resources for Exploitation. Among which are nickel and cobalt
• Petroleum reserves on its continental shelf and the Gulf of Mexico Economic Zone for prospecting and drilling
• Developed infrastructure which translates into 7 international airports throughout the island; 12 ports that can berth large vessels; 95% electrical coverage; and railroad and highway connections across the island
• Skilled labor force. One in 15 workers has some higher education; one in eight has technical school training; and a labor force with a minimum of tenth-grade education
• A modern banking system aligned with international standards
• Trade with more than 170 countries, including throughout the Caribbean where Cuba participates in the following organizations (AEC, ALADI, SELA, CEPAL, ACP Group) as well as tariff agreements with 12 nations in the region that include signed and active Partial Bilateral Trade Agreements.

Source: Ministry of Foreign Affairs, http://embacuba.cubaminrex.cu/Default.aspx?tabid=6077; Accessed April 4, 2011, our translation.

similar strategy. BrasCuba, owned by the Cuban government and the Brazilian firm Souza Cruz de Brasil S.A., surprised everyone with dramatic increases in the sales of its yellow-leaf cigarettes. BrasCuba's Hollywood cigarettes began outselling such renowned international brands as Salem, Camel, Winston, More and Marlboro. BrasCuba also introduced Popular cigarettes into the domestic hard-currency market. Popular had long been sold in pesos on the island and was—as its name implies—quite popular. Sold in hard currency, Popular quickly positioned itself as a top leader in the darker leaf or strong cigarette sector in Cuba. So successful was the new Popular, that by 2011 it was exported to more than 10 countries.

What did Los Portales and BrasCuba's marketing strategies share in common? They are both joint-venture operations, but they operate in different market sectors. The answer is that their market successes stemmed from their brand-planning system and their familiarity with working in a country where radio and TV advertisement, print-media campaigns in newspapers and magazines, outdoor advertising and Internet promotion simply do not exist. To understand how brands are developed without the sorts of tools that prevail globally on the Internet and in this turbocharged new millennium, we present nine case studies: Habanos, Havana Club, BrasCuba, Los Portales, Bravo, Nestlé- Coralac, Coracán, Piñata and Palmares. Although not an exhaustive list, they do provide a wide selection of consumer goods and services as well as branding strategies employed by these European–, Brazilian–, Canadian–Cuban companies, as well as two Cuban state firms (Table 6.1).

Joint ventures have been the entrepreneurial drivers behind enhancing and developing these companies' brands; bringing business acumen to the Cuban market that had not developed, had been undercapitalized or had simply been lost since the 1959 Revolution. Each of the preceding brands, however, has been roundly successful on the island. As we will see, some have even displaced well-regarded international brands in assuming their market position in Cuba. Some brands sold by these companies, moreover, have done well outside Cuba, of which we cite Habanos, Havana Club and BrasCuba.

The study of the kinds of firms we discuss has received little scholarly attention, perhaps because the Ministry of Foreign Affairs and the Ministry of Foreign Investment and Cooperation tend to promote the comparative advantages of the island's national resources that many foreigners associate with Cuba (Table 6.2). Although we are unclear about why natural resource attributes garner more international attention than consumer goods (it may be because there are more profits to be made in extractive industries than attempting to market consumer goods to an island of just 11 million consumers), it is the latter category that more immediately affects the everyday life (*vida cotidiana*) of the populace.

To understand the evolution of the nine case studies in the chapter, we began with some important background about product promotion during the Special Period.

BRIEF HISTORICAL OVERVIEW

It has been over half a century since commercial advertising has had a presence in Cuba. North Korea may be the only other nation that shares that distinction. Advertising expert Mirtha Múñíz summarizes the resistance that commercial advertising on the island has had to confront:

> The content and practice of advertising [in Cuba] has become polemical, and it is not always adequately understood. Often it is underestimated, and in the worst of cases, it is undervalued by those who mechanically identify advertising with capitalism. [Those same critics] do not understand that it is a real scientific workplace instrument, and is an efficient weapon in business . . . [there exists a] sort of mirror reflection in which [advertising is thought to be] an instrument of capitalism and is unnecessary for the socialist process. (2003, 47)

Large-scale advertising was carried out superficially in Cuba in 1998–1999. It occurred when the Cuban authorities allowed sponsorship for the large sporting events held at the World Cup, France 98, World Volleyball League games of 1999 and the Pan American Games held in Winnipeg.

Los Portales, BrasCuba, Mitsubishi Motors and Bodegas Vega de la Reina had the foresight to engage in this unprecedented advertising campaign in a media market that had not carried consumer advertisements in nearly four decades.

Four national TV stations and more than 70 radio stations operate in Cuba, the latter consisting of national, provincial and local broadcasts. In both TV and radio, there is no commercial advertising. In lieu of product and service advertising, viewers and listeners receive announcements that are (1) political in nature (e.g., heralding the accomplishments of the Revolution); (2) promote upcoming cultural and sporting events; or (3) function as public service announcements (PSAs) that cover health and education matters, public-health and natural-disaster events (tropical storms, torrential rains, floods) and related topics. Just a single radio station, Radio Taíno, carries commercial advertising, and it is aimed at Spanish-speaking international tourists. Locals can and do listen to this program but, to our knowledge, no publicly available research exists on the impact this advertising has on Cuban consumption, taste and preferences.

Outdoor advertising in the form of billboards has the potential to be an effective and inexpensive tool for product and service promotion. Nearly 500 billboards exist, though they are heavily concentrated in Havana City, Matanzas and Holguín Provinces. At present, they carry no commercial advertisements (though the area around the passenger pick-up zone at José Martí International Airport does). Although billboards could be used to develop brand images of national, international and joint-venture business, they carry largely political messages that are approved by the government, as well as environmental messages about recycling, saving water, littering, public health, highway safety and related themes (Scarpaci and Portela 2009, chap. 6). Cuban billboards fall under the direct supervision of the Ideological Department of the Central Committee of the Cuban Communist Party. Accordingly, any message that is projected on these billboards (called *vallas*) must be approved by the Party.

Given the almost impenetrable barrier imposed by the government and Party, one can appreciate the challenges of trying to promote goods and services in ways that are much less common in other countries. Investment in marketing promotion, therefore, has to follow different patterns. In Cuba, it is important to enlist an integrated marketing communication strategy for brands that takes full advantage of the scarce opportunities that exist for advertising. The strategies include merchandising; in-store promotion; sales events, business fairs and cultural events; some Internet; public relations; product packaging; and product labels. Research published in the *Harvard Business Review* and elsewhere, however, indicates that in light of new marketing and advertising channels that exist in the twenty-first century, such as Twitter, Facebook and smart phones, many marketers need to rethink their strategies by considering a return to the more traditional means of marketing and advertising that prevailed in the first half of the twentieth century. Brands such as Nestlé's Buitoni, The Body Shop, Cadbury, Häagen-Dazs, Hugo Boss and Swatch—all working in different product categories—are embracing many of the old-school strategies that have prevailed in Cuba in what some have called the 'post–mass communications era' (Joachimisthaler and Aaker 1997). Like Cuba:

> [m]edia options for branded manufacturers in Europe have historically been limited and relatively ineffective. Europeans have had access to fewer commercial television stations, many of which bundle advertisements to avoid program interruptions . . . managers of brands in Europe have found that communication through traditional mass media has been ineffective, inefficient, and costly. As a result, many European-based companies have long relied on alternative communication channels to create product awareness, convey brand associations, and develop loyal customer bases. (Joachmisthaler and Aaker 1997)

The authors go on to cite more traditional promotional venues such as Adidas' and Virgin's urban street culture ads that include stickball and festivals. Related participatory venues such as these are less expensive than mass-media campaigns and afford potential clients more hands-on interaction. This suggests that as many industrial market economies realize that marketing has become extremely fragmented, there may be a need to rediscover some of the more traditional methods (e.g., consumer 'touch' points in contemporary parlance). This is a practice that the small-business sector in post-Revolutionary Cuba has been forced to embrace.

THE ADVERTISING SCENE SINCE 1993

The socialist government's focus on providing a modicum of consumer goods and services has, for a variety of reasons, produced great inefficiencies and obstacles. Until recently, inefficient firms have been allowed to continue producing, even after incurring long-standing deficits. Some of that has changed since the advent of the Special Period. The bottom line, though, is that most Cuban companies have set aside little money for advertising, partly because of the stigma associated with the process (as Múñíz noted earlier) and partly because there has been no open market in which advertising and branding campaigns can be forged. Moreover, a lack of strong competition and carefully controlled gatekeepers that only allow certain international brands to enter the island stifles competition and makes the use of broad marketing campaigns less essential than in market economies.

Decriminalizing the possession and circulation of the dollar beyond the so-called "diplomatic stores" back in 1993 coincided with the collapse of the Socialist bloc, which propelled the Cuban government more quickly into the global market than it probably wanted. Ramifications of this watershed year meant a gradual shift to more decentralized businesses and decision-making. Allowing foreign companies to partner with Cuban entities was also an important modernizing force; Cuban firms were cash-strapped and knew little about marketing and supply-chain issues. New infusions of capital by joint-venture operations enabled Cuban firms to acquire new raw materials and information technologies. Joint ventures gravitated towards tourism, food processing, light manufacturing and construction trades. On the B2C side, dollar-based retailing opened up by state-owned chain stores as did hundreds of small self-employment (*trabajadores por cuenta propia*) outlets who charged in both pesos and hard currency (Peters and Scarpaci 1998). New trades and outlets in the private sector, mostly unseen since the early 1960s, resurfaced: cafeterias, small restaurants, food sellers, artisan outlets, upholsterers, seamstresses and tailors, mechanics and many more. Along with this came a new wave of remittances, tips from the tourist sector, taxi services, non-hotel-based restaurants and related businesses.

The confluence of these forces created a new and budding consumer market in Cuba, and both national and joint-venture companies wanted to tap into it. In the first half of the 1990s, a diverse group of professional Cuban men and women, with different backgrounds (engineering, social sciences, public administration, etc.), began working with foreign investors to create new product and service brands and company names. Promoting these new entities without relying on mass communication outlets was of paramount importance. In the early years of the opening, purchasing power was the central and limiting factor because consumer demand for a variety of goods and services that had been previously subsidized by the Cuban government, the former USSR or the Soviet bloc (CMEA) had disappeared. All stores had to note was that something was for sale and a curious public clamored to find out what it was even if the majority could not buy it. Even a casual foreign observer on the island can hear the standard and methodic way in which Cubans form queues: *Quién es el ultimo?* (Who's the last one in line?) Once apprised, the new joiner silently walks to the end of the line. Cubans have grown accustomed to waiting.

By 1996, a critical mass of firms and products had sufficiently established themselves such that it became necessary for companies to answer the long-standing questions: What makes my product unique? How can I add value for my customers? How can the promotion of my product or service stand out amongst an increasingly crowded retail market? In many ways, this 1990s phenomenon mirrored the transition from the Henry Ford–style days of mere production to thinking seriously about selling the merchandise to customers (see Chapter 2). The key difference, of course, was that this transition took place 70 years later in socialist Cuba.

SUCCESSFUL JOINT-VENTURE BRAND PROMOTION

Many of the successful brand promotion cases described in this chapter drew on the know-how that international companies brought to the island. Their knowledge of marketing management, inventory control, distribution and the marketing mix (price, product, promotion and place) cannot be underestimated. Nowhere was this more evident than in the tourism sector, where Cuba had maintained a fairly low profile in the international circuit, adhering to a belief held by Fidel Castro that Cuba was capable of producing more than an island of chambermaids and bartenders (Scarpaci 2004). Cuba's immediate comparative advantage in 1993 was that it was endowed with sunshine for northern tourists, and it was not heavily visited by outsiders. Ironically, unlike its nearby competitors in Mexico, Central America and the Caribbean, Cuba was widely known in the popular imagination as a relatively small island. Its dance, music, art, athletes, iconic products (cigars and rums) and political history of both revolutionaries and gangsters gave it a certain cachet in an increasingly cluttered worldwide market of tourist destinations that promoted 'sun, surf, sex and sangria' (Scarpaci 2007). Government authorities aimed to graft these uniquely Cuban attributes onto its tourist industry in order to add value to tropical tourism (Scarpaci 2007). To achieve this synergism between tourism and the iconic features of the island, the industry needed to forge heretofore unknown relations with the construction, food, transportation and related industries. In addition, doing so with an import-substitution strategy would help it save the 'leakage' of precious hard currency used for purchasing inputs from overseas.

In the balance of the chapter, we present nine case studies of brand development that indicate how selected Cuban joint-venture firms have handled the marketing management challenges of their industry and, where appropriate, how they have enhanced their brand image nationally and internationally. We realize that these more successful cases cannot be generalized to other firms across the many industrial, manufacturing, pharmaceutical and service industries. They may, however, prove insightful in understanding the comparative advantages, weaknesses and opportunities for sector-specific forays into the Cuban market.

CASE 1: HABANOS S.A. (TOBACCO PRODUCTS)

Habanos S.A. is a Spanish–Cuban joint venture that was created in September 1994. Its equal-share partners are the Cuban government and the Spanish firm Altadis. Cubatobaco, owned by the Cuban government, joined with Altadis (the result of a union of Tabacalera and SEITA S.A., the former French tobacco monopoly) to market and sell all Cuban tobacco products in Cuba and globally. Habanos S.A. is the world leader in selling

Figure 6.1 Original Habano designation.

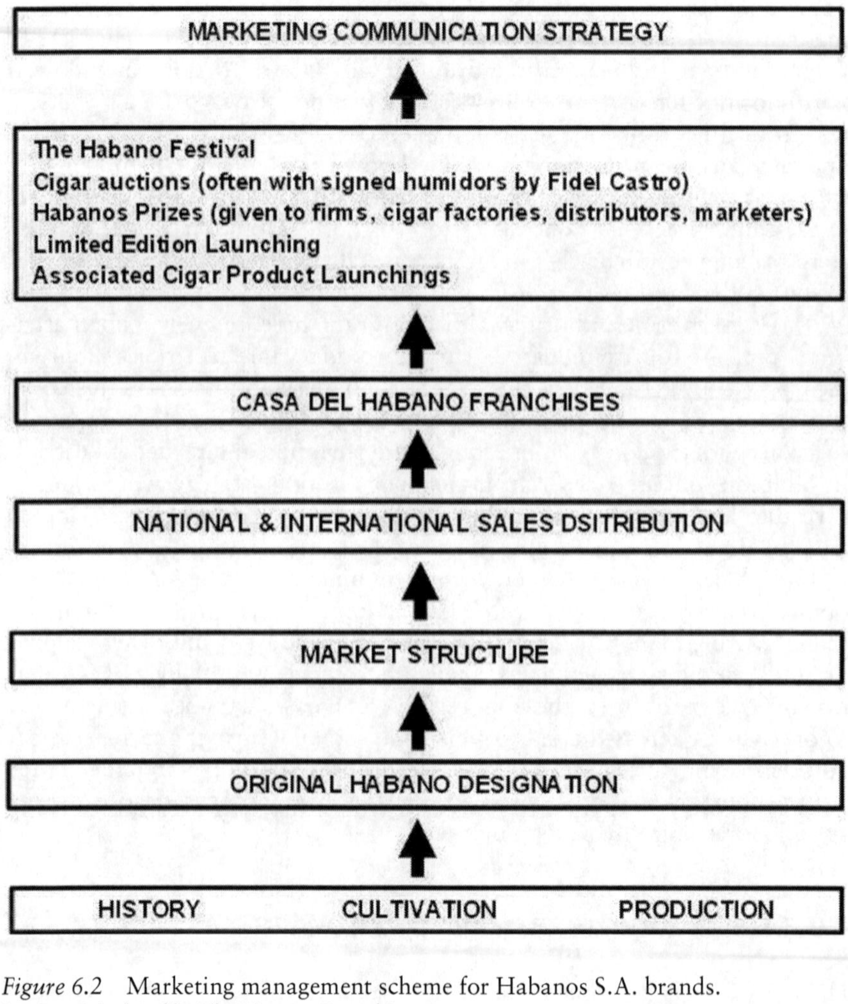

Figure 6.2 Marketing management scheme for Habanos S.A. brands.
Source: Calculated by The Havana Consulting Group

and distributing premium[1] cigars and has a physical (brick-and-mortar) presence on five continents and in more than 100 countries. Ninety percent of their sales come from outside Cuba.

Origin Designation

The company's success relies largely on its origin designation scheme, which allows it to label its tobacco products with the statement "Denominación de Origen Habano" (Original Habano[2] Designation; see Figure 6.1). This label is only given to products made with 100 percent tobacco that is grown in Cuba. For competitors in the Dominican Republic, Honduras, Nicaragua and elsewhere, the only "Cuban" attribute they can promote is whether their cigars are grown from "Cuban seed." Perceptive cigar smokers, of course, realize this, but many novice cigar buyers see the word "Cuba" and often conflate these product features. *Denominación de Origen Habano* also means the product has been subject to quality control at several stages, from planting, harvesting and curing to the final rolling and packaging. Other quality-control measures include the selection of leaf, rolling criteria, size guarantee, flavor and final appearance and packing (see Figure 6.2 and also Chapter 5 on franchising). Brand extension of the Habanos name can be found in cognac (Cognac Extra Cohiba), perfume (Perfume Montecristo) and cologne (Vergueros Perfume Fragrance[3]).

The Habano label draws heavily on the iconic values about the island of Cuba, evident in Cuban consumers' perceptions of the top 10 domestic brands recalled by our national sample (Chapters 3 and 4). The Habano appellation is sustained upon three pillars: history, tobacco cultivation and production. An elaborate hologram system is designed to thwart forgeries.

History

The tobacco plant is believed to have originated in South America and traveled to the Caribbean through the island-hopping migration that took place from offshore Venezuela, along the Lesser Antilles, northward, into the Greater Antilles. Another route of diffusion on the mainland was the Mayan's use of the leaf, which may have spread it as far north as the Mississippi River Valley. The plants were likely cultivated in Cuba by native Arawak, Carib and Taino peoples' or their ancestors, the principle pre-Columbian ethnic groups on the island at the dawn of European conquest in 1492. It is likely that tobacco in the Americas was used for medicinal (including enemas) and hallucinogenic purposes. Spanish scribes describe the use of pipes in what is now Mexico City, where after meals, elaborate ceremonies combined the smoking of various plant resins and tobacco leaf. Columbus and his men were given dried tobacco leaf when they reached San Salvador Island in the Bahamas. His journal recorded that "the natives brought fruit, wooden spears, and certain dried leaves which gave off a distinct fragrance" (Gilman and Xun 2004, 30). When Columbus came to Cuba, he also observed the enthusiastic smoking of dried leaves that were crudely twisted and wrapped into what the natives called *cohiba* (Curbelo Castellanos 1999).

The encounters of the Old and New Worlds revealed that tobacco afforded both physical and spiritual benefits. From the sixteenth century onward, a rage for tobacco was unleashed and took hold strongly in Spain. Spaniards were also the first ones to suffer terrible punishments for engaging in this newfound habit. Fury over this new American plant spread to Persia, Japan and Russia, where even harsher punishments were employed for those who smoked. Curiously, as prohibition against the leaf increased, tobacco's medicinal values became more widely touted.

On April 11, 1717, King Philip V imposed a royal monopoly on tobacco cultivation in Cuba, a decision that became known as the *Estanco del Tobaco* because hardworking tobacco agriculturalists (called *vegueros*) opposed the onerous law and slowed down production in protest. Restrictions and monopoly reigned until June 23, 1817, when another royal decree struck down the monopoly and once again provided Cuba free trade of tobacco with the Western world as long as it passed through Spanish ports.

In Cuba, tobacco production had always been the pursuit of so-called 'free men.' The harshness of sugarcane production was sustained by slave labor. Tobacco planting and cultivation did not require strenuous cutting with a machete or merely sticking cane cuttings in the ground for vegetative propagation (Moreno Fraginals 1964). Instead, tobacco cultivation required (as it does today) a more nuanced treatment or, as José Martí purportedly described it, handling the leaf as if it were a delicate lady. The 'free men' who dedicated themselves to tobacco planting came largely from the Canary Islands, and their descendents, with characteristic blue eyes and fair skin, still reside in Cuba's prime tobacco regions.

In the nineteenth century Cuba firmly reestablished itself as the primary tobacco producer and manufacturer. In 1859, there were close to 10,000 tobacco farms (*vegas*), and about 1,300 tobacco factories (for cigar and cigarette rolling and packaging) in Havana. Cuba started the twentieth century in economic ruins and with weakened markets and supply chains across the island, particularly in tobacco production. It had suffered intermittent independence wars, starting with the Ten Years' War of 1868 and culminating with the Spanish-Cuban-American war from 1895 to 1898 (Rivero Muñíz 1965). Postindependence-war Cuba quickly reestablished its tobacco industry and in North America, the five-cent Cuban cigar became a mainstay in small towns and cities. Rightly or wrongly, cigar smoking has been portrayed as a pleasurable activity and is imbued with mystery and illusion, magic and charm, elegance and power. The centuries-old tradition of cigar smoking, either alone or pairing it with coffee or spirits, is tied to the island of Cuba and all things Cuban. It underpins the origin of perfecting cigars and the saying that Cuba has the best tobacco in the world (Heller and Gold 2002).

Cultivation

Cuba's physical and cultural resources enhance tobacco production. Just below the Tropic of Cancer, at around 23 degrees north latitude, the Cuban archipelago maintains an average relative humidity of about 79 percent and a median annual temperature of 25 degrees Celsius (77 degrees Fahrenheit). The subtropical high pressure over the Atlantic Ocean generates northeast trade winds that carry an adequate amount of humidity and precipitation, especially in western Cuba (where the heart of tobacco production lies). Well-drained soils characterize the tobacco fields, which rest upon a mature karstic or limestone foundation that produces sinkholes, caves, caverns and 'disappearing' rivers.

Centuries of working with tobacco also enhances the human capital base of the island's tobacco industry. Tobacco farmers are known for their meticulous care of the land. Soils are constantly tilled to enhance drainage and minimize weeds. Aerated soils enhance the plants' root system. Only trained oxen are used for tilling the fields as the weight of diesel tractors can irreversibly compact soils. About six months separate planting from harvesting.

Tobacco cultivation starts in greenhouses where seedlings are grown into small plants—a stage that takes about 40 days. Starting in October, the small plants are then transferred and planted in the fields. Over the next two months, each plant will be visited no fewer than 150 times. To ensure it reaches optimum height and maintains the appropriate number of leaves, the *veguero* must weed around the plant and deflower selected leaves to ensure the necessary plant size proportions. Leaf harvesting is an extraordinarily labor-intensive process that is carried out between days 45 and 80, depending on the type of tobacco plant and the use of the leaf in the final production (filler, wrapper, etc.).

After picking perhaps just two or three leaves per plant, the harvested material is then transferred to selection sheds, where mostly female workers choose and classify the leaves. Grouped leaves are gently bundled and placed on overhanging hooks in drying barns and sheds (Figure 6.3) where they undergo a slow process of aging and fermentation.

Figure 6.3 Tobacco drying shed (left) and drying leaves inside (right), Viñales Valley, Pinar del Río Province. Photograph by Joseph L. Scarpaci.

Production

When leaves reach the tobacco factories they are carefully unbundled and lightly sprayed with a mist of water in order to restore to the fragile leaves some of the moisture that was lost during processing. Next *rezagadores de capas* sort the leaves by color and size. The workers moisten their hands as they unfurl, stretch and examine each leaf so that they can separate them into between 18 and 20 leaf varieties, destined to form some aspect of the *habano*.

Cigar rollers, called *torcedores*, are the keystones in the production process. Each roller begins a cigar with about half a leaf that forms the thick inner wrapper, or leaf casing, that will hold the filler tobacco. Leaves are placed inside the binder, or *capote*, and thicker stems and excess leaves are cut away with a small rounded knife called the *chaveta*. Next, the worker gently rolls the leaves into what looks like a very crude cigar. The semifinished cigar is then rolled at one end so that the part that will reach the smoker's mouth is appropriately tapered. From there, the cigar is placed into what appears to be a horizontal guillotine and the lighted end is cut so that all the cigars of the roller's particular production batch maintain uniform length. A ribbon is carefully wrapped around bunches of 50 cigars and they are then transferred to a fumigation unit where they will be immunized against certain molds and pests. Later, the cigars are placed in wooden block presses for three weeks; the process ensures uniform diameter and extracts excess moisture. A final selection process is carried out in a classification department (called the *escogida*) where they are checked again for quality issues such as wrapper luster and hanging leaves caused by the trimming process.

The final production stage entails the placing of the ring on the cigar. A quality-control group samples portions of each roller's cigars and checks again for size, shape, appearance, wrapper luster and thickness. *Habanos* are rejected if they fail to meet the established quality-control criteria, and there are direct ramifications for the rollers because they are compensated partially on how many cigars they roll daily. These production standards are in effect in all of the approximately 80 cigar houses throughout the island, and form the centerpiece of carrying the label Habano and the appellation *Denominación de Origen Protegida de Habanos* (or D.O.P in Spanish).

CASE 2: HAVANA CLUB (RUM)

A happy offspring of sugarcane, rum is a typical Caribbean product. Unlike the famous French cognac or Italian wines, rum is not derived from the cultivation of grapes, which generally do not adapt well to the Caribbean basin. Cuba is well suited to all facets of rum production as portrayed by popular and historic cultural displays of the pleasure of rum and rum-based drinks.

The food and beverage sector was one of the first targets for joint-venture investment following the limited reforms of 1993. Havana Club Internacional was borne from CubaRon in Cuba and the multinational French firm, Pernod Ricard, which at the time was the third largest beverage and spirits company in the world. Havana Club was the most prestigious rum on the island and abroad, at least until the 1980s or so. At that time, its marketing, production and distribution had become weak; it was only exporting about 300,000 nine-liter cases annually, and national sales were low, much lower than exports. To be sure, a worsening economy, low wages and deteriorating purchasing power accounted for tepid national sales, factors that can be traced back to Cuba's larger political economy under socialist rule.

From the outset of the new joint venture, the firm tried to revive the brand value of Havana Club among Cubans by positioning it as a premium rum. The strategy stemmed from the principle that a brand that bases its image on its origin should have its own showcase. As noted earlier, dollar decriminalization in 1993 opened up hard-currency retailing, which provided a platform upon which Havana Club could be marketed to Cubans and the growing international tourist market on the island; it could then be transferred internationally.

Promotional campaigns changed the product taglines from "The Authentic Cuban Rum" and "The Soul of Cuba" into the current (2011) one: "The Rum of Cuba." Each brand phrase attempted to capture the idea that it was

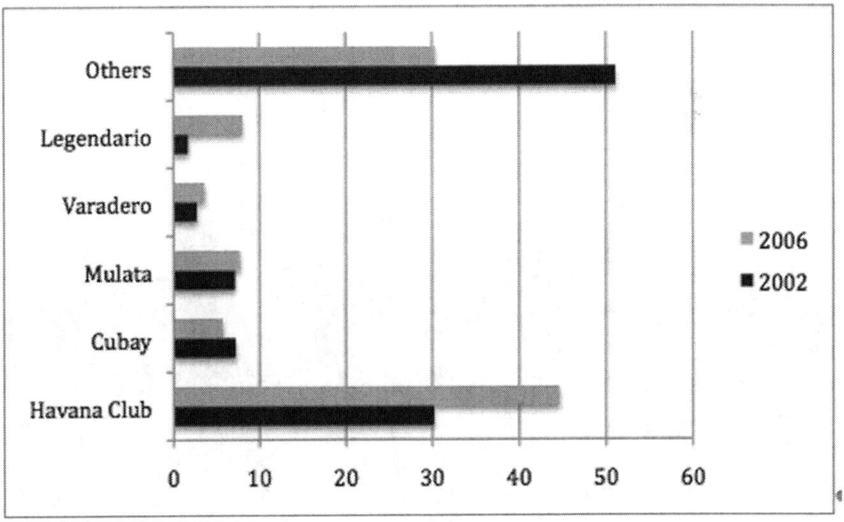

Figure 6.4 Percentage hard-currency Cuban rum sales by brand on the island, 2002 and 2006.

Sources: Calculated by the authors based on unpublished information and interviews with managers and specialists at CIMEX S.A., Tecnoazúcar and Havana Club Internacional S.A.

the most popular rum on the island and that its smooth flavor makes it the highest quality rum in Cuba. To carry out this marketing positioning, a variety of strategies and label and packaging designs were employed. In the early years, the company brought out a new product called Silver Dry, which proved highly successful. It was, in fact, so successful that the competition adopted it as their strategy too. Mulata brand rum, for instance, came out with its own version of Silver Dry, which further enhanced Havana Club's brand value as the reference product in that category.

Havana Club's next strategy was the launching of aged, dark rum—Añejo Reserva—which appeared in late 1997 and early 1998. The new product was well received by the Cuban market. One reason may be that this product launching paralleled a global trend of segmenting various types of aged rums. It also coincided with growing brand recognition of Havana Club on the island and overseas. By 2002, Havana Club had captured 30.22 percent of hard-currency rum sales in Cuba. By 2006, the market share made up of small rum makers dropped markedly, and Havana Club's share rose to 44 percent of the market (Figure 6.4).

Havana Club's strong growth in the hard-currency sector energized a domestic rum market in which more than a dozen major brands had competed. Between 2001 and 2002, these rum sales increased by 16.64 percent whereas rum sales in the peso market dipped by -0.63 percent. That Cubans increased their hard-currency purchasing power at the time accounts for these rum consumption trends. Havana Club then set out to redesign its label and bottle to emphasize various products. In 2002, their new branding strategy guided five uniquely positioned products: Añejo Blanco and Añejo Especial as well as the traditional lines of 3 Años, Añejo Reserva and 7 Años. In October 2010 Havana Club Internacional S.A. launched Havana Club *Selección de Maestros* in response to the value of its "strong

Figure 6.5 Havana Club's 2010 product line.

Cuban heritage . . . [which] is set to drive the emerging ultra premium rum category" (Floating Rum Shack 2011) as part of its diversification with additional brands (Figure 6.5). Moreover, *The International Wine and Drinks Research Magazine* (2010) listed Havana Club and the Dominican Republic's Barceló rum in the prestigious premium liquor's category; only 10 spirits were included in the annual culling of premium brands.

Añejo Blanco substituted Silver Dry and had such an impact on the market that it redefined the premium image of Havana Club which was based on the natural aging of its products. This image turned out to be the key to positioning the brand as the market leader. Havana Club came to be known as the only distiller of rums with a warehousing and distribution system that naturally aged its products. Moreover, it was able to satisfy both internal and overseas demand. Añejo Blanco eventually displaced Silver Dry produced by its competitors, and Silver Dry was discontinued because it was expensive to produce (Havana Club, personal communication, 2005).

The new Añejo Especial responded to a growing market for dark, aged rums. In a market where clear glass was the industry norm, it distinguished itself by using a dark brown bottle. International competitors such as Venezuelan Cacique and Pampero, as well as the Dominican Republic's Brugal, all used the clear bottle at that time.

Other marketing and production efforts set out to highlight Havana Club's new makeover and market growth. The five new rums had self-adhesive labels, metal screw-off tops and more stylish bottle shapes. In the mid 2000s, the firm launched a new product, Barrel Proof, that was being sold for US$35 at duty-free shops only as part of its strategy of positioning Havana Club as a premium spirit. This brand-positioning strategy used promotional mixes such as the creation of the Havana Club Rum Museum in Havana, just a few blocks from two high-traffic tourist centers in Old Havana: Plaza de San Francisco and Plaza Vieja. The museum educates visitors about the stages of rum production and even provides rum tasting events at the end of the visit. Havana Club works with travel agencies in Cuba and abroad in scheduling visits to the museum, which in 2011 was one of the few museums that did not charge admission. Visitors to Cuba will often see Havana Club promoted on travel materials, caps and visors, billboards, in restaurants and bars and where buses and cars are parked; personnel working those areas will often have sun umbrellas and clothing with Havana Club's brand printed on them (Figure 6.6).

B2C efforts are well developed. As international visitors will quickly discover, Havana Club sales promotions are highly visible in places where they, and not necessarily Cubans, visit. Promotional efforts are particularly striking because of the dearth of other types of advertising. Tourist promotional venues include daytime and nighttime settings in bars, discothèques and restaurants. Dining establishments and hotels use raffles, gifts, swimming and dance competitions and other customer-engagement practices to promote the brand. The island's bartender association (*Asociación Cubana*

Figure 6.6 Parking attendants using Havana Club vests and umbrella, Parque Central, Havana, July 2010. Photograph by J. L. Scarpaci.

de Cantineros) has played an important role in developing the brand; bartenders receive information on the history of the product and its features, and are exposed to it when bartender competitions are held. Havana Club sponsors events associated with the International Bartender Association and uses the venues to generate media and industry buzz. One domestic-market promotion aims to get Cuban families to buy a bottle for male household heads at the end of the year through in-store promotion. By 2011, it had become evident that every kiosk, bar, nightclub, hotel and restaurant in Cuba carried at least one of the company's rums.

B2B practices are also noteworthy. The company aims to fill orders to myriad businesses within 72 hours or less. Our interviews with these businesses indicate that this practice has increased trust in Havana Club products. It helps to minimize the amount of stock smaller businesses have to maintain. Such on-time delivery guarantees stand out in a country where distribution and supply bottlenecks characterize many state-run operations (Corbett 2004).

As we discussed in Chapter 4 regarding leading national brands and the embeddedness of *cubanidad* in certain products, Havana Club has become

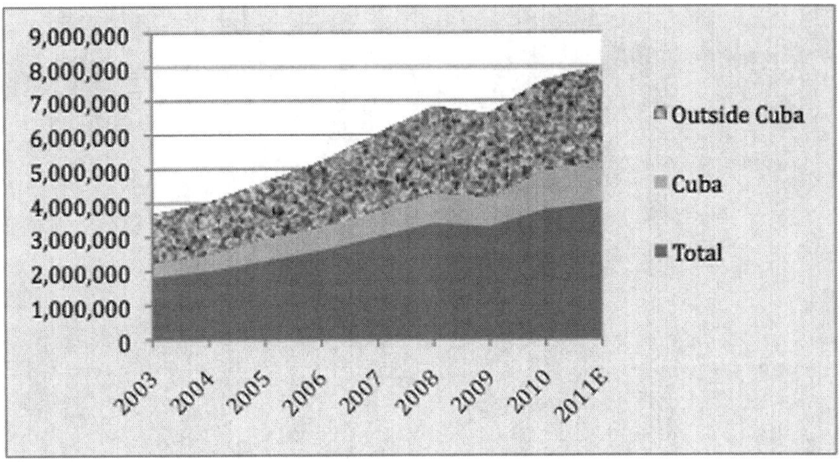

Figure 6.7 Havana Club sales (US$), 2003–2011 (expected).
Source: Calculated by The Havana Consulting Group

iconic in both the world of rums and when thinking about Cuba in general. The company's president, Philip Coutin, remarked (clearly with his own bias) that "there is little doubt that [Havana Club] is a formidable product, one of the best in the world, and everyone knows it. Besides, Grupo Pernod Ricard is actively involved in promoting the brand, and it does so everywhere it currently operates" (de la Rosa 2005).

Havana Club is currently well positioned in a variety of important spirits' markets; it is especially strong in Italy, Spain, Germany, Greece and Switzerland. Its expansion in Latin America includes a toehold in Mexico and Chile; in the latter market Havana Club sales increased by 30 percent in the mid-2000s. In the mid-2000s, the company aimed to produce three million cases a year, which would position it among the top 20 premium spirits in the world. In 2010, the firm sold 3.8 million cases. In the medium term, it strives to increase production to five million cases annually. Between 2004 and 2011, sales were expected to double from about US$4 to US$8 million (Figure 6.7).

CASE 3: BRASCUBA (TOBACCO PRODUCTS)

Recall that BrasCuba is the fruit of a 1995 joint venture between the state-owned Cubatobaco and the Brazilian consortium Souza Cruz. At the time of the merger, the Brazilian company accounted for 80 percent of the country's domestic sales and, like most brands in Cuba, Souza Cruz had not relied on mass communication media.

Strong growth characterizes BrasCuba's sales and its recent 10th anniversary slogan was "Proud to Grow" (*orgullosos de crecer*). In 2011, its

Figure 6.8 Selected BrasCuba brands.

cigarette sales made it the largest producer of cigarettes sold in hard currency on the island. Its main cigarette brands are Popular, Hollywood, H. Upmann, Partagás and Cohiba (Figure 6.8).

BrasCuba has enjoyed steady growth since its inception. It uses more than 5,000 retail outlets across the island and currently exports to 10 countries including Mexico, Spain, Russia, France and Japan. In Spain, Popular is the third most popular brand in the dark cigarette category. In Cuba, it launched a yellow-leaf cigarette for more discerning smokers in an attempt to substitute for imported cigarettes in that same category (Ubeda 2005a). Sacha Ruffier, marketing director for BrasCuba, explains the company's strategy like this: "We depart from the premise that small details make a big difference, and we've worked on that. With the recent introduction of the world famous Rothmans of Pall Mall, made with some of the world's best yellow-leaf tobacco and introduced at the very competitive price of 2 CUC (about US$2), we hope to secure an important segment of the market in a short time, by offering the smoker a different taste" (Ubeda 2005b; our translation).

Rothmans of Pall Mall was created in 1900 in a small tobacconist shop on the small street of Pall Mall in London, by Louis Rothman. In the 1930s, it began exporting to Holland, India, South Africa and Australia. By 2004, it was selling in more than 100 countries on every continent and its sales were over US$2 billion.

Cuban law, Resolution 335, gave BrasCuba the legal right to sell and distribute cigarettes in Cuba, provided that it complied with the law stipulating that health warnings be clearly posted in Spanish on all cigarette packs. BrasCuba then started using Cuban tobacco for manufacturing and selling Rothmans of Pall Mall in hard currency to both the international tourist and the domestic market. Given that it is made with fine (non-Cuban) yellow-leaf tobacco, BrasCuba priced Rothmans of Pall Mall at what they believed was a competitive $2 CUC, above Hollywood, which was selling at $1.20 CUC but below other imports that were selling around $2.40 CUC.

Rothmans helped BrasCuba round out its portfolio and earn a new segment of the Cuban market, as well as expose some international tourists to a brand they might not have otherwise seen back home. At the company's 10-year anniversary, it was widely regarded as one of the more successful joint-venture companies in Cuba. Its 2005 exports were 30 percent higher than the previous year: 550 million cigarettes. Domestically, it was selling 1.4 million, which was 4.6 percent less than in 2004; the decline is attributable to the higher relative costs for Cubans, whose purchasing power is lower than many world consumers, as well as their lower expendable incomes. Only sales of nonfilter (straights) Vega and Hollywood suffered that year, whereas H. Upmann and Hollywood (the latter being the market leader, made with dark-leaf tobacco and sold in packs of both 10 and 20 units) maintained sales levels. By the end of the 2000s, yellow-leaf (*rubios*) Hollywood and Lucky Strikes had continued as the category leaders.

CASE 4: LOS PORTALES (BOTTLED WATER)

Los Portales was established in 1995 as a merger between former competitors: Coralsa, San Pellegrino of Italy and Cubaguas S.A. The latter was a joint-venture that had originally included the Spanish (Mallorcan) company Cavall de Bastos and the Cuban state companies of Unión de Bebidas and Licores de MINAL.

After its creation, Los Portales began investing in the mineral springs it owned in Guane, Pinar del Río Province. Its goal was to bottle and distribute mineral water and call it by the name of the springs (Los Portales) as well as develop soft drinks. Its Italian partner allowed it to import the world-renowned San Pellegrino y Panna bottled water and soft drinks that were exclusively sold in the Italian market: One-One, Arachata and a few other brands. Cubagua's contribution to the merger was a mineral springs in Palmira, Cienfuegos Province, where it operated a bottling works. It sought to develop three soft drink flavors under the brand Ciego Montero using polyethylene terephthalate (PET) technology, which is a combination of plastic resin and a type of polyester that produces a stronger and lighter container than conventional plastics (Napcor 2011).

A government decision in 1999 led to Cubagua's incorporation into Los Portales. Cavall de Bastos sold its operations in Cuba to San Pellegrino, who later sold it to Nestlé Waters. The corporate reshuffling left Los Portales with Coralsa on the Cuban side and Nestlé Waters, headquartered in Paris, on the foreign side. Following these changes, the Palmira spring was dedicated exclusively to bottling water for Ciego Montero, which became the company's premium product. The Guane facility was dedicated to manufacturing Ciego Montero soft drinks in both aluminum cans and with PET technology for plastic containers. Although the material lends itself to recycling (which is then called RPET) no such program operates in Cuba. However, recycling would provide Los Portales with an unprecedented opportunity to become the first company on the island to embark on a recycling program.

Brand Origin

Ciego Montero and Los Portales, then, became official Cuban brands in 1994 and 2002, respectively. Los Portales grew out of the Ministry of Food Industry in the 1970s after they conducted an island-wide search for natural springs from which bottled water could be developed. Ciego Montero has become the premium bottled water because of its quality, market share, success in various market segments and for being the first brand to affiliate with PET in Cuba.

Mineral water is bacteria free and known for its consistent mineral content, which is derived from the geological formation in which the water is found. An entire consumer culture surrounds mineral water consumption. Its health benefits are celebrated as is the purity of its water, which comes from deep underground springs that are assumed to be free of the contaminants commonly found in tap water (Royte 2008). Its product attributes remain consistent over time, regardless of whether there are droughts or heavy periods of rain. The island's two regulatory agencies, Ministry of Food Industry and Ministry of Basic Industry are tasked with certifying the purity and chemical consistency of water coming out of these two springs used by Ciego Montero and Los Portales.

Los Portales bottles water only from one spring and it does so on-site, whereas Ciego Montero does not bottle at its spring. The company introduced Los Portales with two goals in mind. One was to counter encroachment by its competition. A second goal was to take consumers away from the Levísima brand of water that the San Pellegrino joint venture had introduced. In some parts of the island, consumers thought that the word Levísima sounded like the word 'lesbian' and for that reason it became controversial. The misunderstanding convinced Los Portales to withdraw it and replace it with Los Portales brand. Los Portales was touted as a Cuban brand that was bottled at the spring and given a unique positioning and promotion presence. Both Los Portales and Ciego Montero remain the only untreated mineral springs water in Cuba, which separates them from other brands such as Las Lomas, Peña Azul and Copey, which receive some chemical treatment. One national brand of bottled water, La Cotorra (meaning 'the parrot'), was taken off the market because its source waters at the natural spring became polluted.

The company tried to promote Ciego Montero as a brand leader. Its current brands include Ciego Montero for water, soft drinks, TuKola (cola-flavored soft drink) and Ciego Montero Light. It tried developing a series of flavored soft drinks: lemon-lime, orange and cola. Some confusion arose in the minds of consumers over the Ciego Montero Cola and TuKola, the latter being inherited from the Caball de Bastos group noted earlier. This brand dissonance manifested itself when Cuban consumers, mainly in the smaller towns and provinces, began referring to TuKola as the generic 'soft drink' name for all Ciego Montero products, as in the phrase: "Let me have an orange TuKola, please." As a result, the company decided to cannibalize

Ciego Montero soft drinks and use TuKola as its soft drink beverage brand (Ciego Montero, personal communication, 2006).

Ciego Montero developed a variety of soft drink flavors: cola, lemon-lime, orange, maté, lemon and pineapple. In 2001, it launched TuKola Light (using the English term 'light' in its name), which has generated even sales over the years and is not just used by consumers who are concerned about their weight, but also among diabetics. Ciego Montero sales are equally divided between water and soft drinks.

Los Portales' main markets are hotels, restaurants, retail stores and institutional (state) clients. Its competitors can be divided into imported, national and substitute groups. Imported competitors are Coca-Cola, Pepsi-Cola, Mirinda, 7Up, Sprite and Fanta. Cuban competitors include Fiesta Cola, Tilín, Tónico, Tropicola, Cachito, Najita, Jupiña, Fres Cola and Turk Cola (which is made and distributed mainly in Las Tunas Province). The list of substitute competitors consists of instant (powdered) drinks (Piñata, Butti, Caricia, Drinki and Toqui), malt beverages (Bucanero, Caracas, among others), juices (Tropical Island, among others) and ice cream (Nestlé, Flamingo, Coppelia, Nevada, Tolón, Varadero and others).

Brand Positioning and National Marketing Communication Strategy

Los Portales' positioning is based largely on the idea their family of products are useful goods that satisfy a healthy consumer need for beverages and related items. Unlike cigarettes, cigars, beer or spirits, these products used in moderation are generally not harmful; they carry no warnings imposed by the government. In the product's early years, intermediary agents conveyed some information about the products, barmen, waiters and waitresses, clerks in stores, etc. Until a few decades ago, it was common in Cuban restaurants for waiters to place a pitcher of tap water on the table. However, water quality has become an issue (especially the presence of *giardia* parasites, *Giardia intestinalis*, *Giardia lamblia* or *Giardia duodenalis*) and many of these beverages, though relatively expensive, give the consumer confidence about the health benefits of consuming them.[4] *Giardia* and other waterborne illnesses have become a problem in Cuba since the onset of the Special Period (Pelayo et al. 2008). *Giardia* is a tiny parasite that causes diarrhea and can be found in soil, food or water that contain fecal contamination (CDC 2011). Many residents of Cuba, especially in Havana, boil their water or purchase bottled water to avoid this malady. In turn, boiling water to make it potable can concentrate the mineral salts in the tap water and create kidney stones if consumed in sufficient amounts. Young children and the elderly, whose systems may not be immune to these parasites—even at small levels of exposure—are particularly vulnerable to this malady. Los Portales labels emphasize the purity of their springs and the healthfulness of their products, all of which contribute to a healthier life style.

Los Portales soft drink flavors draw on fruit extracts of tropical flavors such as pineapple and a local flavor called maté,[5] which is a tea-based carbonated beverage often called *soda yerba mate* in other Spanish-language markets. Both maté and orange flavors are extracts derived from their original plants. These Los Portales drinks, however, are known for not staining the tongue as do other extracted flavors, thereby offering the consumer another product advantage over other soft drinks.

Recall from the previous discussion that the current advertising outlets are confined to Radio Taíno; the news-oriented weekly *Semanario Opciones*; the international edition of the official Cuban Communist Party publication, *Granma Internacional*; tourist pamphlets and publications approved by the Ministry of Tourism (MINTUR); the airline magazine *Sol y Son* (included in the seat pocket on all Cubana de Aviación [Cuban Airlines] flights); and a few limited outdoor billboards. Some short-lived windows for advertising also cropped up in 1998 and 1999 on Cuban television, the Latin American Film Festival and a few selected international sporting events (1998 World Cup tournament in France, the 1999 Pan Am Games in Winnipeg and the World Volleyball Games). They were unique because they were the first ads to appear in 40 years, and there has not been a repeat of this kind of product placement since then (mid-2011).

The 1998 World Cup games in France were particularly eventful for Ciego Montero because it ran a few TV spots and running headlines at the bottom of the screen on Cuban broadcasts. The TV spots showed the Ciego Montero labels and logos for its water and soft drinks whereas the running headlines lasted just 10 seconds and were transmitted at the beginning and during the halftime of each game. Significantly, the spots were suggestive and never showed anyone consuming the products. Instead, there was just the sound of running water and the text of the brand slogan at the time, which loosely translates as: "unique, for the first time" (*única por primera vez*). Ciego Montero contracted for 22 minutes of airtime over 16 days and 16 games during the World Cup. In all, the brand was mentioned 128 times for a maximum viewing audience of eight million Cubans, though it is unknown how many actual viewers there were because companies like Nielsen do not operate in Cuba.

The 1999 Pan Am Games in Winnipeg carried 120 10-second TV spots for a total of 20 minutes of broadcast exposure. World Volleyball League advertisements consisted of 128 10-second ads for about 21 minutes of promotion. Like the French games mentioned earlier, the estimated viewing audience was set at eight million.

Ciego Montero and Los Portales also used venues at Cuban business expos (called *ferias comerciales*) during this stage of their product placement. Unlike the sporting events, these business shows added B2B targets in their marketing strategy during the first six years of exhibiting at these venues. In the 2000s, though, the marketing communication strategy expanded to include public relations, news releases for the international press and information for consumers that showed product breadth and depth. The broadened communications strategy was helpful in showcasing different products that could then compete for awards in quality categories given at the Havana International Fair Festivals.

Point-of-sale promotions have been regularly used for Ciego Montero and Los Portales products. Posters, beverage coolers, inflatable objects and suspended three-dimensional objects can be seen in many retail outlets, hotels and restaurants (almost exclusively charging in hard currency). Similar promotional objects are displayed at business-training events sponsored by the half-dozen or so state retail stores. An array of objects carrying the companies' logos includes baseball caps, T-shirts, lighters, pens, thermoses, umbrellas, tables, chairs and key chains. Given the scarcity of material goods across the island, these items are particularly valued by Cubans.

In 2007, Ciego Montero's logo and packaging label got a face-lift designed to give it a fresher look. Its logo was redesigned to seem more modern. The quality of the printing improved, giving it a crisper, more contemporary feel. Bottles were redesigned to become more ergonomically friendly and the product became color-coded based on the type of water: carbonated water bottles carry a green tint and regular mineral is blue. Polythene labels replaced the paper ones to prevent mildew stains in a country with high humidity. Printed labels are now generally more aesthetically pleasing, with crisper lettering and background contrast.

Like many new joint-venture companies, external validation of market testing is rarely made available. The reasons may have to do with intellectual proprietary issues and the firms' desires to safeguard in-house practices. Los Portales does, however, try to get a handle on satisfaction and quality-control issues by holding fortnightly meetings with sales and marketing teams. Both teams go over consumer feedback and discuss changes in production, raw-material inputs and related topics.

In the late 1990s, the company relied heavily on third-party wholesalers. Today, though, it has become more involved in distributing its beverages directly, though it also relies on Almacenes Universales, a wholesale company operated by the Revolutionary Armed Forces of Cuba.

Significant Differences among Competing Brands

Table 6.3 compares and contrasts some of the salient features of the bottled water companies operating in Cuba. Besides the 'purified' versus 'natural' water differences discussed previously, bottling sizes vary; Peña Azul carries the larger two- and five-liter containers and only manufactures noncarbonated water. Ciego Montero and Los Portales offer both formats and do not produce purified water.

Table 6.3 Cuban Bottled Water Producers by Format and Type

Brand	Mineral-Natural	Purified	Format			
			Mineral-Natural		With Gas	
Ciego Montero	X		500 ml	1500 ml	500 ml	1250 ml
Los Portales	X		500 ml	1500 ml	500 ml	1500 ml
Las Lomas		X	500 ml	1500 ml	500 ml	1500 ml
Peña Azul		X	2L	5L	-	-

Source: Calculated by authors.

New Products and Exports

Los Portales has tried to design and introduce new products in the course of the firm's operation. Originally, it produced lemon-lime, cola and orange-flavored soft drinks. Slowly, pineapple, maté and TuKola Light were introduced. Ciego Montero recently introduced five-liter plastic containers that afford buyers a greater quality and price value than smaller units. Thus far, the principal clients for the large containers appear to be institutional in nature, with a greater demand from hotels, private bed-and-breakfasts, embassies and foreign businesses than from individuals or households. Larger containers may also find a niche around hurricane season as the island stocks up on emergency provisions.

As of mid-2011, Los Portales was exporting only to neighboring Caribbean countries. It does, though, sell to airline catering companies that service international flights.

CASE 5: BRAVOS S.A. (PROCESSED MEATS)

This joint venture was established in 1996 between the Cuban Ministry of Food and the Spanish firm Proyectos Valencia en el Caribe. Bravos manufactures a variety of cold cuts: pork, turkey, chicken and beef, and brings to the venture high-quality food processing technology. In the mid-2000s, Bravo's revenues stemmed from four sectors: tourism (54.74 percent), the Cuban domestic market[6] (29.97 percent purchased by ministries to provide worker luncheons and afternoon snacks [*meriendas*]), retailers (11.78 percent) and exports (3.61 percent). It is the leading provider of cold cuts and processed meats in the Cuban domestic market and the island's tourism sector. It was the first company in Cuba to incorporate ISO 14000 standards (Verdecia 2005) and to enlist three quality-control measures in its production and distribution systems.

In the mid-2000s, the company underwent a rebranding and marketing exercise designed to dominate the retail market and provide new products that were more affordable to Cubans. The firm recognized that until that time, its products had been geared to higher-end consumers. In the process of repositioning itself, it has earned international awards given at international business expos. It has also won praise for the design of its display booths at conventions and it has been awarded prizes for the design of its product.

Demand for processed meats in Cuba quickly brought Bravo to its production capacity. Bravo's many meat categories meant that it had no immediate competitors. Product depth was due to the Spanish taste for a variety of meats not often found in other countries (e.g., a variety of sausages ([*chorizo* and *morcilla*], pâtés, aged and smoked and cured meats [including the well -known *serrano* ham], multiple kinds of head cheeses and salami). This gave the firm a first-entry advantage in several product categories, and encouraged them to package meats for the fast-food chain El Rápido under the brand *Jamón Rápido.*

Part of Bravo's positioning strategy led them to conduct consumer behavior research. Just over three-quarters (77 percent) of a sample of 303 Havana consumers surveyed in a recent study stated they knew of the brand, but of that same group, only 41 percent claimed that they knew the brand 'well' or 'very well' (Bravo S.A. 2005). The company's follow-up research showed that most consumers of Bravo meats did not realize they were eating its product because it was prepared by a chef or a short-order cook in a restaurant (Morales et al. 2005). Follow-up strategies indicated a need to increase the visibility of the brand and better understand the decision-making process driving consumer choice. Three follow-up questions were put to the sample: "Have you heard of Bravo brands?" (brand recognition); "What brands of cold cuts do you know?" (spontaneous recall), and "What is the first brand of cold cuts that comes to mind?" (first recall). Only one of the three questions was posed to each informant because of the suggestive nature of the question.

As Franzen and Moriarty (2009, 345) argue, "Brands that are introduced at an early stage of the development of a category can maintain a high market share for many years." As consumer purchasing power rises on the island, market entry into the foods sector—a particularly undercapitalized yet high-demand market in Cuba—will not be confined to just joint-venture operations; private wholesalers and retailers will hopefully select brands without government gatekeeping.

CASE 6: CORALAC S.A. (ICE CREAM)

This firm, created in1997, combined the Ministry of Food Industry's entity Coralsa S.A. with the multinational food conglomerate Nestlé, whose 2010 global sales reached nearly US$124 billion (Nestlé 2011). Back in 1996, the Swiss food giant signed a letter of intent with the Cuban government to build an ice-cream factory in Cuba for the local market. Today, the factory produces more than 20 flavors of ice cream, but its output reflects only part of Nestlé's family of products. Non-Cuban-produced products include baby food, breakfast foods, cookies and chocolates, a variety of beverages, bottled water and pet foods.

Introducing foreign ice-cream brands into Cuba was no easy task. To begin with, purchasing power is limited. In addition, the island has a very special (i.e., sweet and tropical) inclination for ice cream, and is attached to a well-known Cuban brand called Coppelia. That company operates a pavilion in the heart of the Vedado district, which is in front of a large and popular movie theater and the large Habana Libre Hotel, formerly the Havana Hilton. Somewhat of a cultural icon, this plaza and ice-cream parlor was the setting for the opening scene of the acclaimed 1995 Cuban film, *Fresas y Chocolate* (Strawberries and Chocolate), produced by the much adored Cuban director Tomás Gutiérrez Alea (known as the Titan or *el titón*), who died the year after the release of the film. At its peak, Coppelia brand ice creams came in 52 flavors and were known for using quality ingredients. However, these pricey inputs led to high production costs, whose overruns were covered by the public sector. Over time, the number of flavors gradually declined, not to mention there were issues of whether a particular retailer had those flavors in stock.

Ice-cream tastes and preferences have changed over the past 60 years or so. Before the Revolution, a wide variety of ice-cream flavors were consumed on sticks, as a single scoop on a cone, in the form of ice-cream sandwiches and other ways. Coppelia's entry into the market in the 1970s changed those habits. The company introduced multiple scoops in ice-cream cones, a three-flavored scooping called *tres gracias* and the so-called ice-cream salad. All of these calorie-charged delights remain popular.

Nestlé faced a double threat in considering its entrance into the island's market. The first was the introduction of its brand into a market where the purchasing power was low, and company products would have to be sold in convertible currency, because the Cuban peso is not traded globally. A second challenge, something that other joint-ventures faced, was how to sell a product without relying on mass communication outlets. After all, Nestlé would have to overcome its low level of brand recognition, surpass the promises and memories of Coppelia's products and convince the public to purchase a minor luxury good in hard currency. The tourist market would be less problematic, as the global food conglomerate holds strong recognition throughout the world, even as a joint venture (Buchel 2003).

In Nestlé's early promotional efforts, it relied on importing its products from outside Cuba, mostly from Mexico. In April 2003, it decided to build a factory in Cuba after being convinced that the venture could be profitable. The logistics process of introducing the product to the island market started with Havana City Province. Nestlé began by superimposing a set of concentric zones centered on the heart of the city. After reaching sales goals of Nestlé's products in hotels, restaurants and retail outlets in one zone it then advanced to the next contiguous concentric zone and so forth.

Such a cautious and incremental approach to capturing Cuba market share proved to be effective. A white oval-shaped logo with red letters and a blue background was eye-catching and somewhat similar to the Cuban national flag (Figure 6.9). Nestlé decided to use a slogan it employed elsewhere in the Caribbean: "An irresistible desire" (*un deseo irresistible*). Hence, both the slogan and the logo played a key role in the marketing communication strategy. This visual treatment of the logo on coolers and refrigerators spread to wastebaskets, tables, delivery trucks, coasters for glasses and other products. These elements helped to deliver a consistent message about the products: quality, safety, modernity and trust; elements that have driven the Swiss pharmacist and entrepreneur Henri Nestlé's branding since its inception in 1868.

Of all the product promotional devices that exist in Cuba, it is perhaps the ice-cream cooler that has done the most to enhance Nestlé's brand. Its effectiveness seems to be that it is functional; customers go to it, open it and select the Nestlé product they seek. In modern retailing across the globe this may not seem so novel, but there are very few self-service products like that in Cuba. The refrigerator units maintain a carefully controlled temperature, which is essential in a subtropical setting where problems with the refrigeration of dairy products carry health consequences. Coolers are also accompanied by a price board where positions, products and prices are carefully segmented. In the lower part, one finds the least expensive items;

Figure 6.9 Nestlé-branded freezer (left) and waste can carry the product logo and remain the major sources of in-store advertising for Coralac's Swiss–Cuban operation. Photograph by Emilio Morales.

the middle lists products for children; and the most expensive items would appeal to adults wanting pricier items. Over 1,000 of these multifunctional coolers (e.g., part refrigerator unit and part mini-billboard) can be found in Cuba. The tourist pole of Havana has 45 percent of them, Matanzas (home to the famous Varadero Beach) has the second most (12 percent) and the rest are distributed across the island (Javier Texido, personal communication, 2005).

Grec Hillman, business advisor from the Strategic Unit of Nestlé Helados (ice cream), highlights the company's careful treatment of the brand in Cuba. He concluded after visiting more than 40 retail sites in Cuba that the coolers greatly enhanced the brand images in ways that other Caribbean sales points had not. Specifically, he pointed out the good condition of the coolers (cleanliness, lack of rusting) and the efficient work of the Coralac sales team driving that success (Texido, personal communication, 2005).

Nestlé-Coralac used two additional strategies to position itself and distinguish itself from the competition. A number of competitors used various-size tubs of ice cream that were packaged in different-shaped containers, and not all these formats were available throughout the year. Nestlé-Coralac standardized ice-cream container sizes and stocked their retail outlets consistently with all flavors. Neither consistent stocking of food products nor providing a variety of flavors has characterized food retailing in Cuba, neither in pesos nor in hard currency. The Nestlé-Coralac supply-chain process was unique and consumers recognized it.

The company keeps its flavors simple, and only three are for sale at any given time. Chocolate and strawberry are the regular flavors, which are rounded out seasonally with a third flavor such as almond, orange-pineapple and shortbread. Additional research is probably required to establish consumers' order of preference for certain flavors and how they vary regionally.

CASE 7: CORACÁN S.A. (POWDERED BEVERAGES)

This joint venture is the result of the union of the Canadian company Reuven International with the Cuban Ministry of Food Industry company Coralsa S.A. Reuven's core competency is to "source premium quality poultry products for the Canadian market from Canada, the USA, and around the world" (Reuven International 2011a). Their relevance to Cuba, however, is that they also provide "product solutions to the retail, food service and industrial poultry market. We offer importation, warehousing, and distribution to food product manufacturers, food service companies, quick service restaurant chains, grocery retailers" (Reuven International 2011b). Coralsa specializes in instant foods and has more than 40 such products in its portfolio. Its flagship product is a powdered soft drink called Piñata, which generates 45 percent of the company's sales.

Background on Powdered Beverages in Cuba

Powdered beverages have undergone impressive market growth around the world and they have evolved from simple, even humble origins. Their convenience, customizability, price, ease of transport and profitability make them attractive to companies attempting to innovate and add new product lines. Baby boomer North American readers will recall Tang and Kool-Aid as two of the original products in this category. Later, Gatorade came out with a powdered sports drink. Today, the global consumer market receives dozens of new powdered products annually, and in 2008, global sales in the powdered beverage category reached a respectable 7 percent growth. Even commodity giant Cargill is eager to tap into the nearly US$1 billion market because it is both profitable and offers a lower-cost alternative to already mixed, liquid drinks, especially in periods of economic downturns when consumers shop for high-value and low-priced products. Gatorade, Propel, AriZona, Zizzazz and Jones Soda have even launched single-portion powder pouches (Beverages Spectrum Magazine 2010). The origins of powdered beverages in Cuba began on a simpler note.

The consumption of packaged instant beverages in Cuba dates back to just before the Revolution, though the mixing of sugar, water and fruit juice has a long history. Instant beverages had a resurgence in the Special Period after the legalization of hard currency and the promotion of new products for the internal market. Powdered beverages rely in good measure on a sugar base and some additives or natural citrus flavor. Before the manufacturing of processed powdered drinks, a popular homemade Cuban beverage combined brown or white sugar with freshly squeezed lemon juice. The dark sugar and lemon drink was popularly called *sopa de gallo* (literally 'rooster soup' even though it was consumed cold or at room temperature) and the white sugar mix was simply called lemonade. Today, both are popular Cuban household drinks. *Sopa de gallo* is associated with working-class, rural and lower-income families (perhaps because the unrefined sugar is less expensive). These instant beverages can also be prepared with natural orange juice, in which case they are locally referred to as *naranjada* and for generations have been mainstays in Cuban households.

Many carbonated beverages existed and were heavily marketed in Cuba before the Revolution: Coca-Cola, Pepsi-Cola, Orange Crush, Materva and Salutaris, among others. However, prerevolutionary Cuban markets also carried natural fruit juices made from melon, orange, pineapple and other local flavors. These juices were sold in restaurants, storefronts and small, often improvised kiosks (*timbiriches callejeros*). Small cane-juice operations called *guaraperas* crushed the juice (*guarapo*) out of cane stock and provided a quick, refreshing and nutritious drink that is served over ice and is topped off by a natural froth created in the mixing process.

Kool-Aid had its trademark registered on the island in 1951 (Kool-Aid Days 2011). Its success was most likely because the 1927 invention by Edwin Perkins in Hastings, Nebraska, offered the same advantages to Cubans as it did to consumers around the world: powdered envelopes were low priced, avoided the breakage of glass containers and kept shipping costs low (Hastings Museum of Natural and Cultural History 2011). Although the soft drink market had many products, Kool-Aid was the only foreign powdered beverage on the island at the time. Its market penetration strategy touted the variety of flavors and its easy preparation. Powdered drinks and foods of another type were already known in Cuba; Kresto and Milo were powdered chocolate beverages and Jell-O instant gelatins had been well received before the 1950s.

The Cuban Powdered Beverage Market Today

Since 1993, the 'dollar' market has unleashed a variety of carbonated beverages, some of which we have discussed elsewhere in the book. The most widely consumed Cuban beverages today are TuKola, Tropicola, Cachito, Najita and Ciego Montero. PET technology has made plastic containers the most economical and popular containers for these beverages, whereas bulk, can or glass-bottle soft drink consumption is less common. The Special Period also unleashed a new set of wholesalers who provided service mostly to the tourism sector. Carbonated beverages manufactured by Ciego Montero as well as juices (orange, pineapple, piña colada, grapefruit) are also distributed by these wholesalers. Domestic producers vying for a piece of the market include Los Portales, CIMEX, Becasa, Locarino, ITH and AT Comercial, among others.

A different market exists on the island quite separate from the tourism sector, and it includes Cuban institutions that provide lunches, afternoon snacks (*meriendas*) and dinners to their employees. The present-day hard-currency producers for this internal market include Piñata, Butti, Caricias, Toqui, Drink and Tang.[7] Price points are the key advantage of the instant refreshment market over bottled carbonated beverages. As noted earlier, they are also practical and easy to store and to prepare.

Marketing research by Morales and Hernández (2005) on the possible introduction of a new product—Piñata Light—assessed Piñata's brand position and that of its competitors in the powdered beverage category within the island's hard-currency market. A product-awareness survey of 2,401 consumers showed that 99 percent had heard of Piñata; almost nine out of 10 had tried the product whereas less than two of three (34.06 percent) had heard of the second-place brand, Butti. To determine the level of consumer awareness, a simple Likert scale question was posed (Table 6.4). Nearly nine out of 10 respondents stated that they knew the product either 'well' or 'very well.'

Table 6.4 Level of Brand Awareness of Piñata

Awareness Level	Number of respondents	Percentage
Somewhat	31	1.3
A little	250	10.5
Well	1,366	57.1
Very well	745	31.1
Total	2,392	100%

Source: Morales and Hernández (2005).

How did Coracán position Piñata as the undeniable leader in the instant beverage category without using mass communication venues? The answer lies in their heavy reliance on alternative means of advertising. Their logo was made over once (Figure 6.10) and their packaging labels were redesigned three times. Apparently, this was done without confusing consumers; on the contrary, it appears to have given them stronger brand recognition. The 1998 image depicted cartoon or outer-space-like orange fruit characters. By 2002, the label had shed its extraterrestrial image and, with what might have been perceived as communication antennae sticking out of their heads, the characters now seemed more like a fruit stem. In 2005, the product image lost one of its juvenile-like characters and opted for images of fresh-cut oranges and the kind of frosty pitcher in the background that Kool-Aid had long used in its packaging and advertising. In so doing, Coracán shifted its labeling from targeting children to including adults as well.

Sales for 2002 dipped slightly (0.28 percent), which was the first time the packaging had changed. Other events transpired that same year: a new competitor (Butti) entered the market and a bootleg product illegally named Piñata began circulating on the island's black market. The manufacturers of the illicit product used an adulterated version of it and were selling it to retailers (the perpetrators were eventually arrested and prosecuted). Nonetheless, the new competition and bad press surrounding the adulterated Piñata—which lasted about two years—seem to have offset any growth sales produced by the new packaging label. Piñata's competitors took advantage of the company's misfortunate and were able to gain market share and better position themselves in the instant beverage market.

Coracán implemented a series of corrective measures in order to recover from the bad press caused by the product tampering and the new competition. They improved their distribution network by eliminating contractors and distributing the merchandize themselves, changed the taste of the product and gave it a higher yield (water to powder ratio). By 2005, Piñata had recovered the ground lost in retail sales from three years earlier.

Figure 6.10 Evolution of Piñata packaging, top, 1998; middle, 2002; and bottom, 2005.

To measure their market position, they commissioned a survey of 2,402 consumers to get their perceptions of seven instant beverage brands (the universe of brands in this category that were sold in Cuba) and seven attributes. Consumers gave Piñata the highest overall scores in their responses to Likert scale attributes about flavor, color, price, image, packaging, quality and market stability (Table 6. 5). Significantly, more than twice as many consumers were familiar with Piñata (2,182) than the second leading brand (Butti); it outperformed the competition in four of the seven product attributes, even in the realm of 'market stability' despite the tampering and falsification scandal a few years earlier. By the mid-2000s, Piñata had regained its lead in the instant refreshment category.

Our final two cases depart from the joint-venture category and represent fully owned Cuban companies, products and services. Of the many unsuccessful state operations that exist, these two—Palmares S.A. and El Rápido S.A.—are worthy of review because they offer an alternative to centrally planned state companies that have not implemented standard business practices.

Palmares and El Rápido belong to Cuban holding companies—Cubanacán S.A. and CIMEX S.A., respectively—that have stockholders and their own accountancy operations and function as private firms within the Cuban government, but they are not publicly traded. Both Cubanacán and CIMEX are partnered in joint-venture operations within Cuba and overseas. Palmares and El Rápido manage advertising budgets and possess investment, marketing and related departments. They are examples of Cuban companies that over the past 18 years have marketed their brands and possess considerable financial autonomy over their operations. We do

Table 6.5 Evaluation of Selected Brand Attributes for Instant Beverages sold in Cuba

Brand	Flavor	Color	Price	Image	Package	Quality	Market Stability	Mean	N
Piñata	4.72	4.81	4.42	4.89	4.80	4.72	4.68	4.72	2,182
Butti	4.76	4.8	4.5	4.88	4.79	4.78	3.54	4.58	818
Caricia	4.44	4.69	4.1	4.77	4.79	4.49	3.68	4.42	795
Toqui	3.89	4.24	4.45	4.40	4.38	4.09	4.18	4.23	586
Drink	4.49	4.6	4.54	4.77	4.74	4.52	3.95	4.52	286
Tang	4.33	4.80	4.43	4.86	4.64	4.79	2.79	4.38	15
Ambrosio	4.29	4.83	4.67	4.0	4.2	4.0	4.17	4.31	7

Source: Morales and Hernández 2005.

Note: 2,401 consumers were surveyed and were allowed to respond on the brands' attributes as long as they stated they were familiar with it. Thus, while 2,182 were familiar with Piñata (90.8%), only 15 had any experience with Tang (.62%) and just seven (0.32%) had tasted Ambrosio, highlighting the disparity of consumer knowledge of this product category.

not know, however, what percentage of profits return to the Cuban government and how much is used for research and development, salaries or other 'discretionary' uses.

Just like the seven joint-venture companies discussed earlier in this chapter. Palmares and El Rápido form part of the business scene that has introduced successful Cuban and international brands. Their human capital contribution to the labor force cannot be underestimated; they have been responsible for training personnel in accounting, finance, management, human resources, information technology, marketing and related fields. Some employees have been trained in Cuba and many have studied abroad, especially in Spain, elsewhere in Western Europe and Mexico. To some degree, they have been at the cutting edge in the emerging Cuban business scene, and they have helped to change the patterns of individual and household consumption on the island.

CASE 8: PALMARES S.A. (RESTAURANTS)

One of the two Cuban cases is Palmares, a successful restaurant chain operated in Cuba. After its formation in 1994, it catered exclusively to international tourism through its mid- and high-range restaurants concentrated in the island's tourist poles. In 2000, it embarked on a campaign to provide hard-currency restaurant services to Cubans by introducing new brands into the market. In 1999, Palmares ranked fifth in restaurant revenue sales out of seven Cuban restaurant chains, with around US$25 million in gross revenues. By 2003, it had the greatest restaurant revenues with around US$48 million in a field of nine Cuban restaurants (Poder Popular, Rumbos, CIMEX, Cubalse, Habaguanex, Artex, Isla Azul and Gran Caribe) (Morales and Hernández 2003). Both its revenue growth (87.59 percent) and market share growth (6.46 percent) suggested that it was doing something right (Table 6.6), but what?

In good measure Palmares' growth stems from their launching of five new restaurant brands: Ditu, Pan.Con, En familia, Dinos Pizza and Dimar, which led to an average US$5 million increase per annum between 1993 and 2003 (Morales and Hernández 2004). Ditu earned US$12.7 million in 2003 with just three years on the market and surpassed middle- and higher-tier restaurants.

Palmares appears to have had gained such rapid growth for the following reasons. First, it quickly captured a share of the hard-currency restaurant market because its main product—roasted chickens—had not been well developed by other franchises. Second, it capitalized on those restaurants that were losing market share because of poor quality, high prices or a combination of the two. Third, its sales venues had little overhead because the aluminum, glass and plastic prefabricated structures are relatively inexpensive and carry a small footprint. Of course, Ditu did not rely on mass

Table 6.6 Cuban Restaurant Market Share and Revenue Performance, 1999–2003

Restaurant chain	Percentage Revenue Growth	Percentage Market Share Growth
Poder Popular	4.63	-3.22
Rumbos	9.4	-2.9
Palmares	87.59	6.46
CIMEX	26.63	-.36
Cubalse	-3.02	-3.18
Habaguanex	11.96	-.82
Puerto Sol	-25.54	-.39
Artex	n.a.	.06
Isla Azul	n.a.	5.99
Gran Caribe	-67.41	-1.42

Source: Palmares, S.A., n.d. Note: Restaurant revenues refer to non-hotel dining establishments, which in Cuba are known as *gastronomía extrahotelera.*

communication outlets. Its name proved to be somewhat innovative and catchy: *ditu* in Cuban vernacular translates loosely as "you tell me" or "whatever you say," and it created a lot of WOM buzz.

CASE 9: EL RÁPIDO (FAST FOOD, SMALL PACKAGE GOODS STORE)

El Rápido was formed within CIMEX, the largest retailing company on the island, in late 1994, and opened its first ketchup-red and mustard-yellow store (Figure 6.11) at the corner of 15th and L Streets, in the Vedado district of Havana. Over the next year, the chain opened 67 stores in 10 (of the 14)

Figure 6.11 Ketchup-red- and mustard-yellow-colored El Rápido fast-food restaurant, the largest chain of its kind in Cuba. Photograph by Emilio Morales.

provinces, with a heavy concentration in Havana City and Varadero, where hard currency was in high circulation because of tourism. El Rápido seems to have enjoyed first-entry advantage because it was the first store of its kind to open in the post-decriminalization of the dollar era.

The chain targets Cuban households with access to hard currency. Its menu incorporates the staples of the global fast-food business: pizza, fried chicken, hot dogs and sandwiches. True to their name, customers expect quick (*rápido*) service, a feature that is uncommon in the peso service market (Scarpaci 1995; Eckstein 2003; Corbett 2004). In somewhat of a 1950s retro approach, the waiters and waitresses had originally skated up to drive-in customers in their cars to take orders for sweets, fried foods (French fries, *empanadas*—fried meat or cheese pies), soft drinks, juices, beer and other beverages. A few years later, though, the roller-skating service ended. But other factors contributing to their success were the standardization of goods and a unique product mix (dine-in, takeout, mixed with an array of convenience items like cigarettes and other low-end sundries common at stores like 7-Eleven). Trays were disposable (cardboard and Styrofoam) and food was cooked or prepared at off-site production centers. This guaranteed a standardized product and quick service, making it necessary only to reheat certain sandwiches, chicken and pizza. No other restaurateur in the emerging nascent hard-currency restaurant sector had delivered fast food this way.

External validation, rightly or wrongly, came through the awards El Rápido earned at the Havana International Fair, which aims to promote service and product excellence across a span of categories. The 2010 event attracted over 1,000 companies from over 50 countries (Feriahavana 2011). El Rápido earned several first and grand prizes for the 'restaurant design' category in the fair's 'Food Festival.' It also earned first place for the best plate competition.

By 2011, the chain operated over 300 establishments on the island with 2006 sales at US$49.1 million. In the first half of the 2000s, its growth rate was above 5 percent per annum. By the late 2000s, the brand was undergoing some redesigning because it had been on the market for 12 years, and there was a sense among the management at CIMEX that its life cycle could be lengthened through a new branding strategy.

CONCLUSIONS

The product assortments discussed in these nine cases range from a single, fast-food convenience store model (El Rápido) to multiple cigar products offered by Habanos S.A. Marketing strategies paralleled the historic production era of the early twentieth century when just 'putting it out there' was sufficient because there was not a lot of competition; witness the account retold of Henry Ford in Chapter 2. By the mid-1990s, the companies reviewed in this chapter realized that just 'putting it out there' was not enough; consumers were beginning to shop around for various product and service attributes. The modestly successful case studies analyzed here show an upward trend in revenues and many of these companies have taken advantage of their first-entry position. Still, these firms encountered a number of problems. Havana Club and Nestlé had to overcome poor supply-chain distribution obstacles. Piñata battled product-tampering issues but in three years regained market leadership. Unlike many state firms that could afford budget over runs and poor sales, at least two products—Ciego Montero Cola and Levísima water—were cannibalized and withdrawn, respectively, because of brand dissonance in the minds of Cuban consumers. And though just 18 years are covered in our review of these products, examples of product cycle are evident; witness, for instance, Piñata's thrice changed package design and how it recast its position from the juvenile market to broader consumer groups.

Regardless of the product breadth (variety) or the depth of the product line, each case needed to demonstrate that their product created value for the newly emerging Cuban consumer market. Cuba's emerging market allows these brands an opportunity to establish loyalty, gain advantage over competitors as first entries and grow brand equity. However, brand awareness, perceived value, brand associations (largely developed during the Castro brothers' tenure) and brand loyalty will face new challenges if a truly unfettered market manifests on the island. Although the short-lived 1998–1999 TV and radio marketing campaigns were nixed, it may have provided a metric against which reforms in the 2011 VI Cuban Communist Party will be assessed. As Sanguinetty argued in the early years of Cuban market reform:

> A more efficient economic system must be de-politicized. Economic considerations, not political ones, must prevail in economic decision making. In order to achieve this, economic agents (consumers, workers, investors, etc.) must have sufficient freedom of choice and economic power, even if their political choice is still constrained. Economic changes in Cuba are so far cosmetic in essence, simply because the government refuses to give a role to the Cubans. (1995, 23)

Although the Cuban retail market has evolved since that assessment, the consumer goods and services market is still controlled by ministerial decisions about which companies—state-owned or joint venture—can enter. Evidence from post-Soviet USSR and Eastern Europe shows that even when free markets emerge, consumer wishes are merely illusory because the purchasing power required to enter these markets remains low, especially among the elderly (Keller and Vihalemm 2005). In essence, the requisite consumer purchasing power in Cuba will have to be coupled with market reforms if real consumer choice is going to be sustained. As Reid (2002, 212) reminds us:

> Consumption is clearly a central issue in the study of post-Soviet culture. But the tastes, desires, and expectations of the new Russian consumer did not emerge on a tabula rasa.

Nor has Cuba's consumer culture been borne out of thin air. That is why understanding new Cuban product promotion and brand development of these companies will be useful in understanding how the, tastes, desires and expectations of the Cuba of tomorrow will respond to a limited yet formidable set of consumer goods and services. There are valid arguments to be made that it is morally reprehensible to market tobacco and alcohol products—occupying six of the top -10 domestic consumer spots—in a country where food, supply transportation and water quality are serious problems (Martínez 1991; Alfonso 1994; Gordy 2006; Bunck 2003). As Julie Bunk (2003, 168) rightly asks in her comparison of Vietnam and Cuba:

> Why should lifelong Marxists be directing a capitalist economy? Why are Marxist societies lagging so far behind their capitalist neighbors? And, why should foreigners but not citizens be given special tax incentives, opportunities to own property with guarantees against expropriation, and—in Cuba—special stores, hotels and restaurants?

Theoretical questions like these appear to be increasingly ephemeral in the Cuban business world as issues of everyday life assume priority for *cubanos* across the island. New discourses may try to mask over this criticism as product promotion in the future uses a dizzying array of new media tools that send Cuba further along the path of consumption. In the meanwhile, the power of remittances will no doubt drive Cubans down that path, a topic to which we turn in our final substantive chapter.

7 Remittances and Brands

Survival and Consumption in the New Millennium

This final substantive chapter examines the impact that the sending of remittances from abroad has had on the development of Cuban businesses and consumer and entrepreneurial behavior since 1993. Recall that the decriminalization of the dollar that year and the subsequent use of the convertible peso have hurried the spread of both international and national brands. Cubans were no longer confined to just subsidized food, clothing, personal hygiene products and household wares. Nonwage income gives Cuban consumers the opportunities to acquire goods and services in greater frequency than a peso-only household income could ever provide. Otherwise, only tips from tourism or under-the-table payment by joint-venture companies are the only other sources available to most Cubans. All of these changes have taken hold since the middle of the 1990s and have continued into the new millennium.

We begin by analyzing the purchasing power of the Cuban population, providing a breakdown of its composition and considering the weight that remittances have. Next, we trace the evolution of remittances over time as well as the changing source of the countries from where they originate. We also describe the major brands that control the transfer of remittances through official channels to the island as well as the unofficial venues. That discussion is followed by an analysis of the role that remittances are likely to play in the national economy—especially the retail sector—and the transforming effect it will have on Cuban society in the next few years. Lastly, we forecast the behavior of remittance transfers and its ramifications on the island to the year 2014 as we take into account different scenarios.

To properly initiate the discussion, however, we begin with a context into which the Cuban case can be situated.

THEORETICAL AND CONCEPTUAL PERSPECTIVES ON REMITTANCES

Several theoretical perspectives anchor the discussion of remittances and their impacts on the sending and receiving nation. At the outset, there are macroeconomic factors that include the advantages and the disadvantages or the costs and benefits of remittances. Balance of payment equations are central to macroeconomic interpretations of remittances and how they influence different sectors of the economy such as the money supply, exchange rates, credit availability, savings rates, housing, business start-ups and related factors. In Latin America, the flow of remittances is uneven, reflecting largely the population size, economic stability and number of migrants working abroad. The United States and Spain are the major source nations for sending remittances to Latin America, and they ranged from a high of US$21 billion sent to Mexico in 2009, to a low of a half a billion in Trinidad and Tobago (Inter-American Development Bank [IADB] 2010[1]). Mexico's proximity to the U.S., the historical pattern of out-migration to jobs that were first in agriculture and now increasingly in services and population size account for such a high figure for Mexico. Trinidad and Tobago, on the other hand, has a relatively developed economy and its low out-migration reflects that. The IADB captures the salience of remittances and migration this way:

> On a macroeconomic level, the volume of remittances transferred to LAC [Latin American and Caribbean] countries dwarfs the combined total of net foreign direct investment flows and official development assistance to the region. In many countries, remittances also represent double-digit portions of gross domestic product.
>
> At the local level, remittances are vitally important to the families receiving them. The funds are used for basic needs, including health and education expenditures, and are invested in assets such as houses and savings, in productive activities (businesses), in social causes, and in community infrastructure. Overall, families that receive remittances are better off than their non-remittance-receiving neighbors. (2010, 2)

So complicated is the measurement of remittances to Cuba, that the IADB study did not even include it. However, as we shall see in this chapter, remittances are the largest single source of hard currency in Cuba, surpassing even the tourist sector.

Remittance research also focuses on a middle level that ratchets the scale of analysis down to specific segments of the economy and market attributes. Socio-demographic and economic variables assess the features of those emigrants working abroad and residents in the developing (receiving) countries. This line of research focuses on the working-age population of the emigrant group and aims to tease out the dependent cohorts at both ends of the demographic spectrum: the elderly and young or school-age children (Orozco 2006).[2] It is difficult to generalize on the profile of remitters. If a popular conception exists that remitters are able-bodied males in their 30s and 40s, there are also exceptions. In Haiti, for instance, "unlike people from other Latin American and Caribbean countries, half of Haitian remitters are women and sixty percent are under thirty years of age" (Orozco 2006, 21).

A third perspective emphasizes the mutual conditioning that exists between migrant streams and remittances, which is a fruitful line of research. In many southern Mexican rural communities, the typical migrant working in the U.S. is middle-aged and male. They leave behind a largely adult female population who look after children, which constrains the kinds of employment women back home can secure. The timing of male migrants' returning to their native villages and towns is a function, among other factors, of the demand for agricultural migrant laborers in the U.S. and Canada, and the seasonality of crops and harvest periods (Jones 1998).[3]

Yet another stream of research places remittances in the literature of globalization and its attendant focus on international migration. Economic adjustments among firms, regions and nations often trigger demand from low-skill sending nations to more industrial economies that seek low-wage workers. Yet, this genre of research on remittances also recognizes the demand for skilled workers in North America, Europe and Australasia. Qualified workers such as engineers, programmers, physicians, natural scientists, college professors and others will remit wages to their home countries (Maimbo and Ratha 2005). Historically, this research stream has been contained within population sociology, demography and population and

Table 7.1 Remittance Guidelines for Sending Money from the U.S. to Cuba

Who Can Receive Money?

Family Remittances

Family remittances are transfers that may be sent to close relatives of the sender in Cuba, up to the third degree of consanguinity, affinity or kinship by adoption (related by blood, marriage or adoption).

Under the new rules, the sender may send money to the following relatives:

- Children, stepchildren, grandchildren and great-grandchildren
- Parents, step-parents, grandparents and great-grandparents
- Spouses, brothers/sisters-in-law, fathers/mothers-in-law, spouses' parents and grandparents
- Brothers/sisters, nephews/nieces
- Uncles/aunts, cousins and second cousins

Remember:

It is not necessary for the last name of the receiver to be the same as the sender. If your husband or wife died, you can continue sending money to their in-laws, grandparents or other relatives.

For more information, call **1-888-984-CUBA (2822)** (in Spanish)

Source: Western Union, http://cuba.westernunion.com/WUCOMWEB/staticMid.do?method=load&pagename=mtSendMoney, Accessed November 28, 2010.

economic geography, but increasingly it is being studied in business and popular culture.

The study of remittances, therefore, spans multiple disciplines. It is a contemporary process with a long history, dating back to the Industrial Revolution when the urban demand for labor triggered a gradual depopulation of many rural settlements. Demand for manufacturing labor in the U.S. accelerated in the first half of the last century whereby European migrants staffed American factories, as did many African Americans who migrated to factories and mills in the 'manufacturing belt' between Duluth and St. Louis, and Pittsburgh and Boston. Sending money 'back home' was a goal among many of those new migrant workers. Today, the focus in the United States is clearly on international migration and remittances; nearly every Western Union station across the 50 states carries bilingual instructions so Spanish-speaking Latin American and Caribbean workers can send money 'home.' Western Union, with more than 380,000 locations worldwide, actually got out of the 'telegram/cable' business (their original core competency) in the early 2000s in order to concentrate on wire or money transfers. Whereas most of the U.S. Spanish-language remittance forms carried by Western Union service Mexican and Central American workers in the U.S., Cuba has a dense network of 150 Western Union stations throughout its provinces. By early 2011, the rules on sending remittances from the U.S. to Cuba revealed very few restrictions (Table 7.1).

INTERNATIONAL MIGRATION PERSPECTIVES

There is common agreement, therefore, that international migrants tend to leave their nations in pursuit of a higher material living standard. The United Nations defines a migrant as "any person who lives temporarily or permanently in a country where he or she was not born, and has acquired some significant social ties to this country" (UNESCO 2010).[4] We can build on this definition by using Everett Lee's (1966) pioneering work on push-pull factors that characterize the origin, destination and intervening obstacles of migration. Essentially, each migrant assesses the positive (+) and negative (–) aspects at the origin and destination. Origin or push factors entail both voluntary and involuntary out-migration, the latter including war, natural disaster, political asylum and even mandatory family reunification of minors with their legal guardians. Destination or pull factors include both material and nonmaterial benefits to the immigrant. Before arriving at the destination, however, the migrant must consider intervening obstacles. These include saving up for the international journey, opportunity costs such as the loss of employment during and after the migration, emotional costs of leaving one's home culture behind and the trauma of the journey itself (ranging from an airline flight or other legal entry on a modern transportation mode, to walking and or rafting across an international border). Figure 7.1 represents the Lee model adapted to the U.S.–Cuban migration conditions.

International migration is defined as the permanent or temporary change of residence that includes residents, seasonal or temporary workers, refugees, students and undocumented persons of various stripes. A variety of factors account for the acceleration of international migration over the past 20 years that bear on our discussion of remittances.

First, technological improvements in global telecommunications allows information to reach sender and receiver nations more quickly than in the past. Theoretically, the positive and negative factors perceived by the migrant should hold greater veracity than in the past, when letter writing or short telephone conversations framed the migrants' decision-making. The Internet, Skype, cable TV, blogs and lower-cost international and Internet-based telephone calls may improve the accuracy about migrating abroad, the attendant job possibilities and a more realistic assessment of the 'pull' factors.

Second, international migration and customs procedures have become more flexible and are easier to verify when crossing borders at customs stations, and embedded bar codes in travel documents and visas are more difficult to falsify. Parallel to this are customs unions such as the European Union, the Andean bloc, Mercosur and other alliances that allow workers to cross borders more freely. More liberalized EU labor laws have been particularly beneficial for 'newcomer' and 'lower -wage' nations of the former Soviet bloc. For Cuban migrants with permanent residence in Spain—the second largest destination of Cuban emigrants—EU documents allows them to more readily secure work in Italy, Germany, France or other nations without suffering lengthy delays in approving the necessary paperwork.

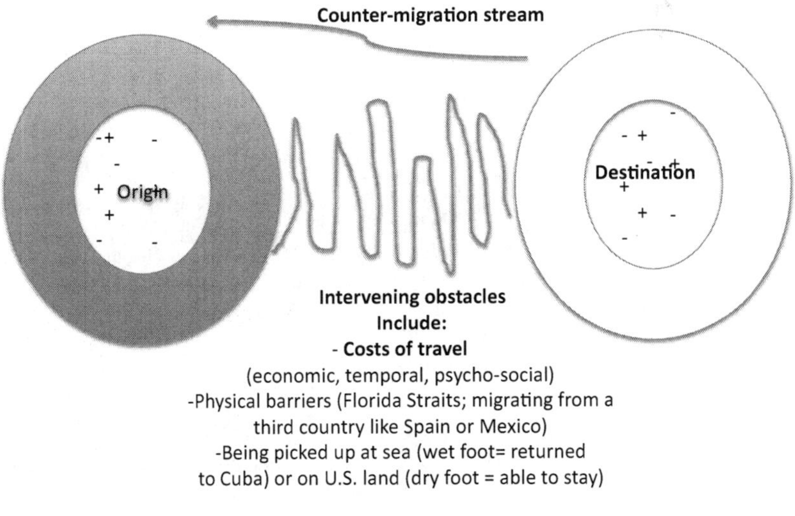

Figure 7.1 Lee's model of migration adapted to Cuba.
Calculated by the author based on Lee's original work.

Third, there has been a resurgence in ethnic, religious, economic, and nationalistic conflict. These tensions create instability that, in turn, encourages the international search for steadier labor markets and settings that are more peaceful. Civil war in Central America in the 1980s, ethnic cleansing in Africa in the 1990s and war in the Middle East in the 2000s characterize this conflict.

Lastly, economic recession has always been a 'push' factor as primary export economies shift or collapse (bananas, tin, coffee), or trade policies hurt certain regions or sectors of the economy (e.g., small Mexican formers after the passage of the North American Free Trade Act in 1994). Remittances and migration continue to function as a tried-and-true means of curbing poverty, however temporary the flow of funds back home might be (Adams and Page 2005). For instance, the demise of the Soviet Union in 1991 sent the Cuban economy into a tailspin that still plagues the economy today. Applications for exit visas (for family reunification or claims of political persecution) and the exit-visa lottery (called *el bombo*) have risen and fallen as economic conditions on the island fluctuate; so too do the attempts to cross the Florida Straits to the United States. Henken (2005a)[5] reports that between 1995 and 2005, some 200,000 Cubans reached the U.S. legally, and at least 10,000 rafters (*balseros*) arrived. A commonly held notion is that only one in four rafters make it, which would imply that at least 30,000 Cubans were lost at sea during that period (Ackerman, personal communication, 2010).[6] Regardless of the accuracy of the data, the

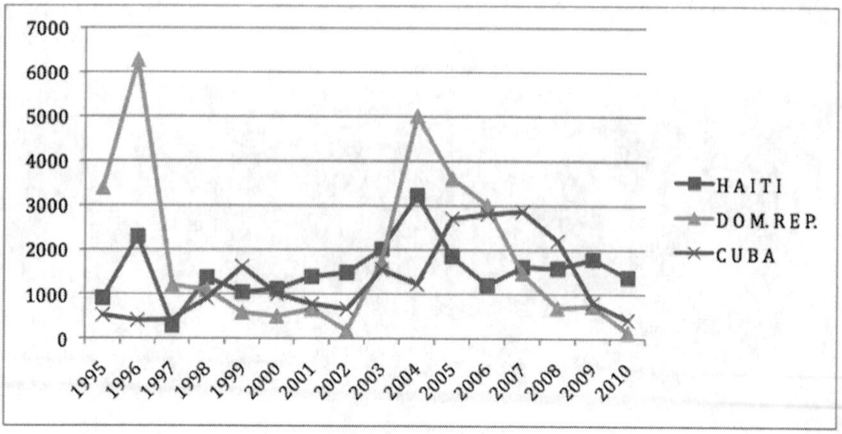

Figure 7.2 U.S. Coast Guard high sea interdictions of Haitian, Dominican, and Cuban migrants headed to the U.S. (including Puerto Rico in the case of the Dominican Republic), 1995–2010 (fiscal years).
Data source: U.S. Coast Guard, Office of Law Enforcement, http://www.uscg.mil/hq/cg5/cg531/AMIO/FlowStats/currentstats.asp, Accessed November 30, 2010

Figure 7.3 Rafters (*balseros*) images. From upper-left-hand corner clockwise: (a) makeshift boat based on 1959 (b) Buick; 1952 truck made navigable; (c) rafters about to be picked up by a tanker; and (d) precarious vessel sinking off the coast of the Bahamas.

out-migration signals the economic pressures of the Special Period. Spikes of interdictions of Cubans in the late 1990s and mid-2000s mirror particularly difficult periods for Cubans on the island (Figure 7.2) and their use of innovative ways to reach American soil (Figure 7.3). The official Cuban government position is that allowing Cubans to remain in the U.S. once they touch foot on land encourages the loss of hundreds or even thousands of Cubans each year who try to navigate the Florida Straits to reach south Florida. One collaborative success that one of us (J.L.S.) has heard in more than a dozen briefings at the U.S. Interests Section in Havana is that U.S. and Cuban authorities work together well and often in Cuban rafter interdiction and repatriation. A less clearly defined yet equally important relationship centers on Washington and Havana policies that influence remittances, gift giving and start-up businesses on the island; all of these factors influence the level of consumption and brand awareness in Cuba.

THE FANDANGO POLICY DANCE BETWEEN WASHINGTON AND HAVANA

How then, are migration, history, geography and international policy tied to consumption in Cuba? The connection, we contend, is not a linear one but the interrelated factors are clear. At the outset, we note that international migration and cooperation talks between Washington and Havana have been highly irregular since the Revolution. It was not until 1977 that President Jimmy Carter established a consulate in Havana. This marked a first step in discussing matters of mutual interest, particularly migration agreements. By the 1990s, the U.S. Consulate office in Havana would regularly report to Americans coming to their building that one of the areas of real cooperation was sitting down periodically with Cuban officials to discuss migration issues. These included how to handle interdictions by either nation's coast guards, transfer of migrants picked up at sea and even drug interdiction information sharing (e.g., cigarette [high-speed] boats running drugs up from South

Table 7.2 Purchasing Power and Consumption Polices: The Washington and Havana Fandago

Year	Barak Obama's Policies	Raúl Castro's Policies	Year
	Stimulating Purchasing Power	Stimulating Consumption	
2010	Easing remittances restrictions and allowing USD $5,000 daily wire transfers to Cuba	Easing computer & DVD player purchases	2007
		Loosening rules on cell phone purchase and purchase	2007
2008–10	Relaxing travel restrictions on Cuban-Americans traveling to the island	Lending more public land to private agriculturalists	2007
	Expanding number of products and value of packages sent to Cuba (from $USD 400 to $800 value)	Broadening private sector jobs Freeing some political prisoners Announcing the laying off a half-million workers (but none were let go as of 4/2011)	2008
		Broadening private sector jobs	2010
	Increasing from $USD 5,000 to $USD 10,000 the maximum remittance allowed per transaction	Freeing some political prisoners Announcing the laying off a half-million workers (but none were let go as of 4/2011)	2010
2010 2011	U.S. Treasury drafts guidelines following President Obama's directive to allow people to people travel that had been prohibited in 2004	Changing the Cuban economic model to an irreversible process Creates more jobs and access to hard currency for workers in tourist sector and allied fields	2010
	Results	Results	
2008 2009–11	Lowering shipping/wiring costs for some firms	Increase in consumer expenditures	2009–10
	Significant increase in travel of Cuban Americans to the island; exceeds 400,000 in 2011	Rise in entrepreneurs' working capital	2009–11
2010	Rise in remittance	Greater private-sector investment; 171,000 private-sector work licenses are approved in just 4 months.	2009–10
2009–11	Increase in packages sent	Greater independence from government	2009–11
2009–11	Enhanced communication among families	Enchanced communication among families	2009–11

Source: Calculated by The Havana Consulting Group

America, past Cuba and along the Bahamian islands chain). These relations were not always harmonious: the Cuban Air Force's 1996 shooting down of a small airplane that had violated Cuban airspace (while dropping leaflets over Havana) killed four Cuban Americans, and the Elián González saga between 1999 and 2001 deeply marred bilateral relations.

Nevertheless, Washington and Havana seem to have engaged in a series of quid pro quo policies that might signal rapprochement. Whether derived from the Spanish fandango, the seguidilla or a Caribbean version of them, both governments have behaved like couples in dances where the partners approach and move away from the other one. In doing so, they send messages of intent. Nowhere has this odd policy dance been more evident than in recent years as the administrations of Barack Obama and Raúl Castro strengthen Cubans' purchasing power and stimulate domestic consumption (Table 7.2).

Significantly, the global downturn of the mid-2000s and late 2000s crisis has not reduced money sent to Cuba. Money that was wired there in 2010 was expected to rise by 16.2 percent over the previous year. Not since the economic opening of 1993 had the dollar amount—approximately US$2 billion—reached this high-water level.

This unusual choreography of policy positions on both sides of the Florida Straits moved in tandem. The allowable daily wiring of money increased to US$10,000. Later, instead of allowing Cuban Americans to travel once every three years, they were allowed to visit even extended kin as often as they liked. Disseminating this news in Cuba has also been helped by unrestricted (though relatively expensive) access to cell phones as well as calling loved ones abroad (Table 7.2).

DECRIMINALIZING CELL PHONE SERVICE

Permitting Cubans to own cell phones without fear of breaking the law increased remittances by 14.24 percent in 2009 compared to 2008. In just the three years since the prohibition was eliminated, cell phone use increased by nearly 250 percent; from about 400,000 in 2008 to nearly a million in 2010. By 2013, assuming a constant rate of growth, there could be 1.4 million cell phones on the island (Table 7.3). These will be essential tools for small retailers to track supplies, sources and related small-business matters.

ETECSA (the Italian–Cuban joint-venture telecommunications firm) earned nearly $US684 million in gross revenues from cell phones alone (without considering landlines and fax lines); 90 percent were paid for by remittances. By 2013, we expect cell phone use will add another $US737 million to ETECSA. Cell phone activation and service rates should fall by 2013 as cell phones become an essential tool in B2B transactions.

The new economic model approved by the April 2011 meetings of the VI Cuban Communist Party Congress underscored the importance of new

Table 7.3 Cell Phone Use and Expenditures in Cuba, 2008–2009, with Projections for 2010–2013

Year	Lines	Service Contact Fees $USD	Service Activation Fees $USD	Cell phone Purchases $USD	Cell phone accesory Purchases $USD	Total $USD
2008	431,861	103,646,640	19,306,112	20,685,120	2,585,640	146,223,512
2009	785,324	188,477,760	21,207,780	42,415,560	5,301,945	257,403,045
2010*	1,007,000	241,680,000	8,867,040	26,601,120	3,325,140	280,473,300
Projections for 2013						
2013	1,405,903	674,833,440	14,156,120	42,468,360	5,308,545	736,766,465

Data source: Reports filed by ETECSA. S.A and various news reports. Calculated by The Havana Consulting Group. Note: 2013 figures are based on ETECSA estimates, which anticipated the approximately three-quarters of a billion $USD revenues by 2014. However, we revise that figure based on recent liberalizations on the island, about which ETECSA was unaware when they made the forecast in August 2010. *Data based only on late August totals.

measures to stimulate private entrepreneurs. Just announcing there would be a laying off a half a million public employees generated over 100,000 applications to start new businesses in late 2010. Downsizing the public sector will test to what extent the Cuban government is willing to meet the challenge of changing the economic model. Recent announcements to liberalize the buying and selling of cars and trucks will be an important supply-chain mechanism in distributing agricultural goods and industrial inputs for private firms. Before 2011, most new car buyers faced a byzantine state-controlled car lot of older vehicles; current car and truck owners have more flexibility in selling their cars to individual prospective buyers. Remittances from overseas will help Cubans purchase thousands of vehicles in the next few years. We expect about 80 percent of the cars and trucks would be used, but the new–used ratio should shift over time as private businesses add to household incomes and increase consumer purchasing power.

M. Orozco (2003) reported in the early 2000s that two-third of remittances sent from the U.S. to Cuba originated in Florida, with New York and New Jersey each contributing 6 percent, California 5 percent and other states the balance (17 percent). Undetermined amounts of individual travelers (called *mulas* or mules) also bring in merchandise. Upon arriving in Cuba, the *mulas* proceed to visit designated households and distribute the money: "Customers feel assured that they can trust the safety of the money and that it will arrive in a short period of time" (Orozco 2003, 9). Orozco describes the *mula* network this way:

There is no single type of mula and their numbers may run in the thousands (exact numbers of mulas cannot be calculated). Some mulas are salaried and employed by particular entrepreneurs who hire them to travel back and forth to Cuba. There are also mulas who are sole proprietors of their informal remittance businesses and who work with family networks in the United States and Cuba. (2003, 5) We know very little about what these *mulas* send, though clearly their brand selection is driven by cost and weight. Charters between Miami and Havana—all U.S. owned—charge US$2.00 per pound. Cuban American economist Mario Gonzalez Corzo describes the relationship with his *mula*—who brings Corzo's mom packages, this way:

> "It's almost like he's telemarketing," Gonzalez Corzo said. "He called me two times to just let me know, 'Hey, Mother's Day is coming up, and I am able to bring anything you need.'" (quoted in Weissert 2008)

Unbeknownst to them, *mulas* act as first-entry retailing marketers as they introduce new products to Cuban consumers.

Recent work on remittances by Orozco (2011) and a team of researchers at Baruch College assessed the impact remittances are having on present and future microentrepreneurship activities in Cuba. Several findings are germane to our study of remittances and consumption in Cuba. First, although the U.S. continues to be the largest source of transfers, Europe and Latin America have increased their contributions. Cuban doctors and nurses working in Venezuela account for the largest increase from the Latin American region. Second, despite President Obama's increase of allowable wire transfers of up to US$10,000 daily, no new remittance transfer operators have entered the market. In fact, *mulas* constitute half of the venues by which money reaches the island; paid individuals simply deliver the money in person. For the purposes of our research, it also means that they are bringing a host of consumer goods. In a survey of 300 receivers of remittances in Cuba, 45 percent said they would be interested in starting a business, 34 percent did start a small enterprise because of remittances and 23 percent were already operating a business (Orozco 2011, 4). The frequency of receiving remittances from abroad rose from six times per year in 2005, to nine times in late 2010 and early 2011. This implies a steadier of flow of cash and the receipt of goods for household or business use and, by extension, more visits to state stores as well as greater exposure to 'branded goods.' Although these branded goods might not all be available in the island's state-run outlets, they are indirectly contributing to Cubans' knowledge about brands, and are shaping their preferences for products, which has expanded since 1993.

18 YEARS OF REMITTANCES

Chapter 2 of this book explained how the government of Fidel Castro eliminated both a middle class and a dense network of retail operations. Within the first eight years, the revolutionary government tried to create an egalitarian society, at least by decree. From the perspective of consumer behavior, Castro was able to make nine million Cubans rely on the state for both jobs and goods and services. Now that all companies were owned by the state, inefficiencies and cost overruns could be 'absorbed' by the government because Soviet subsidies could partially remedy fiscal problems. Thus, it was not until 1993 that the allowance of remittances and small private businesses began changing consumption patterns. In sociological terms, 1993 marks a shift from an egalitarian society to a classist one. For the first time since the early 1960s, Cubans were allowed to make individual decisions that not only reflected their purchasing power, but, perhaps more importantly, their lifestyles and ways of life. Far from unleashing a pattern of conspicuous consumption, Cubans were able to manifest some aspects of individual behavior that previously had been discouraged and were even illegal.

Wealth, well-being, consumption and self-expression have slowly become untethered from the paternalistic welfare state, and have begun relying more heavily on relationships forged on kinship, fictive kinship (*compadrazgo*) and friendship. What had from 1959 until 1993 been used to describe the exile community—worms (*gusanos*), scum (*metralla* or *chusma*) and counterrevolutionary—had, ironically, become the economic lifeline. Exiles were rescuing both the Revolution from material and political failure as well as offering salvation for millions of Cubans on the island. We dare say that since the 1990s, remittance sending from the exile community has not only been the economic lifeline for the islanders, but it has spawned a world of individual ideas and opportunities that transcends mere brand recognition.

The economic and sociological transformations unleashed by remittances carry repercussions that are largely 'underground' and therefore pose a series of methodological challenges in analyzing advertising without marketing. Nonetheless, two parallel processes are at play here. One is the manifest rise of consumer purchases in state stores and the allowance of consumer goods to be brought to the island by Cubans who visit and work abroad and the exile community coming back for short periods to visit family. A second and more profound process surrounds the phenomenon of the double moral (*doble moral*) about which we have written elsewhere in this book. This means that millions of Cubans on a daily basis spend hundreds of thousands of dollars outside the state-retailing network via their forays into the black market and private sector. These daily patterns are devoid of political protest, for the state system would quickly snuff out any such expression. Even the most 'revolutionary' of families—those of military officers or politicians in the National Assembly—silently accept this behavior as a rational coping mechanism in the face of what can only be deemed a catastrophic economic failure. Without this private-sector space where basic material needs are satisfied, mass pauperization would develop. Put another way, the market reforms have evolved in 18 years from a mere temporary release valve to a mainstay of daily living and survival.

RESHAPING THE SOCIAL AND ECONOMY SPHERES

This onslaught of basic supply-and-demand economics is evident, superficially at least, at the street level and just inside many houses. It is largely a remittance-driven process from the once hated exile community. Buying houses on the black market (or paying lawyers and government officials 'under the table' to have deeds changed), home repairs and remodeling, home restaurants, small bed-and-breakfasts and other forms of petty commerce are now the lifeblood of everyday living. Our argument is not just that consumption has changed, but rather lifestyles and social values have too. Specifically, four spheres of Cuba's economic and social fabric—(a) family, (b) workplace and professional, (c) consumption and (d) lifestyle—capture the impact of remittances.

Family Sphere

Nearly two million Cubans have left the island since the 1959 Revolution. Their motivations were largely political and economic, but they now play a saving role in keeping the islanders in good material stead. The political and social connotation of having a relative abroad is no longer what it was in the first few decades of the Revolution. At that time, career and educational advancement could easily be curtailed if a 'deserter' was in the family. And although that sentiment still exists, official and unofficial attitudes about families with relatives abroad have become much more relaxed. One still reads and hears official pronouncements and the demonization of the "Miami mafia" (a reference to practically any activity conducted by Cubans in South Florida), but the irony is that their role in sustaining the island has been essential since the implosion of the Soviet Union and collapse of the Berlin Wall.

The family ties have been strengthened between islanders and exiles; a sort of reunification has been the result of the post-1993 economic reforms. Cubans abroad have been inserted into a different reality that has unleashed a process of transculturation. In turn, solidarity between exiles and family members on the island ruptures the ideological divide that officially exists. A widely held value and generational difference is that Cubans born after 1959, who then migrate, feel a special bond and obligation in sending remittances back home. Among the 'older' exile groups who left in the 1950s and 1960s, there appears to be less support for extended family members on the island (see Grenier and Pérez 2003).

Workplace and Professional Sphere

In Cuba's contemporary economy, remittances and a dollarized economy invoke a hierarchical process in the workplace in which some professions are more likely to benefit than others. Those trades include tourism, restaurants, hotels, taxis and artisans, among others. Both a human resource and social values imbalance stem from these preferential group of workers. Crossover workers from education to tourism, for example, characterize this imbalance. Educators can earn many times their monthly salary of roughly US$22 to $25 dollars by working in tourism where gratuities are the main draw. The social values imbalance arises when educators, originally committed (who perhaps still are) to the ideals of universal education, realize that material needs in the home take a priority over their original career choice (something quite common in the United States as well). This brain drain out of the educational sector has been pronounced, and the country has not been able to retain and train young educations as it did before 1993. Perhaps the most uncanny social value imbalance to appear is that, suddenly, taxi drivers and bartenders can earn more than the leading neurosurgeons, university professors or legal scholars. In 2011, a kind of 'inverted labor-force pyramid' exists where waiters, porters and chambermaids are earning 30 or 40 times what an engineer or surgeon takes home. Official interpretations of this market 'distortion' are that no one in Cuba needs to earn more; the state provides a basic set of services that avoids any level of penury. Instead, the state might counter, those leaving the education sector need to reassess their personal moral compass and recognize the lifelong contributions the socialist government has provided in the area of housing, health care and education.

Consumption Sphere

Throughout this book we have attempted to show the breadth of information that consumers have about national and international brands. We have argued that the knowledge Cubans have about these matters is noteworthy because of how information reaches them. Remittances and working in tourism or self-employment drive consumer retailing, and tilt the scales from being a window-shopper to becoming a consumer. In less than two decades, consumption has shifted from a world of brandless products to one where brands influence what and how much households will purchase. Brands now matter in what Cubans consume.

It is also noteworthy how remittances in the form of products and money have had a deep impact on changes in individual and household consumption. Cash remittances increase consumers' purchasing power and not only determine what, where and how to buy a product or service, but also force consumers to consider product attributes such as value, quality, durability, aesthetics and price. To individuals acculturated in market economies, this phenomenon may seem axiomatic. However, to Cubans raised on the island, the process has shifted from being an illegal or socially frowned-upon process to practically a norm. In-kind remittances (gifts) create a branding culture on the island that was quite limited before 1993. Today, clothing, household appliances, medicines, personal hygiene products and other goods allows Cubans to compare those goods with what is available in state retail stores, and ultimately shape tastes and preferences. Remittances, then, enable Cubans through WOM to disseminate information about product quality and to compare those products with comparable national and international brands.

Gifts of material goods also influence what state stores stock, what *cuentapropistas* make and what national producers manufacture for the domestic market. State companies will launch copycat products that assume some of the features of a gifted product; the changes may be superficial in terms of the name or packaging, or they may be substantive in nature. Self-employed workers may also emulate established brands or modify their products based on what they see from in-kind remittances. The shoe, clothing and related sectors lend themselves particularly well to this kind of product emulation. For instance, whereas Nestlé is widely popular, its flavors are quite limited. We know of an ice-cream maker in Old Havana who cannot keep enough mango-flavored ice cream in stock. When the harvest comes in May and June, she buys as much as she can, slices the mangoes and places them in plastic bags, which are then frozen, and gradually releases the ice cream to the market over the course of the year. In brief, remittances drive competition and encourage product innovation in ways that centralized planning has not.

Lifestyle Sphere

Product and brand diversity driven by the post-1993 rise in remittances have, to the chagrin of some, reinserted individualistic and materialistic values into individual lifestyles. Cubans on the islands in the realm of commerce—previously referred to as comrades (*compañeros*)—are gradually being referred to as consumers (*consumidores*), clients (*clientes*) or users (*usurarios*). Whereas this is far from the social maladies invoked by brand consciousness and 24/7 advertising (Quart 2003), brand fetishism (Klein 2000), anything approaching the conundrum of the 'overspent American' (Schor 1998) or the locking of children into a world of excessive consumption and branding (Schor 2004), there is no doubt that the 'collectivist' narrative of socialism is gradually being diluted by small-scale capitalism.

Although we discuss our own conceptualization of the different types of Cuban consumers in the final chapter of the book, it will not be surprising that age and gender are important features in defining lifestyle expressions. Hip-hop, reggaetón, salsa and other forms of music and artists carry a particular clothing style that young people find appealing. Dockers and wrinkle-free cotton-polyester pants lend themselves especially well to men on the island because of the lack of a need for an iron (which is expensive to buy and use), their durability and the island's climate. For each consumer cohort, remittances take on a 'life-saving role,' much like the national patron saint (Our Lady of the Charity of Copper). Hardly ostentatious, gifts from overseas can be as subtle as determining what a child brings to school for lunch, and in what kind of backpack or lunch box, paying for photographs of a wedding or a *quinceñera* celebration or having a supply of sanitary napkins versus the use of rags or old clothes. That an estimated seven of 10 Cubans receive direct or indirect benefits from remittances is a testimony to their reach across the island, a topic discussed in the following.

THE EVOLUTION OF REMITTANCES, 1993–2010

The Cuban exile community has continually sent remittances to the island since 1993, despite the vicissitudes in the world market (Figure 7.4). Only in 2004 was there a negative annual change in remittance rates (–6.3 percent). The dip stemmed from the Cuban government's elimination of the dollar as the official hard currency. As a result, exiles shifted to other hard currencies (Canadian dollars, euros) to avoid a 20 percent fine/processing fee (Morales and Hernández 2006). Payments between hard-currency retail stores and by customers buying in those stores also shifted from dollars to CUCs. Another factor responsible for the 2004 dip was President George W. Bush's draconian reduction of remittances to just $US300 quarterly, and then only to immediate (e.g., nuclear) family members. The president also confined Cuban Americans visits to a single visit every three years. By 2005, the Cuban Central Bank (Banco Central) took charge of all hard-currency bank accounts and established new exchange rates between the CUC and the Cuban peso. Shortly thereafter, the CUC was adjusted by 8 percent vis-à-vis the U.S. dollar, euro and other hard currencies.

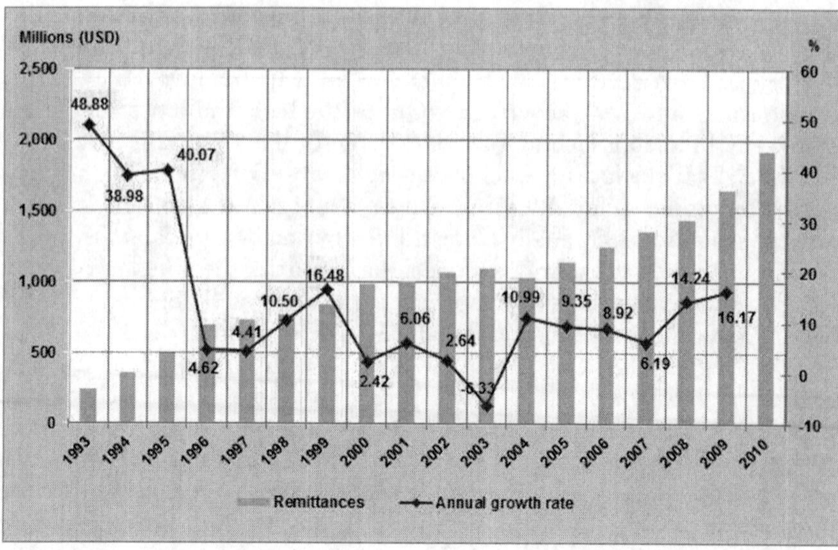

Figure 7.4 Evolution of remittances to Cuba, 1993–2010 (2010 projected).
Source: The Havana Consulting Group.

Remittances have mitigated the problems created by the material scarcity and trade imbalances that have plagued the Cuban regime for half a century. In bad years, Soviet subsidies remedied revenue shortfalls, but by 1993, the so-called Soviet 'lungs' had disappeared. Our argument is that the new 'artificial lungs' to revive the economy were the direct result of the Castro regime's efforts to divide the family in the first place. How did this come to pass?

Most of the Cuban emigrants since the 1980s have been individual as opposed to family moves (Grenier and Pérez 2003). A common strategy is that once they get established in a new country, they aim to save to get their loved ones off the island. Some exiles have been able to reunite with their families in a couple of years, whereas for others it takes decades. The key point is that, in a Faustian bargain of sorts, the Castro brothers are now reliant on the exile community for salvaging the island; the same individuals who were scorned for betraying the Revolution.

More than one million Cubans have left the island since the start of the Revolution, and about 1.8 million Cuban Americans (first, second and third generation) reside in the United States (Martínez 2011). Furthermore, a new Spanish Historical Memory Law may allow up to half a million Spanish passports to be issued to Cubans of Spanish ancestry if they can prove that their parents or grandparents left Spain between 1936 and 1955 because of the conflict of the Spanish Civil War and the regime of Generalísimo Francisco Franco. Cubans have until December 2011 to document the matter at the Spanish embassy in their home country (in this case, Havana), which will add to the number of Cubans sending remittances back to the island. Not unlike emigrants who work in Europe, Australasia and North America and send money back to Latin America, Africa and Asia, the Cuban exile community is driving this process back home. Suddenly, the once "evil capitalist dollars" now revive cities, place the once-forgotten traditional carmel sauce (*dulce de leche*) on Cuban tables and bring a bit of color back into daily lives that were once lived in black and white.

Changes in household consumption have been paralleled by transformations in both the private and public business sectors as well. Remittances reinvigorate retailing, much like a phoenix rising from its ashes. Recall from Chapter 2 that more than 6,000 retail stores operate from one end of Cuba to the other, providing employment (some of which has access to hard-currency bonuses) to workers who would otherwise be confined in jobs that pay in pesos. Business in the black market, about which much as been written (Pérez López 1995; Henken 2005; Peters and Scarpaci 1998), has also been bolstered. In short order, previously empty showcases now carry consumer goods, granted at very high prices. The key point is that the stocking of these goods is not the result of the 'glorious achievements of the Revolution,' but because of the hard work and sacrifice of the once 'despised' exile community who strive to bring a modicum of material comfort and dignity to family and friends.

HARD-CURRENCY CONSUMER PURCHASING POWER: CHARACTERIZING ITS SOURCE

For more than 50 years Cuban and international economists have faced a daunting challenge when trying to find out information about consumer purchasing power on the island (González-Corzo and Larson 2007). Politicians, business people, sociologists, geographers, marketers and others have sought this information in order to understand the material and economic well-being of the population. If market mechanisms are the venues through which goods and services are distributed, their essence is even more important to Cubans (Blue 2004).

Remittances have also been a key source in understanding Cubans' purchasing power, but thus far only a few studies from the UN's Economic Commission on Latin American and the Caribbean (Fajnzylber and López 2007), the Inter-American Development Bank and a few Cuban institutions have been able to tackle this methodologically difficult endeavor. In this section we aim to make a modest contribution towards filling this void.

One of us (E.M.) worked for several Cuban and foreign companies that operated in a number of sectors of the dollarized economy. Significantly, one of those positions was for six years as director of strategic planning in the marketing division of CIMEX. The experience offered a close-up look at the challenges, experiences and methodologies used in marketing research analysis, as well as the estimation of remittances and consumer purchasing power at the county (169), provincial (14 at that time) and national levels. It is upon this experience (Table 7.4), plus those acquired by Morales as a freelance consultant outside of CIMEX, that we develop the section that follows.

Working in the areas noted in Table 7.4 allows us to identify 10 major sources of hard currency in Cuba. The thickness of the arrows in Figure 7.5 corresponds to the relative magnitude the source or hard currency uses.

Because retailing sits at the end of the supply chain, the intersection where the consumer meets marketing, managers must monitor their inventories carefully. Cuban retail managers operate on the assumption that between 3 and 5 percent of their goods will be unsellable because of damage or perishability issues, which create pricing and distribution problems. If employee theft is added to that, then another 10 to 15 percent combines for a total Cuban retail shrinkage rate of between 13 to 20 percent across the island. Whether in hard currency (retail 'dollar stores') or the peso market (a state company's construction site), Cuban workers have adopted the bad habit of stealing from their employers (something that is not unique to Cubans[7]) as part of their subsistence philosophy. It derives from a rationalization[8] and material need. Because Cuban retailing is not a self-service operation in most instances, retail theft by consumers is not a major problem. Our sense is that the only way to mitigate inventory shrinkage is to grow the private retail sector, pay workers livable wages and begin imposing a cul-

Table 7.4 Sources Consulted to Determine Cuban Purchasing Power

Organizations & Entitites (Spanish name in parentheses)	Nature of Consultancy
Ministry of Economy and Planning (*Ministerio de Economía y Planificación*)	· Workers and sectors enhanced by hard-currency (bonuses, tips) · Tourism: Number of arrivals · Number of workers in tourism · Number of workers in maritime, port, and longshoremen endeavors
Ministry of Tourism (*ministerio de Turismo*)	· Foreign tourists and Cubans residing overseas who return to the island · Country of origin · Tourist breakdown by venue (camping, hotels, bed and breakfast, conferences, business fairs) · Mean tourist expenditures
Foreign Affairs Ministry (*Ministerio de Relaciones*)	· Accredited diplomatic and consular corps in Cuba · Cuban workers in foreign embassies and consular offices · International organizations with offices in Cuba · Cuban workers in international organizations · Foreign journalists · Cuban diplomatic corps overseas
Ministry of Foreign Investment (*Minsterio para la Inversión Extranjera*)	· Statistics about overseas technical assistance
National Institute of Sport, Physical Education and Recreation (*Instituto Nacional de Deporte, Educación Física y Recreación*)	· Coaches, specialists and athletes under short-term contract to work overseas
Ministry of Culture (*Ministerio de Cultura*)	· Estimates of Cuban artists contracted to work overseas
Ministry of Education (*Ministerio de Educación y Educación Superior)*	· Cuban professors and teachers contracted by foreign institutions · Foreign professors and teachers working in Cuba · Foreign scholarship recipients studying in Cuba
Port Maritime Union (*Unión Marítima Portuaria*)	· Number of workers in these sectors
Chamber of Commerce (*Cámara de Comercio*)	· Foreign companies operating in Cuba

Continued

Table 7.4 Continued

Civil Aeronautic Institute (*Instituto de Aeronáutica Civil*)	· Flight crews
Self-employed workers (*cuentapropistas*)	· Home restaurant operators (paladares).· Artists · Bed & breakfast operators · Others
National Tax Office (*Oficina Nacional de Administración Tributaria* (ONAT))	· Tax collectors · Inspectors
State providers of products and services	· Managers · Warehouse operators · Accountants · Employers and their staff
General Population	· Household heads · Prostitutes · General population

Source: Developed by the authors

ture of honesty centered on a sense that workers have a significant stake in a company's business performance.

The principal source sustaining purchasing power—remittances—accounts for about two-thirds of all hard currency in circulation (Table 7.5). About US$1.9 billion was sent to Cubans in 2010, part of a 1993–2010 total amount of nearly US$27 billion. With 11.2 million residents, this equals a type of 'foreign-aid package'—despite the long-standing U.S. trade embargo, of US$2,378 dollars for every man, woman and child over the 18-year period. If we breakdown the 2010 remittance level (US$2.64 billion) on a per capita basis, we get about US$235, which is more than twice the amount of the Latin American and Caribbean average of US$102 (Fajnzylber and López 2007, 2).

The life cycle of Cuban purchasing power between 1993 and 2010 reveals an ascending rate in absolute amounts (Figure 7.6). Annual rates of increase between 2008 and 2010, despite the global economic downturn, have reached double-digit levels. Unlike other Latin American and Caribbean nations, until 2011 Cubans were not allowed to buy houses or sell their automobiles to whomever they wanted (the purchasing and buying of cars has traditionally been handled a by a single state dealership and the state set the prices). Houses and cars are, of course, some of the largest consumer purchases anywhere in the world. Until 2007, cell phones could not be freely purchased, Cubans could not lodge in tourist hotels and air conditioners and DVD players/burners were off-limits. These restrictions meant only a limited number of consumer goods and services—mostly retail products—were possible uses of remittances.

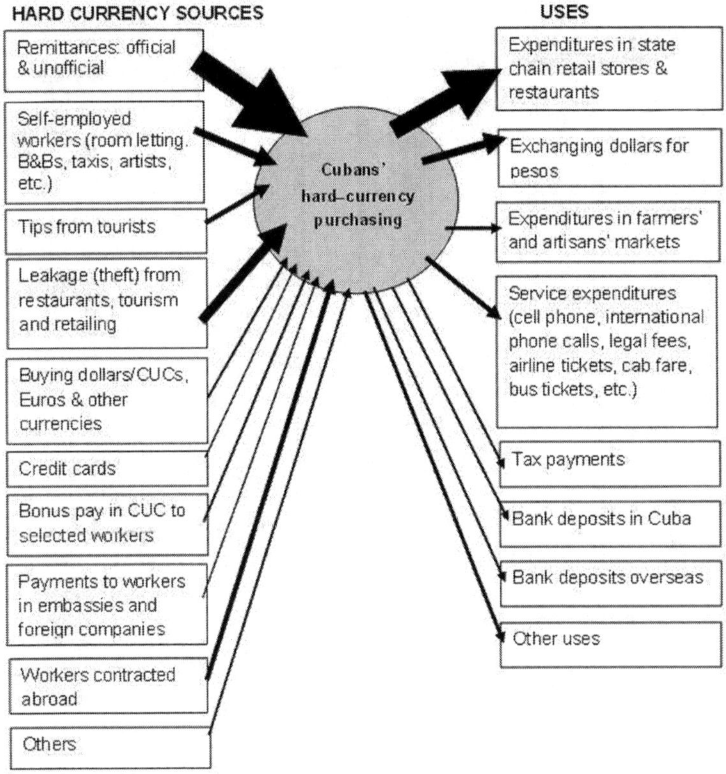

Figure 7.5 Hard-currency sources and uses. Based on the authors' fieldwork.

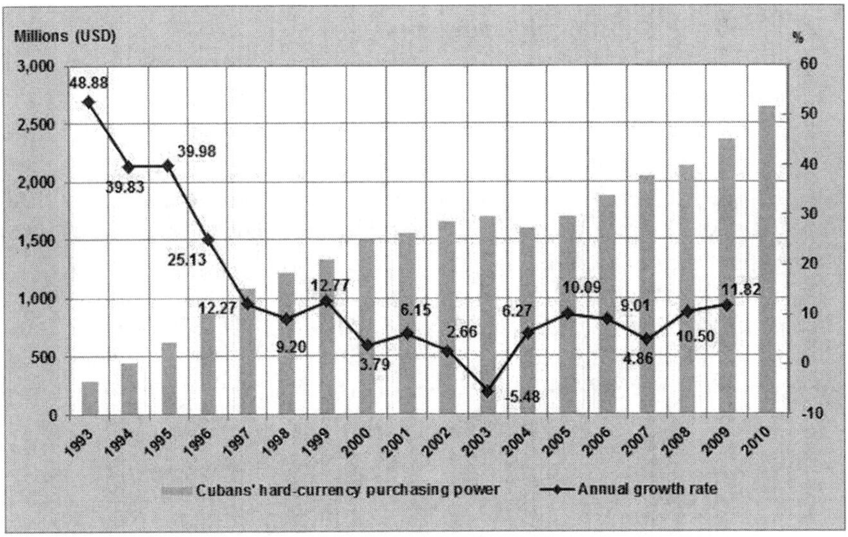

Figure 7.6 Life cycle of Cuban purchasing power, 1993–2010.
Source: Calculated by the authors. See also text.

Table 7.5 Evolution of Cuban Hard-Currency Purchasing Power, 1993–2000

Year	Other Sources	Remittance Total	Purchasing Power Total
1993	47.60	242.24	289.84
1994	82.12	360.64	442.76
1995	117.89	501.21	619.10
1996	164.60	702.02	866.62
1997	350.01	734.43	1,084.44
1998	450.67	766.85	1,217.52
1999	482.13	847.35	1,329.48
2000	512.34	986.96	1,499.30
2001	545.23	1,010.87	1,556.10
2002	579.61	1,072.15	1,651.76
2003	595.29	1,100.46	1,695.75
2004	572.06	1,030.84	1,602.90
2005	559.26	1,144.12	1,703.38
2006	624.15	1,251.15	1,875.30
2007	681.52	1,362.71	2,044.23
2008	696.57	1,447.06	2,143.63
2009	715.57	1,653.15	2,368.72
2010	728.31	1,920.44	2,648.75
Total	8,504.93	18,134.65	26,639.58

Source: Developed by The Havana Consulting Group. All figures in thousands of U.S. dollars

Figure 7.6 also shows a tapering off of remittances in the early 2000s at just over US$1.5 billion. From 2005 onward remittances increased notably, to which we attribute the travel restrictions over Cuban Americans visiting Cuba that was imposed by the administration of George W. Bush, as well as capping remittances at US$300 quarterly.

The VI Cuban Communist Party Congress held in April 2011 took the unprecedented action of legalizing the sale of homes and the free-market purchase of automobiles for ordinary Cubans. Now that such large household purchases have become available, we expect the exile community to increase their wire transfers so that loved ones on the island can obtain these goods.

MAJOR SOURCE COUNTRIES FOR SENDING REMITTANCES

Earlier in this chapter we highlighted the universal nature of international migration with the goal of providing financial support to family back home. In some Latin American and Caribbean countries, remittances even account for more than 10 percent of the gross domestic product and have become as important a source of hard currency as exports. In 2005, for example, migrants from Latin America and the Caribbean working overseas sent a total of US$48.3 billion back to their homelands. In the previous year, remittances accounted for 70 percent of foreign direct investment in Latin America and the Caribbean, which was 500 percent greater than official development assistance to the region (Fajnzylber and López 2007).

As in many countries, measuring remittance amounts exactly is difficult, if only because the 'unofficial' means (e.g., not wiring the funds) are difficult to assess. However, because of the 'ceilings' imposed by both the U.S. and Cuban governments, we are confident that this unofficial amount is greater than in other countries. Transfer fees for sending money to Cuba were, until late 2010 or so, one of the highest in Latin America and the Caribbean. Wire transfer companies have secured a relatively small portion of the Cuba remittance business because of these high fees. Traditionally, about 20 to 30 percent of remittances sent to Cuba were done by unofficial means (e.g., the use of third-party 'mules,' family members or friends bringing cash directly to the island). Today, for a number of reasons, about 70 to 80 percent of remittances reach the island through the unofficial route. To better understand the remittance process that drives consumer purchases, brand preferences and small-business activities, it will be helpful to define a few concepts.

> *Remittances.* Transfer of money by emigrants to their family members who remained in the country of origin. Includes that portion of emigrant income sent home that constitutes a means of financial support for family members.
>
> *Sending of packages.* Transfer by emigrants of high-demand consumer goods such as clothing, shoes, food and medicines back to the families in the country of origin.

Cuba is like most countries in the western hemisphere in that most of the remittances received come from the United States. Although more than a dozen countries constitute the main sources from where remittances reach Cuba, 80 cents on every dollar sent to the island comes from the U.S. (Table 7.6). A number of countries host temporary Cuban workers in the health-care, education, sports and construction sectors, and they send a portion of their earnings back home. The case of Cuban health-care and education professionals working in Venezuela, where one intelligence company calculates that up to 60,000 Cubans labor, is the best-known example (Stratfor Global Intelligence 2011).

A number of approaches can be used to estimate remittances coming to Cuba. One source derives from the level of dollar-store retail sales.

In-country surveys have also been conducted by the Cuban government, probing the amount and frequency of remittances received. To the methodological mix we can add economic estimates based on the propensity of Cubans who are likely to migrate, the numbers of Cuban American arrivals at airports across the island and the number of Cubans traveling abroad who both need hard currency to conduct transactions overseas and may actually earn foreign currencies that come back to the Cuban economic system. Lastly, the most reliable source—data gathered by money-transfer companies—also serves as a key dataset.

Other published sources exist regarding remittances to Cuba. These include publications by the National Bank of Cuba and the National Statistics Office of Cuba. The latter office classified US$743.7 million of remittances as "net current transfers" in 1996. By 1998, the figure ascended to US$813 million (ONE 1998). Our estimates, therefore, assume that the sending of remittances to Cuba is inconstant and annual rates of change

Table 7.6 Major Source Countries from Which Remittances are Sent to Cuba, 2007

Country	%
United States	80.0
Spain	9.0
Italy	1.75
Mexico	1.2
Puerto Rico	1.05
Canada	0.81
Germany	0.78
Argentina	0.62
Dominican Republic	0.6
Venezuela	0.56
Brazil	0.56
Chile	0.5
Sweden	0.42
Honduras	0.36
Panama	0.36
Ecuador	0.35
South Africa	0.35
Total	**98.91**

Source: Calculated by the authors based on various studies conducted by them, particularly with CIMEX and the Cuban Ministry of Foreign Affairs

Table 7.7 Remittances Sent to Cuba by Official and Unofficial Means, 1993–2010 (US$ millions)

Year	Official Means	Unofficial Means	Total Remittance
1993	11.53	230.71	242.24
1994	13.92	346.72	360.64
1995	15.67	485.54	501.21
1996	16.12	685.90	702.02
1997	18.22	716.21	734.43
1998	24.95	741.90	766.85
1999	47.83	799.52	847.35
2000	95.83	891.13	986.96
2001	83.53	927.34	1,010.87
2002	100.42	971.73	1,072.15
2003	105.39	995.07	1,100.46
2004	141.04	889.80	1,030.84
2005	231.87	912.25	1,144.12
2006	312.37	938.78	1,251.15
2007	377.97	984.74	1,362.71
2008	442.22	1,004.84	1,447.06
2009	513.94	1,139.21	1,653.15
2010	685.78	1,234.66	1,920.44
Total	**3,238.60**	**14,896.05**	**18,134.65**

Source: Developed by The Havana Consulting Group. All figures in thousands of U.S. dollars

reflect such variables as the rates of out-migration from the island as well as the contracting of Cuban workers overseas. These disparate data sources, however, lead us to what we believe is a fairly accurate estimate on the amount of money sent to Cuba between 1993 and 2010 (Table 7.7).

Table 7.7 shows that the unofficial or 'informal' means of sending money has been the predominant venue of getting back home, though the gap between unofficial and official had narrowed somewhat in recent years. In 2010, official amounts (US$658.78 million) accounted for about 35.7 percent of all money reaching Cuba.

SENDING MONEY THROUGH FORMAL ROUTES

Several factors account for the rise in sending money through formal routes in recent years. These factors are supported by better technology whose key

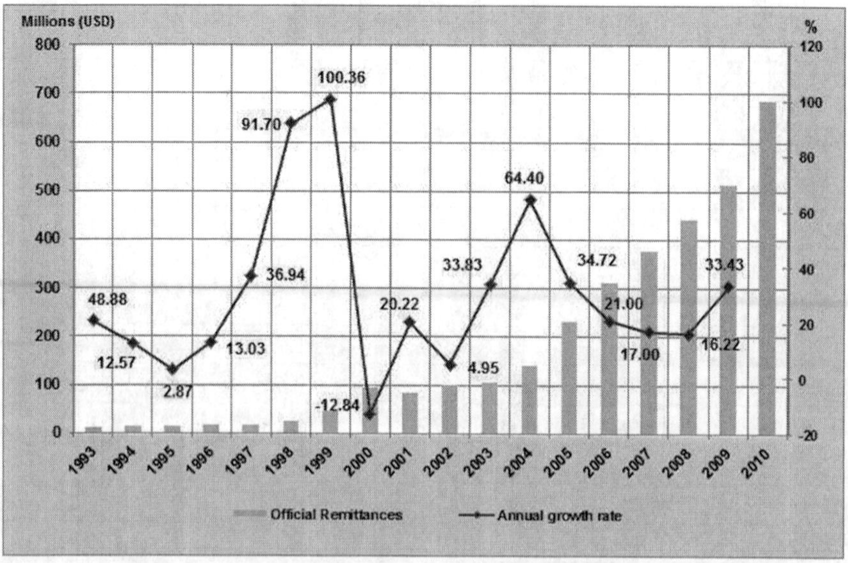

Figure 7.7 Official remittances sent to Cuba and annual growth rates, 1993–2010 (millions of $US).
Source: Calculated by The Havana Consulting Group

attributes include speed, security, lower transfer costs and the ease of both sending and receiving money. Every year except one over the past decade witnessed double-digit annual rates of increase (Figure 7.7).

Cost is perhaps the most complex and determinant attribute, and just four firms control it: American International Services (AIS), Transcard, Western Union and Caribbean Transfer. AIS has about 120 agencies around the world, but the majority are located in the United States (Figure 7.8). It collaborates with Cubapack, a company owned by CIMEX S.A., which distributes official wire transfers that reach Cuba, as well as packages sent from abroad. Transcard is a Canadian company that focuses wire transfers mainly from Canada and the United States to many points around the world. It began operating in Cuba in 1997. It entered the market by selling personalized debit cards in North America that could be used for sending money to the island. On the island, that same card is also used in

Figure 7.8 Transcard logo.

Figure 7.9 Western Union logo.

hard-currency state retail establishments as a debit card, and with a 2 percent discount from the purchase price. The card carries no service fee and the owner does not have to have a savings account in Cuba to use it.

Western Union is a U.S. company that has great brand recognition and operates as the world leader in wiring remittances (Figure 7.9). It entered the Cuban market in July 1999 and the word quickly spread among Cubans. Today, over 150 Western Union offices are distributed throughout Cuba.[9]

Until early 2011, Western Union was unique in Cuba because it was the only transfer company that delivered remittances to recipients in U.S. dollars. Recall that between 2004 and 2011, the maximum wire transfer was set at US$300 based on laws imposed during the Bush administration. In late 2010, the Obama administration raised the ceiling from US$300 quarterly to US$5,000 daily, and in early 2011 it was doubled to US$10,000 daily. Departing from the Bush era, money can now be sent to any family member (e.g., extended members such as cousins and aunts). Unlike its competitors, Western Union delivers cash only, which is a disadvantage because its competitors use the debit-card system that requires that proper identification be used when making transactions; such guarantees cannot be used with lost or stolen cash.

Caribbean Transfers is a Cuban remittance firm belonging to CIMEX S.A. that offers several modalities and advantages in this growing remittance market (Figure 7.10). Its chief competitive advantage is that it presents the recipient with a Caribbean Transfer debit card that is charged in CUCs. Unlike the use of U.S. dollars, there is no 10 percent penalty for using the debit card. Some 8,500 retail outlets on the island accept Caribbean Transfers' debit cards, making them the most widely accepted card of their kind. The company took the lead in the Cuban remittance market in 2005 with 37.19 percent of the market share, overtaking Western Union (20.42 percent, which had been the market leader until that time), Transcard (25.49 percent) and AIS (15.86 percent). This ranking held steady until late 2010 when the Obama administration changed the frequency of Cuban American visits and remittance levels. Late 2010 was also when Western Union was authorized by the U.S. government to send money in CUCs (The Havana Consulting Group 2011).

Western Union embarked on a strong advertising campaign across South Florida in which it announced its authorization (granted by the U.S.

Figure 7.10 Caribbean Transfers logo.

Table 7.8 Wire Costs Charged by Money Transfer Companies Operating in Cuba, 2005

Agencies Wiring Remittances to Cuba	Wire costs	Money Exchange	Amount Sent	Amount Received
Western Union	29.90 USD	—	300 USD	240 CUC
Transcard	19.90 USD	24.00 USD	300 USD	300 CUC
Caribbean Transfer (except in USA)	19.90 USD	24.00 USD	300 USD	300 CUC
Caribbean Transfer (agencies authorized in USA)	23.90 USD	24.00 USD	300 USD	300 CUC
AIS	19.90 USD	24.00 USD	300 USD	300 CUC

Source: Calculated by the authors

Table 7.9 Transfer Fees Charged by the Principal Remittance Transfer Companies Operating in Cuba, 2011

Company	Costs in 2011 for each $300
Western Union	24 USD /300
Competition	24-48 USD/300

Source: Calculated by The Havana Consulting Group

Treasury's Office of Foreign Assets Control) to send CUCs. It also promoted that it was lowering its transfer rates to Cuba by 50 percent. This strategy aimed to help them regain the market lead they had lost in 2005. As Table 7.8 indicates, Western Union was at a clear disadvantage a few years ago because those at the receiving end would lose 20 percent of the original amount sent due to fines and exchange fees. Thus, of US$300 wired, only $240 reached a Cuban on the island. Under Bush era regulations, it was the Cuban government that skimmed off a US$60 profit. New guidelines issued by the Obama government have created more competition and lower prices, giving the U.S.-based Western Union more competitive pricing in Cuba (Table 7.9).

Western Union aims to recapture its leadership position in Florida through its new price structure, the dense network of its offices throughout the state and a concentrated advertising campaign (Table 7.10). The company dominates 83.7 percent of the Florida wire transfer market (to

Figure 7.11 Self-employment in Cuba.

Table 7.10 U.S. Distribution of Western Union Offices and Those of Its Competitors that Send Money to Cuba, 2011

City	WU	Competition	% WU	% Competition	State
Florida	490	95	83.76%	16.24%	FL
Fort Lauderdale	24	1	96.00%	4.00%	FL
Hialeah	64	33	65.98%	34.02%	FL
Key West	7	1	87.50%	12.50%	FL
Lake Worth	12	1	92.31%	7.69%	FL
Miami	204	45	81.93%	18.07%	FL
Naples	15	3	83.33%	16.67%	FL
Orlando	66	1	98.51%	1.49%	FL
Port Richey	3	1	75.00%	25.00%	FL
Tampa	67	8	89.33%	10.67%	FL
West Palm Beach	28	1	96.55%	3.45%	FL
Rest of the Country	724	18	97.57%	2.43%	
New Jersey	130	6	95.59%	4.41%	NJ
California	412	7	98.33%	1.67%	CA
Puerto Rico	83	2	97.65%	2.35%	PR
Minneapolis	1	1	50.00%	50.00%	MN
Chicago	42	1	97.67%	2.33%	IL
Las Vegas	56	1	98.25%	1.75%	NV
TOTAL	1214	113	91.48%	8.52%	

Source: The Havana Consulting Group LLC.

all destinations, not just Cuba) and 97.57 percent of the national market. It remains a matter of speculation whether Western Union can keep up with the demand from operators of Cuba's small businesses (which reached 300,000 in the first few months of 2011) who will need support from relatives in friends in the U.S. Any wire transfer company will likely move aggressively to position itself in Florida so it can gain a toehold in the wire transfers that will be used to support new businesses on the island.

The number of job descriptions for self-employment increased from about 154 to over 178 (Figure 7.11). This Cuban policy aimed to capture those downsized public workers. Sources of capital for these new entrepreneurs are coming from the Cubans in exile in the U.S., Spain, Mexico and elsewhere. President Raúl Castro declared on December 20, 2010, that these policies would be irreversible (Morales and Scarpaci 2011c).

Relaxed Obama travel rules for Cuban Americans also led to more charter flights to visit family and friends on the island (Table 7.11). Between 2006 and

Table 7.11 Passengers Carried on U.S.-Based Charter Flights to Cuba, 2006–2011 (estimate)

Charters to Cuba	2006	2007	2008	2009	2010	2011E
Mean number of weekly flights	10	12	15	32	52	70
Number of passengers	80,000	94,000	100,000	200,000	410,000	546,000
Growth (%)	2007/06	2008/07	2009/08	2010/09	2011E/10	2011E/08
Growth in flights	20.00	25.00	113.33	62,50	34.62	366.67
Growth in passengers	17.50	6.38	100.00	105.00	33.17	446.00

Source: Calculated by The Havana Consulting Group

Table 7.12 Shipping Costs (US$) per Pound for Food, Medicine and Clothing Sent to Cuba from South Florida, 2008–2011

Sipping costs for:	2008	2009	2010	2011
Medicine	10–12	10–12	8–10	2.5–5
Non-perishable food	10–12	10–12	8–10	2.5–5
Clothing	12–15	12–14	10–14	2.5–10

Source: Calculated by The Havana Consulting Group

2010, the average number of charter flights increased fivefold, and the number of passengers also rose in tandem (from 80,000 to 410,000). These increased flights mean that more hard currency will circulate in the Cuban economy. Purchasing power will rise as will exposure to consumer products carried over as checked and carry-on luggage. Family reunification visits will also enhance the amount of money reaching the island via nonofficial means.

Our interviews with bag handlers at charter companies that fly out of Miami International Airport to Cuba in April 2011 revealed that the average Cuban American charter passenger brings between six and eight checked bags that weigh up to 70 pounds. An indeterminate amount of medicine, food, clothing and other items fill those suitcases.

Rates for shipping packages from South Florida to Cuba have also fallen; shipping charges for clothing fell from US$15 to $2.50 per pound, and the cost of sending medical goods also fell (Table 7.12). On top of these lower costs is the reality that Cuban Americans can now reunite with their families as often as they wish, thereby increasing the 'informal' or 'unofficial' means of sending consumer goods.

SENDING REMITTANCES INFORMALLY

Thus far we have shown how the majority of remittances reach Cuba through informal means: friends, family members or hired 'mules' deliver the cash (Figure 7.12). In the Latin American and Caribbean context, Cuba stands out as the nation receiving the largest percentage of remittances sent through these informal routes. In addition to the so-called 'mules'[10] or 'backpackers' who carry cash and deliver it directly, there are also tourists, diplomats and members of the international business community providing the same service (M. Orozco 2003).

Several hypotheses exist about why these informal routes prevail. Some believe they are popular because residents do not want the Cuban government to know who is receiving how much money and how often (Puerta 2003). Related to that is the assumption that informal routes disallow the Cuban regime from earning a percentage through commissions and processing fees. Many islanders are unfamiliar with rates, pricing, types of formal-sector wires, the variety and location of the agencies and other market identifiers. As a result, they rely on the tried-and-true method of person-to-person delivery (Grupo de Estudios del Mercado 1999). Clearly, the lack of advertising through modern communication channels keeps a segment of the island uninformed, leaving Cubans to rely on WOM—as they do for other products and services—to decide.

By the end of the last decade, a trend had developed showing a gradual deceleration of unofficial remittances sent to Cuba. The ease, lower cost and security of formal mechanisms made that possible. Whether more relaxed travel for Cuban Americans will drive informal remittances upward remains to be seen, but the 'lifeline' into island households is clearly on the rise.

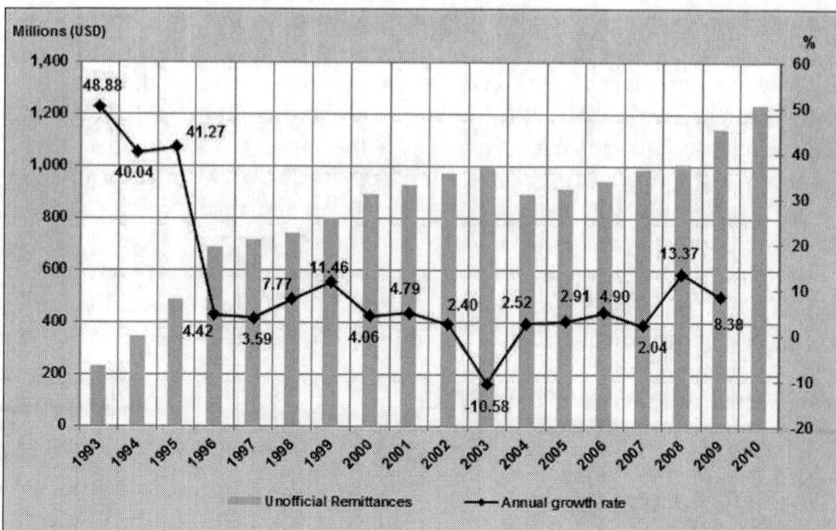

Figure 7.12 Unofficial remittances sent to Cuba, 1993–2010.
Source: Calculated by The Havana Consulting Group.

CONCLUSIONS

Cubans' access to hard currency through working in tourism and receiving money sent from abroad is now in its second decade. By 2011, remittance levels approached about US$2 billion annually, surpassing gross revenues in tourism. These funds are used to sustain Cuban households in basic goods such as food, clothing and medicines, but they are also providing capital to start up small and medium enterprises and to sustain self-employment trades (Scarpaci 2004). Washington, D.C., and Havana have developed policies to stimulate production and consumption. Though the ramifications of these policies are difficult to disentangle, they are driving both the frequency and variety of purchases that Cubans are making in dollar-retail establishments, and gradually shifting consumers to the dollar-retail outlets when they can afford it (Figure 7.13). If remittances are now the development mantra of the new century, then they can only be sustainable if money used 'back home' goes beyond providing basic needs, and gets invested in productive retailing and manufacturing (Kapur and Mchale 2005). Microenterprises are generating brandless products and services that serve as a metric against which branded goods and services can be assessed. Who knows how many budding Cuban versions of Black and Decker, Old Navy or Swanson Foods are out there?

How can we measure the social effect of remittances and visits by Cuban Americans to their homelands? What is the cumulative effect of those millions of conservations?

Figure 7.13 Window-shopping and browsing. Cubans spend a lot of free time window-shopping (*vitriniando*; left), and like consumers around the world, their purchasing power lags behind their ability to acquire many goods and services. The island's peso retail stores usually sell lower-quality Cuban or Asian products, and the store spaces are crowded and notably less attractive (right) than the so-called 'dollar stores.' Photographs by J. L. Scarpaci.

> [I]t is worth asking whether a less visible, quantifiable, and tangible form of remittances—namely, social remittances and the flow of ideas—have a more critical impact than their pecuniary counterpart. The overseas experience must have some cognitive effect on migrants. At the same time, the communications revolution has led to an exponential growth of transnational calls and e-mail, as well as a sharp increase in international travel. As a result, not just elites but social groups at the lower end of the social spectrum are exposed to new information, not just new ways of making or selling things, but also new views of what is acceptable in terms of service standards. (Kapur and Mchale 2005, 357)

The ramifications of these encounters for services marketing extend beyond Cuba and into the rest of the Caribbean and Latin America, Africa and Asia.

In a perfect marketing research setting, it would be rewarding to know the content of those bulky bags (called *gusanos* or worms because of their elongated duffel-bag shape) that Cuban Americans lug to airports, often layered in tamper-proof shrink-wrap. What are their contents? Do they contain items commonly used by the diaspora in their own households, or were they recently advertised goods on sale at Costco, Sam's Club, CVS, Walgreen's, Sears, JCPenney or Amazon.com? Although Deshpande et al. (1986) argue that the Hispanic preferences in the U.S. of one group cannot be generalized to others (e.g., Mexican Americans to Puerto Rican Americans), less is known about cross-border influences of similar Hispanic groups. In a less restricted setting an interesting research question would be the extent to which these gifts shape the tastes and preferences of Cubans on the island. For international marketers, those *gusano* bags contribute to the product placement and promotion in the minds of prospective buyers. Ironically, the term *gusano* was hurled at Cubans who wanted to seek exile; it was a derogatory term to indicate how cowardly they would slither away from the achievements of the Revolution. A half a century later, survival and consumption in the new millennium means that remittances and those *gusano* bags are highly coveted because they bring modest relief and material comfort in ways the Revolution has not.

8 Conclusions

In our final chapter, we outline the key points that our review of Cuban brand preferences and consumer choice has revealed and then position them in a broader marketing management context. We anchor our discussion around four themes:

1. Regulatory framework
2. Advertising, branding and consumer behavior
3. Cuban retailing (yesterday, today and tomorrow)
4. Situating the Cuban consumer in the global marketplace

As the 'ink on these pages dry,' unprecedented announcements by the Cuban government regarding marketing regulations hold promise for a new regulatory framework, to which we turn in the following section.

REGULATORY FRAMEWORK

The marketing regulatory and political environment necessarily consists of laws, legislation, political parties and government organizations, as well as civil society groups (unions, lobbies, advocacy groups, special interests) who serve as stakeholders for their respective parties. For 52 years, the Cuban government has assumed it knows what products and services to sell, at what price, and how to market them throughout its convoluted retail system. It has crowded out other stakeholders in large measure because of its fear of a threatening bourgeoisie (Domínguez 1992); that is, a class that does not own the means of production and can only sell its wage labor in the marketplace. As a result, consumers have had to cobble out a hodgepodge information base about brand quality and reputation. Even the simplest advertising medium—print—is curtailed in a society whose own government, on the one hand, heralds its people's literacy but, on the other hand, curtails the dissemination of print media. Contrast this with the U.S. magazine industry's campaign promoting the strength of, and consumer commitment to, magazines:

> We're *lucky* to have *more* free media than ever, a *parade* of never-ending *wired* options. Yet most of *us* will spend our *money* on magazines. Readership is up among young *people* as well as their *parents*. Why? It's *real simple*. Magazines have an *essence* and *vibe* like no other medium. From *New York* to *Los Angeles*, folks just can't imagine *living* without them.[1]

Created by Young Rubicam of New York and spearheaded by the leaders of five major magazine companies (Charles H. Townsend, Condé Nast; Cathie Black, Hearst Magazines; Jack Griffin, Meredith Corporation; Ann Moore, Time Inc.; and Jann Wenner, Wenner Media), the text from the preceding ad (Table 8.1) is part of the "Magazines, the Power of Print" campaign (PR Newswire 2010). Few governments around the world disagree with the fundamental premise of the ad, but the Cuban government believes it knows best. This is why a revamped regulatory environment with unrestricted commercial, political and economic speech needs to develop in Cuba to strengthen civil society. Accordingly, the French international nongovernmental organization Reporters without Borders (2011) ranked Cuba just 10 places from the bottom; 167 out of 178 countries in its 2010 Press Freedom Index. Cuba's 98 percent literacy rate puts it in good stead for a return to a time-honored and technology-appropriate medium for advertising and the exchange of ideas: print.

The regulatory framework will also require an independent, third-party assessment of Cuban businesses and products. For instance, various ministries now award management certificates to state companies that perform well. This award, called *perfeccionamiento empresarial* (business perfection), is particularly important in the hotel and tourism industry. Establishments that receive this placard prominently display it in their hotel lobbies. For services marketing in Cuba to reach the next level, Cuban tourism businesses need to receive assessment from the World Travel and Tourism Council, Fodor's, Michelin, Zagat's and AAA (of Canada, at present), and not their own in-house evaluations. Up-to-the-minute websites like Trip Advisor[2] also allow consumers to assess facilities, and at the same time, the property's manager can respond. Consumer-driven service-quality websites are timelier than hard-copy printings of service assessments. A Cuban version of Angie's List—where consumers assess the quality of local service providers—would mark a huge step in revamping the framework.

Two popular Cuban brands are also in need of independent assessment: Cristal beer and the El Rápido fast-food chain. An ad that appeared bundled as part of ETECSA's telephone directory (the joint-venture telecommunications company) praises the awards that Cristal has garnered, but at *Cuban* taste competitions (Figure 8.1). Because all of the awards were given on the island, the appeal of the beer's quality seems parochial and less meritorious than if it were earned internationally. Likewise, El Rápido may be a successful chain in Cuba, but without any foreign, domestic or private competition, it has no *real* competition. External validation, rightly or wrongly,

Table 8.1 The Enduring Value of Print as Reflected in "Magazines: The Power of Print" Campaign Applied to Cuba

Author	Affiliation	Statement	Relevance to Cuba
MRI Fall 2009 MRI Fall 2005	Readership research firm	Magazine readership has risen 4.3% over the past five years	Cubans love to read; annual Book Fair show (Feria del Libro) has been selling out; advertising will subsidize printing costs and satisfy latent demand
MRI Fall 2009	Readership research firm	During Google's first 12 years, magazine readership rose 12%	Only 2% of Cubans have access to the Internet, let alone computer terminals (BBC 2011). Print will be a more affordable medium than on-line information
Cathie Black	President, Hearst Magazines	"Magazines are the most effective medium at both ends of the purchase funnel. They drive consumer attitudes and intended behavior more effectively and efficiently than viewing television advertising alone or when TV is combined with online advertising."	Cuba's 98% literacy rate. In the early 20th century, Havana City alone had 32 daily newspapers at one time.
Jann Wenner	CEO, Wenner Media	"Magazines have enduring values for readers and advertisers that have gotten a little neglected and misunderstood in the era of Internet instant buzz and chatter."	Cuba has a rich culture of weekly magazines such as *Archivos de Folklore Cubano*, 1924–1930; *Bohemia*, 1911–present; *Carteles*, 1911–1960; *Havana Post*, 1913–1960; *El Mundo*, 1901–1969; *Otro, revista de difusión cultural*, 1912–1956; *Social*, 1916–1938
Jack Griffin	President, Meredith National Media	"The campaign reflects the vitality magazines have now, and will continue to have with audiences of all ages . . . Clearly, magazines continue to resonate on many levels with consumers, and this is reflected in the enormous trust and value readers have their favorite magazine titles."	High literacy levels; culture of periodical reading

Data source: Newsire 2010; Cuban Heritage Collection on the web at www.library.miami.edu/umcuban/cuban.html

comes through the awards El Rápido earned at the Havana International Fair, which aims to promote service and product excellence across a span of categories. The 2010 event attracted over 1,000 companies from over 50 countries (Feriahavana 2011). Still, it was not a Madrid-based, Paris-based or Mexico City–based venue.

Moreover, like all state companies, profits return to the state coffers with little financial and accounting transparency about the company's fiduciary health. The cold-cut- processing Cuban joint-venture Bravos S.A. earned ISO 14000 standards and should be a model for other Cuban firms considering overseas expansion. The implications this ISO qualification will have for B2C and B2B communication strategies are many and serve as an independent metric for potential business performance despite the regulatory constraints on the island.

Overseas and at home, Cuba faces regulatory challenges in the form of the long-standing U.S. trade embargo (even though 700 U.S. businesses sold goods to Cuba in 2010), but also in other export and franchising contexts. It is unlikely in the short or medium term that the Cuban government will tap into franchising unless there is a radical political and economic shift that could remedy the weak economy. Franchising opportunities exist for leisure pursuits, music, restaurants and hospitality services, to cite just a few. For many Cubans on the island, the much-anticipated 'great opening'—a pronounced Cuban-style *perestroika*—has yet to develop even though the VI Cuban Communist Party guidelines (*lineamientos*) hint at them. The April 2011 Congress used the word 'private' (*privado*) just twice, and it referred only to water consumption by private entities. The word 'market' (*mercado*) appeared 25 times, and the term 'consumer' showed up four times. On the one hand, Guideline 311 hinted at a new approach in achieving a market economy when it proclaimed the government's intent to "create and structure the supply of goods and services to the population so that it relates to solvent consumer demand, including post-sales services" (*Lineamientos* 2011, Guideline 311; our translation). The devil, however, remains in the details, because we do not know the meaning of 'solvent consumer demand' (Morales and Scarpaci 2011b). On the other hand, the guidelines indicate that the state has a duty in supply-chain management, which would negate the potential benefits of Guideline 311. To wit, Guideline 312 proclaims that the state will "[e]xercise effective control of sales management and rotating inventories throughout both the wholesale and retail networks with the aim of minimizing idle resources and losses" (*Lineamientos* 2011, Guideline 312; our translation). The word 'choice,' however, appears just once, and it refers only to consumer policy and not consumer choice in a marketing management context.

As we completed this book, we learned that the Cuban government (May 2011) relaxed certain taxes and regulations to encourage private-sector employment. The move comes on the heels of recommendations from international experts as well as learning from the experience that has unfolded

Figure 8.1 Cristal beer ad. The title reads, "National industry committed to quality and freshness." The lower-right-hand corner lists the prizes it has won in Cuba: Gold Medal in the Havana Fair of 1999; Quality Prize in the Alimexpo (Food Expo) Fair of 2000; First Prize for Advertising. None of these prizes is validated off the island, a prerequisite to building brand equity at home as well as brand recognition in a future export market. Ciego Montero and Havana Club, too, will have to move their prize-winning acclaim from island-based awards to international venues as well.

from the recent economic openings. Among the measures introduced are the lowering of taxes on hired wage or salaried laborers and increasing the seating capacity at the emblematic home restaurants (*paladares*; see Leyva 2011).

The measures were approved by the Council of Ministers, headed up by Raúl Castro, with the goal of "smoothing out the increase of private-sector jobs as alternative employment," according to *Granma*, the official newspaper of the Cuban Communist Party. The newspaper stated that new changes will go into effect "starting this month and until the following June (2012)." Some 314,538 Cubans now work in the private sector, a figure that reflects the increase of approved private-sector occupations to 178, up from 154.

Among the more noteworthy measures is increasing the number of place settings from 20 to 50 at the island's famous *paladares*. Prior to the change, no more than 12 customers could be seated and only household members could work at the restaurants. There is little doubt that the new measure will help increase the quality and competition between the private sector and the roughly 2,500 chain restaurants operated by the Cuban government. These chains cater to both international tourists as well as Cubans (Leyva 2011).

A large number of home restaurants and allied food service businesses (Henken 2008) have opened up throughout Havana and major cities since these private-sector measures were announced. Formerly prohibited items such as beef and lobster will now be on the *paladar* menu. New measures also call for a lowering of business taxes by 25 percent. High monthly taxes have been a major complaint voiced by those who rent rooms in their homes. Also being considered is a temporary tax holiday—possibly from three to six months—for commercial drivers and homeowners who are carrying out repairs for renting rooms on their premises.

The Council of Ministers also "agreed that identifying low-producing public retail establishments, mostly in the food sector, and allowing them to work as private entities, would increase their business sales," a measure that the government started applying to barber shops in 2010, according to *Granma*. "The extent to which the number of self-employed workers (*cuentapropistas*) increases will make it necessary to continue adopting and putting into practice measures that enhance their work," *Granma* stated, adding that "correcting the course (*rectificar el camino*)" is the premise driving the expansion of the private sector (Leyva 2011).

The cumulative effect of these regulatory changes may signal a gradual transfer of state activities in production and services to the private sector, but those activities have yet to be touched by the reforms. Many business professionals would benefit from these reforms. For instance, new private-sector laws governing self-employment call for rigorous accounting procedures that will be subject to audits. Accountancy professionals could secure an important role in providing auditing and tax services, as would marketers, brand designers, webmasters, advertisers and other experts. These business skills will be indispensible for thousands of ordinary Cubans starting private companies who lack experience and training in business administration (Morales 2011).

ADVERTISING

Recall the sage advice given by advertising expert Mirtha Múñíz, who worked in the industry before the Revolution and during it, when she argued that the practice of advertising in Cuba had become polemical because it was automatically associated with capitalism. It can, as she rightly argued, be an "efficient weapon for business" and need not lead necessarily to conspicuous consumption. Múñíz had been a lone voice in trying to advertise Cuban government-made consumer products before her retirement.

Marketing without Advertising allows us to revisit theories about how advertising creates an effects hierarchy that starts when exposure to advertising ends with a consumer purchase. Brand managers in many industries have championed consumer purchase of the product as the single most important metric in assessing advertising strategies (Franzen and Moriarty 2009). Much of this was subsumed under the so-called AIDA model, which contends that the final *A* could result in nonpurchasing behavior; 'action' might translate into finding out more about a product or service, going online to read corporate websites and consumer reviews or reading blog postings (Grewal and Levy 2010). The Cuban case aligns with Ehrenberg (1997) and Castleberry and Ehrenberg (1990) in that users of a brand have a broader network of associations than nonusers. Our findings in Chapter 3 show that consumer decision-making in Cuba is greatly influenced by reference groups and retail personnel because of the lack of conventional advertising strategies. Perhaps because of Cubans' limited purchasing power, their search and decision-making processes are more methodical and thoughtful than previously assumed. Future research should try to separate these complex relationships if more contemporary marketing channels open up there.

Our findings also corroborate an age-old axiom that no amount of advertising can mask a poor-quality product or service. Cubans are not, in local parlance, *bobos* or *tontos* (fools), who have been logo-starved in a frenzied consumer world. To be sure, they are unjustly denied a market wage that allows them to acquire simple goods that are widely available elsewhere in the Caribbean. We believe that the recent trends in the past few decades of engaging consumers through interactive settings and local sponsorships—venues of a more grassroots or 'guerilla' setting—would be an appropriate marketing communications strategy to pursue should modern media channels become available on the island. Joachimsthaler and Aaker's work (1997) about building brands without mass media show that corporate social responsibility practices by Body Shop and Häagen-Dazs, or product placement in unexpected venues such as Swatch's sponsorship of 'unusual events' (i.e., the 1992 UN Earth Summit in Rio de Janeiro; *perestroika* in Eastern Europe, the passing of Halley's comet) strengthened brand equity and deepened brand awareness. Who is to say such nontraditional media campaigns are not appropriate in Cuba? "Providing extensive information, especially using media advertising, cannot duplicate the impact of customers' personal experience with a brand" (Joachimsthaler and Aaker 1997, 7).

Part of the experience that Cubans have had with the limited array of goods to which they have been exposed is, we argue, tied to the 'Cubanness' of the product. In that regard, our findings show that iconic brand potential for Alicia Alonso perfume exceeded other national brands. Advertising and marketing communication strategies will have to carefully tease out iconic brand potential for the domestic versus the international markets. The national–international iconic schism suggests that iconic attachments would play out differently in domestic and international markets. Alicia Alonso promoted overseas would have to use different brand awareness or 'Cubanness' strategies to reach non-Cubans than for, say, campaigns designed to laud the island's premier rum and cigars. Scores of Cuban artists, athletes, actors and actresses could easily promote national goods in a deregulated setting. Consider, for instance, the implications of Naranjada (orange-drink) and guarapo-based drinks promoted by a Cuban athlete, artist, musician or dancer. The combination of sponsorships and promotions that tap into iconic Cuban values are seemingly endless.

Foreign brand awareness in Cuba will likely expand in Cuba as purchasing power rises. Recall that in 2006, only 80,000 Cubans had cell phones yet more than half of the respondents were able to recall a cell phone brand. By early 2011, the number of cell phone users on the island had risen to over one million users, underscoring the rise of remittances, purchasing power and brand awareness in this crucial telecommunications sector.

Advertising on the island in the future could come through corporate and nonprofit sponsorships. Reflect upon, for example, promotion of the island's national sport: baseball (González Echeverría 1999). There is great potential for local churches and private businesses to sponsor the hundreds of baseball teams across the island. What about U.S. minor league (farm) baseball teams on the island, and the cable TV promotion of those games? Havana Club's product use of the bartender association (Asociación Cubana de Cantineros) has played a key role in getting that brand in front of tourists. The same could be done for auto parts personnel, hardware store clerks or pharmacy employees so that they become familiar with different product lines. The island's huge stock of old automobiles (Baker 2006) could readily attract auto parts sponsors (e.g., Pep Boys, Advanced Auto Parts, Auto Zone, O'Reilly) and auto club shows to support the makeshift changes to 1949 Plymouths and 1957 Chevys. Playing baseball and driving automobiles are not insignificant components of everyday life (*la vida cotidinia*) in Cuba.

Advertising Cuban brands will be able to tap into the rich tapestry of iconic symbols such as revolutionary figures and logos, musicians, colonial landscapes, cigars and rum, 'fiery mulattas,' Cuban artists, athletes, dancers, palm trees and sandy white beaches, just to name a few. The marketing campaigns of the few Cuban franchises operating overseas—Casa del Habano, La Bodeguita del Medio and Cohiba Atmosphere—will offer valuable lessons on finding the right mix of *cubanidad* in product and service promotion, on the one hand, and local cultural tastes and preferences, on the other. In the end, Cubanized versions of the Colombian Juan Valdez will no doubt emerge as the country projects itself outward and reenters the global marketplace. Cuba's comparative advantages are many.

Pronouncements published in *Granma* in May 2011 also suggest that the use of mass communication media may be just around the corner. Advertising would jump-start some of the reforms and generate greater market competition, which are essential if these reforms are going to be successful, especially in the realm of services marketing. Broad-scale advertising already exists in the work that the Cuban government carries out with foreign companies in the tourism sector. However, it will have to increase if mass U.S. tourism, absent from the island for 50 years, is on the horizon.

Advertising will also play an important role in transforming the consumption habits of Cuban society. One way or another, Cubans are going to find out about new services and products. There may be no other way to do so except through advertising that goes beyond the conventional in-store promotions, the occasional product placement or WOM. In other words, the model of marketing tourist services already exists, and it would be an appropriate model to pursue to inform Cubans about new items beyond tourism. Full-fledged advertising would not only help the island's nascent private sector, but it would reaffirm the government's proclamation that these economic reforms are irreversible. A return to advertising would make the nation more attractive to foreign investment, something the island's economy so desperately needs.

BRANDING AND CONSUMER BEHAVIOR

Little empirical evidence exists on the impact of advertising in Cuba using mass communication media and consumption per se. Recall that the Ciego Montero ads in 1998 were daring. However, the spots were suggestive and never showed anyone consuming the products. We do not have information on whether product purchases rose, fell or remained flat during this short foray into TV advertising. This relationship between 'evil' advertising and retailing ties into broader questions about the understudied nature of consumption and consumerism in Cuba. Cuban consumers are neither the counterparts of their Miami cousins nor the hard-core revolutionaries of pre-reformist China. Much has changed in the realm of consumption since 1958 when, according to Falcoff (2003), more Cubans had visited the United States than Americans had visited Cuba. Survey results from Chapter 3 indicate brand recall of U.S. products has not been eradicated entirely. We concur with Weinreb (2009, 83) in that the Cuban leadership is inching towards 'citizen-consumer desire' as it reformulates its economic policies. Perhaps out of necessity, Cubans have become pragmatic consumers who face a yawning gap between their wants and needs. What sets them apart from the rest of the world—emerging, Third World or global nations of the 'South'—is that the stigma about consumer consumption has dissipated since the 1960s.

If there is a universal wish to consume global goods and services, it seems reasonable to assume that it is conditioned by local political, economic and social conditions (Appadurai 1986; Simmel 1978). Today, Cuban small farmers need reliable machinery and parts; women want to use affordable cosmetic products that hold up in the island's climate; young people consider new fashions and trends in music, art and entertainment. In the future, Cuban youth *fashionistas* may be able to use a smart phone application about Mango clothiers while mechanics read consumer reviews of one brand of brake pads versus another. In the end, everyone gains because a more efficient and rational use of limited household income minimizes risk and uncertainty.

The branding literature tells us that consumers assess novel stimuli (in the case of free-market Cuba, this amounts to almost any advertising) in order to gain knowledge of the brand (Sujan 1985). Thus, advertisement for unfamiliar brands (which will be many), may seem more novel and interesting to Cubans, but may also demand greater processing than in the pre-ad era, which has reigned for half a century. Alternatively, Cubans will probably engage in simpler decision-making and rely on more confirmation-based processing when exposed to marketing of familiar brands, such as the top-tier domestic brands discussed in Chapter 4.

Perhaps no sector of Cuban culture and economy has been so expressive, has challenged the socialist order so much and has been disseminated so broadly as the island's contemporary music scene. To be sure, the global reach of Cuban music goes beyond the film and soundtrack of *Buena Vista Social Club*. Cuban rappers, such as Las Orishas and Las Krudas, as well as hip-hop artists often express their strong criticisms of neoliberal globalization as well as their belief that Cuba is really a black nation struggling for justice in an unjust domestic and world order (Fernandes 2003). The European-based Cuban rap group Orishas was one of the first global Cuban bands to forge an identify with the African diaspora and present glimpses of urban street life from their Cayo Hueso neighborhood in Havana. Although Fidel Castro met with them and celebrated their music in 1999, some suggest it was an attempt to co-opt the band from criticizing the regime. At the same time, their global success has signaled to some their "selling out to commercial pressures to evoke Cuban nostalgia" (Basu and Lemelle 2006, 168). Anthropologist Sujatha Ferndanes's study of Cuban hip-hop underscores how one aspect of Cuban consumers' foray into the global marketplace is as much a political statement as an economic one.

> The hip-hop movement in Cuba reflects trends within American hip-hop such as conspicuous consumption, and the use of American clothing has also been used to make certain political statements. It is undeniable that the wearing of designer label clothes such as Fubu and Tommy Hilfiger that forms part of hip-hop movement in the US has also become

> incorporated into Cuban hip-hop. The majority of audiences at a peña [party or musical gathering] during the festival are attired in baggy pants, sweatshirts and baseball caps or stocking caps brought by relatives in Miami or from tourists. Moreover, this style is not simply an adoption of American styles and capitalist culture; it is also a gesture of defiance that signals a refusal to conform to the dominant society. (2003, 598–599)

It is noteworthy that Chapter 3 argued that one weakness of conventional psychological theories of branding is that they fail to generate the brand symbolism that adds brand value based on how consumers in certain societies envision themselves. In the preceding example, international brands are an affront to the Cuban socialist establishments. Nevertheless, some young Cubans will also interpret using these brands as a sellout of sorts to international capitalism. In the following, Fernandes relates an interview she had with a Cuban music producer (Herrera) who explains how he was ambivalent about whether to accept free clothing in a promotional recording deal:

> Herrera felt conflicted over whether to accept it, because he said that on the one hand he felt it was a symbol of multinational capitalism, and he recognized the attempt of the producer to take advantage of a present opening in Cuban society to market the Edge label in Cuba. But on the other hand, Herrera felt that the clothing was very fashionable, and he added that it is difficult to find good clothing in Cuba. Networks of fashion labels and transnational record companies . . . provide multiple options for Cuban rappers to draw on outside of the state, and alleviate the difficulty of their current circumstances. Like African-American rappers who may see hip-hop, as well as sport, as an activity that "embodies dreams of success and possible escape from the ghetto." (2003, 601)

Thus, darker-skinned Cuba is no mere twinning of lighter-skinned Miami. Consumer preferences and tastes will be shaped by age, race and lifestyle (Taylor 2009).

Our findings also extend Yadong and Peng's (1999) work on competition and learning in emerging economies. One of their conclusions was that a "country-specific experience is more important to performance in the early stage than in the late phase of overseas operations. This requires that multinational enterprises (MNEs) attach particular importance to experience during the early stages" (1999, 289). In the Cuban case, this may mean relying on the business acumen and expertise of the South Florida diaspora community.

We posed several questions in Chapter 2. "To what extent could Cuba today (2011) be considered a consumer society?" It is noteworthy that the CBBE model is founded on repetition and modern communication channels to deliver brand message. These channels, however, have not reached the three-quarters of the population born after 1959. Moreover, with mean public salaries in the range of US$22 to $30, there would seem to be little discretionary income available for nonessential goods, even factoring in remittances. However, as Chapter 7 makes clear, remittances are making a huge difference in expanding consumer purchasing power.

A second question we asked was: "How has the socialist system prevented Cuba from becoming a consumer society?" One way is that it has kept advertising to a minimum and in its place there are political messages. Yet, the decriminalization of the dollar in 1993 is changing that, and window-shopping and gifts from abroad deepen consumers' knowledge about the world of brands. In short, the beginnings of a consumer society have taken root.

A final question we posed was: "To what extent has consumer behavior shifted from passive socialist consumers to consumers who take cues from signals in a limited retail market?" Survey findings from Chapter 3 and content analyses of focus groups in Chapter 4 indicate that a rich cultural and historic thread underlay iconic brands. When the early twentieth-century cigarette ad (Figure 2.3) read, "The three things a *guajíro* (Cuban cowboy or farmer) loves: his girl, his horse, and Flor de Tomás Gutiérrez cigarettes," it underscored a cultural value that resonated with consumers. Put another way, there existed an early Cuban version of rugged individualism long before the iconic U.S. Marlboro man of the 1960s. Fast-forward nearly a century to our 2010 focus groups where we learn that Cuban consumer references to an agrarian past still characterize much of what consumers think about the 'Cubanness' of Cuba's top 10 brands.

How, then, might B2C ventures into the Cuban market conceptualize and operationalize the segmentation, targeting and positioning of the island's consumers? Based on our knowledge of consumer behavior and brands we outline Cuban consumer profiles as a potential starting point (left-hand column of Table 8.2), some widely accepted consumer categories from the industrial North Atlantic economies and the necessary adjustments for the Cuban case. The segment profiles mesh both demographic and lifestyle elements that are germane to the island's consumer culture.

If the economic reforms of 2011 are to be successful, then, Cuban firms will need to use their competitive intelligence to synthesize information about their position in the market with regard to their rivals. They should know better than multinational companies, at least in the short run, their national culture, which includes the visual nuances of dress, behavior, ceremonies, the use of Cuban Spanish, tastes, food, color and other cultural attributes. As Cuban consumers become 'time-poor,' it follows that they will take the shortcut cues that branding allows shoppers to follow. At one extreme, is the time-strapped and brand-saturated North American and European whose day might unfold like this:

> Lunch is Taco Bell at your desk while you work on the Lucent account, followed by Altoids to kill the taste. By five o'clock, you're running on

Table 8.2 Comparison and Contrast of North Atlantic and Cuban Consumer Profiles

Cohort	Tweens & Millennials	Gen Y	Gen X	Baby boomers	Seniors
Range of Birth Years	1996–2000	1977–1999	1965–1976	1946–64	Before 1945
Age in 2011	11–15	22–34	35–44	45–64	65
Characteristics	Rely on their parents for purchasing power. Begin desiring "grown up" products and services. Prone to viral (a.k.a. buzz) marketing.	Realistic and optimistic, seek killer lifestyle, institutions are irrelevant, Multitaskers, assume technology	Analytical and pragmatic. Live killer life, reject rules, distrust institutions, multi-taskers, use new technology	Idealistic, conformist, created institutions, participated in social movements, task & technology specific,possess new technology	Control the majority of discretionary income; share many of the product and service 'likes' of younger cohorts; value oriented

Cuban Consumer Generational Cohorts

Cohort	Survivors	Revolutionary babies	Reared in the revolution	Straddlers	Seniors
Range of birth Years	1993–2000	1977–1992	1959–1976	1946–1958	Before 1945
Age in 2011	11–18	19–34	35–44	45–64	65
Characteristics	Born during the Special Period. Know only nascent market reforms. The most exposed to mass commu-nication marketing media. Aware of global styles & trends. Notice 'brands' worn by classmates such as Thaba or Nike backpacks.	Lived childhood during modest prosperity of 1980s before collapse of Soviet bloc. Some familiar-ity with global styles and fashions before advent of technology used by 'survivors.'	Reared as youth in times of sacrifice and scarcity but knew some modest prosperity of 1980s. Parents of survivors.	Straddle the early years of the revolution and pre-revolutionary period as well. Have lived adulthood with the hope of promised yet unfulfilled consumption in both quality and quantity.	Have vivid recollection of market mechanisms, rewards, and weaknesses before 1959; now relying on lean state social security and pensions in a mainly weak peso economy

Source: Calculated by The Havana Consulting Group

> Yoo-Hoo, Visine, and M&Ms, so on your way home you decide to reward yourself with a Domino's pizza and a six-pack of Heineken. Midnight finds you asleep in front of a commercial for Chia Pets—with one hand still buried in a bag of Cheez Doodles. (Morris 2004, 2–3)

A Cuban version of tomorrow could read something like this:

> Lunch is a franchised *sandwich cubano* (hot grilled pork sandwich) while you work on the (Cuban hotel chain) account, followed by any *chicle* (chewing gum, once common but scarce for many years) to kill the taste. By five o'clock you have your *merienda*, which consists of a *café cubano extra fuerte*. On the way home you decide to reward yourself with a local roasted chicken (*pollo asado*) from a new franchise and a few bottles of Cristal beer. Midnight finds you asleep in front of a commercial with one hand still buried a in a bag of fried pork rinds (*chicharrones*).

Ease and economy, framed by recognizable brands, solve simple, everyday problems in a modern world.

In this regard, work by McDonald et al. (2000) in their comparative study of Vietnam with China and Eastern Europe is germane to Cuba, once private supermarkets enter the island in force. The researchers found that Vietnamese would shop often but buy little and attributed that behavior to "a combination of novelty seeking, a preference for fixed pricing and the desire for foreign brands. The high level of shopping frequency and low number of purchases resulted from a genuine enjoyment of shopping, a lack of planning and status seeking, not infrastructure or economic factors suggested by past researchers" (McDonald et al. 2000, 53). Given the problem of food prices and availability, it is reasonable to expect similar 'novelty seeking' in Cuban retailing.

CUBAN RETAILING: YESTERDAY, TODAY AND TOMORROW

Retailing in the early Republic years described in Chapter 2 revealed robust service and advertising sectors in the island's large cities. These sectors relied on export-trade journals, direct-by-mail advertising, newspapers, motion pictures, streetcar advertising, billboards, handbills and sample packages, in-store demonstrations and other venues (Sanger 1919, 3). A century later, however, and all that remains in the early 2010s are window displays and in-store demonstrations (Morales 2009). *Advertising without Marketing* has attempted to trace that transition and cast light on the simplistic analyses that dichotomize life in Cuba as self-sacrificing and noble, and portray Cuban Americans as mired in mindless consumerism. However, our findings suggest otherwise. Although casual observers will still hear "Quién es el último?" (Who's the last in line?) in retail settings, Cubans' familiarity with waiting may have created a steadier information search when assessing brand value than other Caribbean and Latin American consumers. Future research will need to assess this.

The roughly US$4 billion (roughly equal in terms of cash and merchandise) in economic support that reaches about two-thirds of Cubans annually is the economic engine driving Cuban retailing today. That amount is likely to increase by 2020. About US$18 billion in cash and US$19.5 billion in merchandise have entered Cuban households since 1993. Put another way, that represents an average annual rate of US$2.2 billion or US$37.5 billion in less than two decades. Supplemental 'gifting' from family and friends overseas does not detract from the amount of time that Cubans spend window-shopping. Like consumers elsewhere, their purchasing power lags behind their desires. Cuban peso retail stores generally offer lower-quality national or Asian products, providing consumers an option of substituting name brands when hard-currency items are unavailable (Griffith, Cavusgil and Xu 2008).

That substitution effect of national peso and hard-currency-imported items will no doubt shift, particularly if the move to a single convertible currency unfolds. Whether that convertible currency will be the U.S. dollar or the euro remains to be seen, but the costs of conducting retailing with multiple currencies has been problematic. However, the switch to a single hard currency is unlikely to produce a full-fledged 'invasion' of foreign retailers. U.S. law must be changed by an act of Congress to allow direct foreign investment by U.S. companies, and Cuban law must change to permit foreign retailers to operate without a Cuban counterpart. Despite potential regulatory change in retail operations, lessons have been learned elsewhere as U.S. chains move into emerging economy markets. Recall that Best Buy and Home Depot reduced their presence in China because of consumer push back. In just five years, Best Buy closed all nine of its branded stores (by 2011) as well as its headquarters in Shanghai. That Home Depot purchased the local Chinese chain Home Way in 2006 poses interesting options for Cuban retailing, where home improvement is one of the top social concerns among Cubans, who must seek out Portland cement and paint on the black market or from expensive state stores (Scarpaci et al. 2002). Might CIMEX, the island's largest owner of hard-currency retail outlets, become a partner some day with Wal-Mart, Lowe's or Home Depot? If that were to happen, will consumer wishes become illusory because their purchasing power—especially among the elderly—lags behind market conditions (Keller and Vihalemm 2005). As recently as a decade ago, almost *any* product would satisfy consumer needs just because there was such scarcity of basic goods. That sentiment was expressed well by Cristina García's character Felicia, in *Dreaming in Cuba*, where the protagonist laments the lack of variety among exterior latex paints:

> Last fall, the line at the hardware store snaked around the block for the surplus paint, left over from a hospital project on the other side of

> Havana. Felicia bought the maximum amount allowed, eight gallons, and spent two Sundays painting the house with borrowed brushes and ladders.
>
> "After all," she said, "you could die waiting for the right shade of blue." (García 1992, 38–39)

Today, there are glimmers of hope that waiting for the right shade of blue is a less onerous, though still costly, task. If waiting is a form of powerlessness and a message the state sends to its people about who is really in charge, one can only hope this small-scale capitalism gradually does away with it.

Throughout this book, we have shown how Cubans adapt readily to market change, particularly technology. We presented cell phone adoption data to show that. In an unfettered market and technological setting, retailers will experiment with Twitter, Facebook and smart phone applications to capture the island's consumers. However, we have shown that WOM and in-store demonstration—the tried-and-true methods of 'old-school' marketing, still hold promise. Joachimsthaler and Aaker's (1997) review of Nestlé's Buitoni, The Body Shop, Cadbury, Häagen-Dazs, Hugo Boss and Swatch has found that multiple communication strategies in this so-called 'post–mass communications era' may be necessary to capture and retain loyal customers. Loyalty, moreover, can only come about when customers believe that the retailer trusts the customers (Figure 8.2). Nestlé's use

Figure 8.2 Cuban retailing store. Most Cuban retailing does not allow for self-service. Instead, clerks will show customers products one item at a time, causing delays and congestion. Photograph by Emilio Morales.

of self-service ice-cream coolers has proven to be quite popular given the traditional 'clerk-behind-the-counter' method of showing the customer one item at a time.

SITUATING THE CUBAN CONSUMER IN THE GLOBAL MARKETPLACE

Cuba in 2011 has largely rid itself of the stigma once associated with certain types of consumption. If 'big-box' stores come to the island, it would mark a radical change from the neighborhood-based stores where sales staff members in private and public businesses have forged a relationship with clients (Hirt and Scarpaci 2007). Scenarios such as these were remote possibilities only a few years ago, but today they appear to be more plausible.

Our basic research has challenged the conventional assumptions about brand equity, brand extension and brand loyalty because of Cuba's unique marketing conditions. Consumption on the island falls uniquely between the conspicuous model found throughout the 'developed North' and the more modest levels found in the so-called 'developing South.' Flaunting a consumer purchase as if it were the trophy from a long-fought hunt seethes of the kind of individualism that the current socialist government abhors, but it would be unfounded to assume that all Cubans are bent on that behavior. Indeed, their needs are much more modest, and having cash to purchase anything is the challenge most Cubans face today. A 62-year-old construction worker from Artemisa described it this way: "Look, I could talk all day about the pros and cons of TuKola over Coca-Cola, but at this point, it would just be nice to have either one regularly."

We suggest that this tempering of consumption may be one of the lasting contributions of the revolution on the social and moral fabric of Cubans. Islanders are neither rabid consumers nor ignorant simpletons in a congested world of brands. Angelina Corso of Centro Habana, a 43-year-old factory worker, describes the infrequent moments of pleasure she gets from spraying on Alicia Alonso perfume. "For me [the perfume] is a real treasure. I don't use it a lot and I take care that it does not evaporate by keeping it in the refrigerator in the original box." With a slow and widening smile, she added, "When the moment is right, either alone or with my husband, I'll put it on." She lifted her hair off the back of her neck and acted like she was spraying some perfume there. "It transforms me, you know, it takes me to another place! [*tú sabes, que me lleva a otro sitio!*]"

The connections about brand awareness that we have shown in this book contest a few tenets that drive globalization theory. Globalization theorists often assert that we are living through a new postnational order in which economic and cultural globalization weaken national identify and homogenize consumer tastes (Appadurai 1996; Bhabha 1990). Yet, in Cuba, the spread of transnational cultural flows in the form of imported brands has strengthened the socialist government in the new millennium by earning billions of dollars from its retailing while keeping its role as the benevolent and paternalist gatekeeper. Our review of Cuban brand awareness (Chapter 3) and the iconic potential for Cuban brands and *cubanidad* (Chapter 4) shows that Cubans appropriate transnational cultural and material values in many ways. TuKola has to be sweeter than Coca-Cola, Alicia Alonso exudes the best of the Cuban woman in ways that Carolina Herrera perfume cannot and Rolex may be the most identifiable brand of watches, but for Cubans, a Seiko will do just fine (thank you very much).

Situating the island's consumer in a broader global economy does not automatically mean that they will adopt Miami-style tastes. Our literature review revealed that Hispanic tastes and preferences in the U.S. cannot be generalized to other Hispanic subgroups. Moreover, even less is known about cross-border influences of similar Hispanic groups such as Mexican Americans in the U.S. and their relatives in Mexico, El Salvadorans in Canada versus those back in San Salvador and so forth. A robust area of research remains in exploring how gifts condition the preferences and tastes of Cubans on the island. For international marketers and brand managers, the contents of those *gusano* bags offer valuable insight into this tiny, yet growing, market of 11 million Cubans.

Cuba has been the object of huge social and economic experiments over the past 120 years. From Spanish colony and young republic, it evolved into a market in the 1950s with a highly skewed income distribution. Over the last half century, private enterprise was all but eliminated, and only in recent years has it made a tepid and limited return. This may bode poorly for a government about to downsize its public workforce by one million workers and trust that a nascent private sector will gainfully employ them. These reforms develop piecemeal in a setting where, as marketing guru and entrepreneurial star Gary Vaynerchuk (2010) has been heralding, the importance of customer loyalty is essential. This first-generation Belarus immigrant to the U.S. learned old-school retailing experiences while working at his father's liquor store. Today, he aims to blend the old (knowing your customer, good in-store service) with the new (Twitter, Facebook). Whereas these new technologies are a long way off in Cuba, the core of the message is essential to Cuban marketing: business owners (private, not public ones) need to start acting like small-town shopkeepers so that they shape the WOM about them. This new work ethic can start at the humblest of *timbiriches callejeros* and spread from there. Only by treating each Cuban as though he or she were the most important customer on the island can future retailers begin to restructure the island's economy. Cuba is not yet the victim of a time-starved consumer culture, but it is on the eve of recreating itself so that millions of simple wants can be satisfied.

Notes

NOTES TO CHAPTER 1

1. In 2009, a desktop publisher in Miami, Alexandria Library, published *Cuba: Tránsito silencioso al capitalismo?* (ISBN978–1–934804–55–1), by coauthor Emilio Morales. Only 120 copies of the Spanish-language work have been printed, and the tome is limited to Spanish readers. This English-language text not only enhances the work by providing a broader contextual framework on consumption, branding and international marketing management, but it excludes three chapters and includes one that was not included in the 2009 book.

NOTES TO CHAPTER 2

1. Ramón Areces Rodríguez, a Spaniard born in Asturias, migrated to Cuba in 1919, and then was for a short time in New York. At the age of 23, Areces returned to work in Cuba for six years before returning to Spain to set up his own business. Even though Spain was on the verge of civil war, Areces invested in retailing nonetheless. He established himself in Madrid and invested his Cuban savings to purchase a tailor's shop. In 1940, as the store grew and various services and offerings were added, the Corte Inglés was incorporated, and today is the largest retailer in Spain with over 55 stores. It is the largest private company in Spain and the third largest Spanish firm (Funding Universe 2011).
2. CDR (*Comité para la Defensa de la Revolución*) remains a government-sanctioned organization that functions at the neighborhood block level to monitor neighborhood activities, including sanitation, crime and safety, social issues, public-health and civil-defense programs, as well as reporting on possible antigovernment (e.g., anti-Revolutionary) behavior among neighbors. Since the 1990s, it has served an important citizens-watch function, chiefly to prevent burglarizing state stores.
3. 1 CUC equaled about US$1.08 at the time.
4. *Un cubanote dice a otro: "¡Chico estoy harto de estar siempre haciendo una cola, cola pa`la comida, cola pa`la medicina, cola pa`las cosas de la casa. Sabes, mejor voy a ir a matar a Fidel y todo esto se va a acabar!"A los tres meses vuelve y su amigo le pregunta: "Bueno y como te fue con lo de matar al comandante". A lo que el otro le responde: "Mal chico, que para matar a Fidel uno tambien tiene que hacer cola!"*
5. *¿En qué se parecen el Vaticano y la Reforma Agraria Cubana ? En que en 50 años, solo han producido cuatro papas.*

NOTES TO CHAPTER 3

1. See *Asistencia al empresario El mercado minorista y la franquicia*, 24 de Julio del 2006 Guillermo de la Cuesta, http://www.opciones.cu/leer.asp?idnuevo=2130, Accessed June 2, 2010
2. In all, there were about 2,400 brands because some, like LG, Sony and Sanyo, were listed in various product categories.
3. In early 2011 there were official announcements about eliminating multiple currencies and moving towards a single currency, but at the time of this writing, the details had not been disclosed. The specific recommendations appear in the office "Guidelines" (*lineamientos*) published after the April 2011 SVI Cuban Communist Party, but the implementation of these recommendations is not yet clear.

NOTES TO CHAPTER 4

1. Other derogatory terms used during the era were *yoni*, *yuli*, *cuchi*, *bebi*, *yeyo*, *envaselinados* (for using a lot of Vaseline in the hair), *modositos* and *femeniles*, among others. According to Sierra Madero (2006, 82), those displaying mannerisms that violated the codified and socially accepted norms of heterosexual male behavior were "persecuted in the name of moral and good customs; but most of all, in the name of the nation." These values appear to have continued at least a half century as displayed by the autobiography of Cuban author Reinaldo Arenas (1993), and as brought to a broader public by Julian Schnabel's film, *Before Night Falls*, which shows the contradictory behavior of the Cuban Revolutionary Armed Forces in the 1960s and 1970s. Homosexuality was both condemned but also seemingly common among a segment of the troops, and the Cuban Revolution of the 1960s implemented brutal crackdowns on homosexuals, who faced incarceration and even rehabilitation for antirevolutionary and bourgeois behavior. In the 2000s, the daughter of Raúl Castro, Mariela Castro, director of Cuba's Center for Sexual Education, has become an advocate for gay, lesbian and transsexual rights and even hosted several gay pride parades that received her father's approval. One news analyst in 2008 wrote, "Prejudice against homosexuals remains deeply rooted in Cuban society, but the government has steadily moved away from the Puritanism of the 1960s and 1970s, when homosexuals hid their sexuality for fear of being ridiculed, fired from work or even imprisoned" (Rodríguez 2008).
2. Born in 1921 as Alicia Ernestina de la Caridad del Cobre Mártinez Hoya, Alonso's middle name—Caridad del Cobre—is the name of the island's patron saint, the Virgin of the Charity of Copper. She is undoubtedly one of the preeminent ballerinas and choreographers of the twentieth and twenty-first centuries. Following World War II, she founded the dance company Ballet Alicia Alonso. For more than half a century, she has gained fame as one of the best-known Latin American artists affiliated with theoretical dance (Concepción 2003).
3. "Ella, como el mismo producto, representa lo mejor de Cuba . . . lo que la tipica cubana aspira a realizar en su vida: el éxito, la elegancia. Y eso vale tanto aqui' como afuera."

NOTES TO CHAPTER 5

1. In Cuban Spanish, a *Habano* (or Havanan) refers to cigars; not to be confused with a *Habanero* or *Habanera*, a man or woman from Havana. Cigars

in Cuba are generally referred to as *puros* and should not be confused with the false cognate among English-speakers, which is *cigarros* (which in Cuba means cigarettes).

2. La Bodeguita del Medio and Cohiba Atmosphere are also internationally franchised, but they are smaller operations than Casa del Habano.
3. We draw on the works of Dinnie (2008), as well as Levi and Heller (2002).
4. Cigar producers outside the island (mostly in the Dominican Republic, Honduras and Nicaragua) compete with island-grown tobacco by promoting their *Cuban-seed* cigars; a product differentiation that the Casa del Habano exploits to their advantage.

NOTES TO CHAPTER 6

1. The term 'premium' cigar is more than a simple adjective describing a cigar. Specifically, premium cigars use many varieties of tobacco for both the wrapper and the filler. Long filler cigars, for instance, are generally considered a high-quality product because they rely on long leaves throughout the cigar. They also contain a third kind of tobacco leaf, which is called a "binder." This binder is placed between the outer wrapper and the filler, which allows the cigar maker to use more attractive and delicate leaves because it is the wrapper, or the outer layer, that touches the smoker's tongue and lips. In most cases, premium cigars always blend varieties of tobacco leaf. Cuban cigars are no exception; top brands such as Cohiba, Montecristo and Trinidad frequently mix tobacco from different tobacco regions around the island to create multiple and distinctive flavors.
2. Remember that the term *habano* in the cigar business refers to the Cuban word for Cuban-origin cigars, and should not be confused with just *Havana*, as in "made in Havana." It is somewhat analogous to the use of the word *champagne*, which, if not produced in the original French region of the same name, must be marketed and sold as sparkling wine.
3. See 'related products' of the official Habanos S.A. website at http://www.habanos.com/relatedproducts.aspx?lang=en.
4. The irony that a socialist government is making money on the sale of bottled water because its tap water may not be safe is not lost on us.
5. Those who are unfamiliar with maté may find the following description useful: "A golden brown soda. It smells much like a champagne cola and the taste is somewhat akin. No its [*sic*] not really: this tastes like a crisp apple juice, sweet and light. But it has some of the sweet tart taste over that and ends in an earthy bitter flavor . . . It's not very fizzy at all. The flavor doesn't have great complexity, mostly just the appley sweet and then the herbal bitterness" (Delicious Sparkling Temperance Drinks 2011).
6. The term employed to indicate public agencies' purchase of food is *alimentación social*. Thus, for example, if the Ministry of Education purchases food products in hard currency for student luncheons or afternoon snacks, the figure and category would include this kind of expenditure on food.
7. Tang was originally developed by General Foods in the late 1950s. Its popularity was boosted by its use in the Gemini space program at NASA. Later, Tang was purchased by Kraft Foods. Although Tang is, according to Kraft, sold in more than 30 countries, Cuba is not listed as one of them, though Mexico and Canada are listed (see Kraft Foods 2011). Like many U.S. products, Tang (and its 38 flavors) can be imported to Cuba from third countries despite the long-standing U.S. trade embargo against the island.

NOTES CHAPTER 7

1. In the U.S., for instance, the 22nd Annual Retail Theft Survey in 2009 found that among 25 retailers alone, over one million shoplifters and dishonest employees were apprehended, which produced US$163 million in stolen goods. (Jack L. Hayes International, 2010).
2. There is a common saying in Cuba that reflects this rationalization: "They act like they pay me, and I act like I work."
3. A database listing this and related information for all 169 counties is available at www.thehavanaconsultinggroup.com.
4. Anecdotally, one of us (J. S.) traveled to Cuba six times within a five-month period in 2000 and found himself on the same flight with the same two *mulas* in Miami and Nassau, Bahamas. Clearly, there is a steady and informal industry of transfer agents.

NOTES TO CHAPTER 8

1. The ad is particularly effective because the 14 underlined words in the ad are actually magazine titles that circulate in the U.S. In the original ad, the magazine names appear in their original cover-page font and color type.
2. A recent set of postings by tourists about their stay at a hotel in Santiago de Cuba, the safety of valuables in one's room and possible romancing between young local women and men ("holiday romances between young Cuban girls and men old enough to be their granddads and vice versa") appeared on Trip Advisor in May 2011. The defensive response by the hotel's general manager underscores this pressing issue of services marketing in Cuba. See http://www.tripadvisor.com/Hotel_Review-g147273–d252230–Reviews-Melia_Santiago_de_Cuba-Santiago_de_Cuba_Cuba.html, Accessed June 1, 2011.

Author Biographies

Emilio Morales is the former Director of Strategic Marketing Planning Department for CIMEX, S.A., the largest Cuban company in the retail and wholesale sectors. Born, raised and educated in Cuba, he worked there until 2006 before moving to Miami. He holds a B.S. in Computer Science from the José Antonio Echevarría Higher Polytechnic Institute in Havana, and a Masters in Marketing from the University of Havana. He also earned an MBA from the Higher School of Marketing in Madrid, Spain.

Morales worked for more than 10 years in marketing research and authored or co-authored more than 50 marketing studies on products and services in health care, tourism, cell phones, retailing, medical equipment, tourism, and investment strategies. He provided technical service for the Cuban government in a variety of binational projects in South Africa, Argentina and Canada.

He is the author of the recently published marketing monograph *Cuba: tránsito silencioso al capitalismo?* and serves as President of The Havana Consulting Group LLC.

Joseph L. Scarpaci is Associate Professor of Marketing in the Gary E. West College of Business, West Liberty University, West Liberty, WV. Recent books related to Cuba include *Cuban Landscapes: Heritage, Memory and Place* (Guildford, 2009, with Armando Portela); *Plazas and Barrios: Heritage Tourism and Globalization in the Latin American Centro Histórico* (University of Arizona Press, 2005); and *Havana: Two Faces of the Antillean Metropolis* (University of North Carolina Press, 2002, with Mario Coyula and Roberto Segre).

Scarpaci serves as Executive Director at The Center for the Study of Cuban Culture + Economy and as Vice-President of The Havana Consulting Group, LLC.

Glossary

acopio—A farmer–state production agreement about agricultural output that farmers and ranchers promise to the state at a preset rate.

AIDA—*A*ttention, *I*nterest, *D*esire, *A*ction. Common set of communication stages in promoting product and brand awareness in market economies. Frequently used in settings where modern mass communication channels can repeat advertising messages often.

assisted recall—Asking consumers to respond to a specific brand or product question by providing them with a list of brands or product options (see also unassisted recall).

B2B—Refers to Business-to-Business marketing activities.

B2C—Refers to Business-to-Consumer marketing activities.

bodega—Spanish for a small store or corner grocer. Today in Cuba it refers to the state-run grocers where the libreta food ration booklet can be redeemed and subsidized food can be sold to Cuban households. Commonly found in most neighborhoods, urban and rural.

brand awareness—The extent to which consumers recognize the availability and awareness of a service or product. Creating brand awareness is a fundamental step in promoting a brand to customers.

brand equity—The power coming from the name recognition and goodwill accumulated by a brand over time. Brand equity increases over time should translate in greater sales volumes and profits compared to the competition.

CADECA—Also known as the *casa de cambio*, they are the official state-operated money exchange houses where Cuban pesos, U.S. dollars, CUCs and other currencies are traded and exchanged. Prices are set by the Cuban government. They are an important service outlet for the increasingly dollarized retail sector.

capote—The binder leaf used in cigar rolling.

CBBE—Consumer-based brand equity. When consumers hold a more favorable impression of how a brand, product or service is marketed a certain way than when it is not. This may result when the brand, product or service is attributed to an unnamed or fictitiously named version of the product. Such equity may also be attributed to national myths or folklore that can endow a product with iconic potential.

chaveta—A cigar-making tool/knife with a rounded blade.

choteo—Refers to a particular brand of humor specific to Cuba. Sometimes associated with street humor, it serves as a window to the political and economic opinions of the people.

CIMEX—The largest Cuban retail outlet operating in hard currency and controlled by the highest level of government: the Council of the State (as opposed to a Cuban ministry or joint-venture operation).

clientes—Spanish for customers or consumers.

CMEA—The now defunct Council of Mutual Economic Assistance, also known as Comecon, was spearheaded by the former USSR in 1949. In the late 1980s, its members included Soviet Union, Bulgaria, Czechoslovakia, the German Democratic Republic (East Germany), Hungary, Romania, Poland, Cuba, the Mongolian People's Republic (Mongolia) and Vietnam. It aimed to share resources and market preferences as a counter to capitalism's hegemonic grip on global markets. The USSR provided most of the material and financial support.

cubanidad—Cubanness (see also lo cubano).

CUC—Convertible Currency Units. Used in Cuba exclusively as a hard-currency unit (as opposed to pesos). In 2011, there was talk of eliminating the 'dual-currency' (CUC and pesos) monetary system on the island and moving towards a single currency.

diplotiendas—Before the decriminalization of the dollar in 1993, this was the term used to refer to retail stores charging in hard currency or setting prices in U.S. dollars. Only diplomats or selected authorized Cubans could purchase retail items there, items usually not available to Cubans seeking goods in Cuban pesos. The term was gradually dropped after 1993 when a spate of hard-currency stores sprung up around the island, and anyone having hard currency could enter and buy goods.

divisas—Spanish for hard currency. In Cuba this means most any other unit of currency other than the Cuban peso, which is a soft currency and is therefore not traded. Cuban *divisas* generally refer to the CUC, euros and the U.S. dollar.

doble moral—A condition in Cuba where some members of society are accused of hypocrisy by espousing one set of principles but act in a way that is inconsistent with those beliefs. It may be applied to individuals who are government or Party officials yet also participate in illicit activities involving the black market. Literally, "double morals" or "dual morality."

empresas mixtas—Joint-venture businesses between Cuban and foreign companies.

fulas—Cuban slang for dollars.

guarapo—Freshly pressed sugarcane juice consumed with ice in a frothy mixture or at room temperature. Often sold at kiosks called *guaraperías*.

habanos—Refers to all Cuban cigars (versus those produced elsewhere with Cuban seed). Despite the name, the cigars do not have to be grown in Havana (most are not, though most are rolled there).

iconic brands—When a particular product or service seems to exceed the value of other brands in a similar category by becoming associated with popular culture and by representing a particular lifestyle that is widely and readily recognized by consumers.

Ley de Cierre—Retail law in the first half of the twentieth century that mandated the hours of retail operations.

libreta—Spanish for 'small book' or 'booklet.' In Cuba it refers to the official food ration book introduced in 1960, which, as of 2011, is likely to be phased out. It was allocated to each household in Cuba so that subsidized food staples could be provided. The *libreta* lists all legal residents in the household unit and when presented at the state food store (*bodega*), entitles the bearer of the book a certain amount of food per household member.

lo cubano—Cubanness (see also cubanidad).

machismo—A socially constructed definition of acceptable and even expected male behavior that values strength, assertiveness and stamina.

marcas—Spanish for brands.

marianismo—A socially constructed definition of acceptable and even expected female behavior that values beauty and strength. One could argue that in Cuba, the passivity often associated with marianismo elsewhere in Latin America is absent or greatly reduced.

mercados agropecuarios—Spanish for agricultural markets. A Cuban-style farmers' market in which produce and other farm products can be sold by private producers or agricultural cooperatives that have satisfied their contractual agreements with the government (*acopio*). Most of these markets operate in Cuban pesos and remain expensive for most Cubans but offer a retail outlet less expensive than the hard-currency *shopping*. Also known as *agros*.

merienda—An afternoon snack common throughout Latin America and Spain. In some ways, analogous to British afternoon tea. In Cuba, it refers to a snack but also refers to state-sponsored snacks for public workers.

MINAL—Ministry of Food.

MINBAS—Ministry of Basic Industry.

MINCIN—Ministry of Internal Commerce (Ministerio de Comercio Interior). Handles all matters of retailing.

mulas—Literally mules, but in Cuba it generally refer to those travelers who carry cash and merchandise from Cuban Americans abroad and deliver it to their relatives and friends on the island. They are usually paid for this service. In the rest of Spanish-speaking Latin America, the term often implies those who smuggle drugs.

pesos—The official Cuban unit of currency. In 2011, the official exchange rate for one CUC unit was about 24 to 1, as it was for the U.S. dollar (excluding a penalty/service surcharge for cashing the dollar). Most Cuban workers are paid in pesos those working in tourism may receive hard-currency as gratuity, and Cubans working for joint-venture operations may receive bonuses or under-the-table payments in CUCs.

product breadth—The number of product lines a firm provides; sometimes referred to as variety. Cristal, the most popular beer in Cuba, for example, has no product breadth as it does not offer a light, lime- or wheat-flavored beer.

product depth—The number of categories within a particular product line. Havana Club has considerable product depth because of the many types of rums in its product line (clear rum, various aged rums, dark rums, etc.).

product and service categories—Clusters of like products or services under which particular brands are listed. Examples might include alcoholic beverages and spirits, business services, personal hygiene goods or legal services. Essential for marketing research and sales and distribution studies.

quinceñera—Commonly held Latin American rite of passage for girls celebrating their fifteenth birthdays. Often associated with a transition to womanhood and is embraced by family and friends through parties, special gowns and dresses, photographs and gifts.

shopping—Used in Cuba as a noun to refer to hard-currency retail outlets as opposed to peso-based stores; as in 'los shopping.' Not used as a gerund/verb.

SKUs—Shop-keeping units; the smallest retail item coded and inventoried at retail outlets.

Special Period (in a Time of Peace)—Coined by Fidel Castro Ruz in the early 1990s to refer to the economic shocks incurred in Cuba by the dissolution of the Soviet trading bloc (Council of Mutual and Economic Exchange) and the demise of Soviet subsidies to the Cuban economy. By 2011, the Cuban leadership contended that the Special Period was largely over, though the economy in many sectors has yet to recover to 1989 levels.

timbiriches callejeros—A Cuban term for small, improvised kiosks and vendor stands that were widely found before the Revolution. In recent years, they have become more abundant as small-scale vending expands.

unassisted recall—Asking consumers to respond to a specific brand or product question without providing them with a list of brands or product options (see also assisted recall).

vallas—Billboards and other forms of large, outdoor advertising in Cuba, most of which are used for political and civic messages and not product or service advertising.

villas—The original frontier and military outposts established in the first decades of the sixteenth century.

WOM—Word of mouth. How consumers everywhere, but especially in Cuba, pass on information about product and service attributes such as value, price, style, quality, taste and related features.

References

Aaker, D. A. 1991. *Managing Brand Equity.* New York: The Free Press.

———. 1996. *Building Strong Brands.* New York: The Free Press.

Aaker, D. A., and Joachimisthaler, E. 2000. *Brand Leadership.* New York: The Free Press.

Adamas, R.H. and Page, J. 2005. The impact of international migration and remittances on poverty. In Maimbo, S. M. and D.Ratha. Eds., 2005. *Remittances: Development Impact and Future Prospects.* Washington, D.C.: The International Bank for Reconstruction and Development, The World Bank. Chapter 14, pp. 277–306.

Alba, J. W., and Hutchinson, J. W. 1987. Dimensions of consumer expertise. *Journal of Consumer Research* 13: 411–454.

Alger, C. F. 1992. Local response to global intrusions. In Z. Milner, Ed., *Globalization and Territorial Identities.* Aldershot: Avebury, pp. 77–104.

Amaral, F. 2010. Franchise statistics in Brazil, http://www.franchiseek.com/Brazil/Franchise_Brazil_Statistics.htm, Accessed July 12, 2010.

Appadurai, A. (Ed.) 1986. *The Social Life of Things: Commodities in Cultural Perspective.* Cambridge: Cambridge University Press.

Appadurai, A. 1996. *Modernity at Large.* Minneapolis and London: University of Minnesota Press.

———. 2004. Disjuncture and difference in the global cultural economy. In F. Lechner and J. Bohli, Eds., *The Globalization Reader.* London: Routledge, pp. 100–109.

Arenas, R. 1993. *Before Night Falls.* New York: Viking.

Artero, J. P. 2009. The media in Cuba, Dominican Republic and Puerto Rico. In A. B. Albarran, Ed., *The Handbook of Spanish Language Media.* London: Routledge, pp. 189–200.

Auyero, J. 2011. Patients of the state: An ethnographic account of poor people's waiting. *Latin American Research Review* 46:5–29.

AZFranchies. 2010. Franchising facts, franchising industry statistics ,http://www.azfranchises.com/franchisefacts.htm, Accessed July 12, 2010.

Baker, C. 2006. *Cuba Classics: A Celebration of Vintage American Automobiles.* Northampton, MA: Interlink Publishing.

Basu, D. and Lemelle, S.J. 2006. *The Vinyl Ain't Final: Hip Hop and The Globalization of Black Popular Culture.* Ann Arbor and London: Pluto Press.

Belk, R. W. 1995. Hyperreality and globalization: Culture in the age of Ronald McDonald. *Journal of International Consumer Marketing* 5: 27–68.

Belk, R.W., Ger, G. and Askegaard, Sl. 1996. Metaphors of consumer desire. *Advances in Consumer Research* 23:368–373.

Berkowitz, S. 1997. Analyzing qualitative data. In J. Frechtling, L. Sharp and Westat, Eds., *User-Friendly Handbook for Mixed Method Evaluations* (Chapter 4),

National Science Foundation, Directorate of Education and Human Resources Web, http://www.ehr.nsf.gov/EHR/REC/pubs/NSF97–153/CHAP_4.HTM, Accessed June 21, 2006.

Betancourt, R. 1992. The Distribution Sector in a CPE: CUBA. Department of Economics University of Maryland College Park, MD. Available at http://econweb.umd.edu/~betancourt/distribution/cpedistribution.pdf, Accessed July 3, 2011.

Bettinger-López, C. 2000. *Cuban-Jewish Journeys: Searching for Identify, Home and History in Miami*. Knoxville: University of Tennessee Press.

Beverage Spectrum Magazine. 2010. Powdered Power. http://www.bevspectrum.com/cover-story/2008/powder_power/, Accessed October 23, 2011.

Bhabha, H.K. 1990. *Nation and Narration*. London: Routledge.

Blue, S. A. 2004. State policy, economic crisis, gender, and family ties: Determinants of family remittances to Cuba. *Economic Geography* 80: 63–82.

Bogdan, R. B., and Biklin, S. K. 1998. *Qualitative Research for Education: An Introduction to Theory and Methods*, Third Edition. Needham Heights, MA: Allyn and Bacon.

Bourdieu, P. 2000. *Pascalian Meditations*. Stanford, CA: Stanford University Press.

Büchel, B. 2003. Managing Partner Relations in Joint Ventures, MIT Sloan Management Review (July 15). Accessed at http://sloanreview.mit.edu/the-magazine/2003-summer/44412/managing-partner-relations-in-joint-ventures/ October 30, 2011.

Cardoso, F. H. and Faletto, E. 1979. *Dependency and Development in Latin America*. Berkeley and Los Angeles: University of California Press.

Castleberry, B. S., and Ehrenberg, A. S. C. 1990. Brand usage: A factor in consumer beliefs. *Marketing Research* (June) 2:14–20.

CDC (Center for Disease Control) 2011. Parasites—Giardia.http://www.cdc.gov/parasites/giardia/, Accessed October 23, 2011.

Concepción, A. 2003. Alonso, Alicia (1921–). In L. Martínez-Fernández, D. H. Gugeredo, L. A. Pérez and L. González, Eds., *Encyclopedia of Cuba*, Volume Two: People, History, Culture. Greenwood, CT: Greenwood Press, pp. 378–379.

Corbett, B. 2004. *This is Cuba: An Outlaw Culture Survives*. Boulder, CO: Westview.

Coyula, M. 2011. Personal communication, Havana, Cuba.

Curbelo Castellanos, J. L. 1999. *Cuba y La Habana*. Madrid: Limite Visual.

de la Rosa, A. "Pormayoresventas de Havana Club". *Opciones, SemanarioFinanciero, Comercial y Turistico de Cuba* (Noviembre 2005) http://www.opciones.cu/cuba/2005-11-27/por-mayores-ventas-de-habana-club/, Accessed October 30, 2011.

Deshpande, R. Hoyer, W.D. and Donthu, N. 1986. The intensity of ethnic affiliation: A study of the sociology of Hispanic consumption. *Journal of Consumer Research* 13(2): 214–217.

Deutch, E. 2008. A sportscaster reveals a dictator's human side. *New York Times*, June 15, http://www.nytimes.com/2008/06/15/sports/15mckay.html, Accessed October 11, 2010.

Dicken, P. 2011. *Global Shift: Mapping the Contours of the World Economy*. New York: Guilford.

Dinnie, K. 2008. *Nation Branding: Concepts, Issues, Practice*. London: Butterworth & Heinemann.

Dominguez, J. 1992. *The secrets of Castro's staying power*. Foreign Affairs (Spring), 97–107.

Eckstein, S. 2003. *Diasporas and Dollars: Transnational Ties and the Transformation of Cuba*. Cambridge, MA: Massachusetts Institute of Technology, Mellon-MIT Center on NGOs and Forced Migration, Paper #16, Februray, 31 pp.

Ehrenberg, A. S. C. 1997. Repetitive advertising and the consumer. *Journal of Advertising Research* 37 (6): 7–14.

Espinosa Chepe, O. 2010. *La economíacubana: Tiempos de esperanza?* In Cuba in Transition, Volume 20, Edited by Jorge Pérez-López. Washington, D.C.: Association for the Study of the Cuban Economy, 17–24.

Falcoff, M. 2003. *Cuba the Morning After: Confronting Castro's Legacy*. Washington, DC: AEI Press.

Fajnzylber, P., and López, J. H. 2007. *Close to Home: The Development Impact of Remittances in Latin America*. Washington DC: World Bank.

Featherstone , M. 1990. *Global Cultural and Post-Modernism*. London: Sage.

———.1991. *Consumer Culture and Post-Modernism*. London: Sage.

Feriahavana 2011. Memories. http://www.feriahavana.com/en/memories, Accessed October 23, 2011.

Fernandes, S. 2003. Fear of a Black nation: Local rappers, transnational crossings, and state power in contemporary Cuba. *Anthropological Quarterly* 76:575–608.

Fernández, W. *La Habana en los años 50*. Miami: Fernandez Productions (video: lahabanaenlosanos50.wmv),

Figueredo, D. H. 2003. Zoé Valdés. In L. Martínez-Fernández, D. H. Gugeredo, L. A. Pérez and L. González, Eds. *Encyclopedia of Cuba: People, History Culture*, Volume 1. Westport, CT: Greenwood Press, pp. 393–394.

Floating Rum Shack. 2011. Havana Club Rum: Showcase de los maestros. http://thefloatingrumshack.com/main/index.php?option=com_content&view=article&catid=24:press&id=289:havana-club-rum-seleccion-de-maestros, Accessed October 23, 2011.

Focualt, M. 1979. *Discipline and Punish*. New York: Vintage Books.

Fox Piven, F. and Cloward, R. 1971. *Regulating the Poor: The Functions of Public Welfare*. New York: Vintage.

Frank, M. 2006. ABC News. Castro's Cohiba cigar feted in Havana, http://abcnews.go.com/International/story?id=1691759&page=1, Accessed September 15, 2010.

Franzen, G., and Moriarty, S. 2009. *The Science and Art of Branding. Armonk*. New York: M. E. Sharpe.

Friedman, J. 1994. *Cultural Identity and Global Process*. London: Sage.

Funding Universe 2011. El Corte Inglés Group. http://www.fundinguniverse.com/company-histories/El-Corte-Ingleacute;s-Group-company-History.html, Accessed October 22, 2011.

García, C. 1992. *Dreaming in Cuba*. New York: Random House.

Gilman, S. L. and Zun, Z. 2004. *Smoke: A Global History of Smoking* (Editors). London: Reaktion Press.

Gimeno Chocarro, J. 2003. Corporaciones Cubanas. Havana: OficinaEconómica y Comerical de la Emajada de España en La Habana, ICEX (Instituto Español de Comerico Exterior). Havana: Spanish Embassy.

Gjelten, T. 2008. *Bacardí and the Long Fight for Cuba: Biography of a Cause*. New York:Viking.

Goldenkoff, R. 2004. Using focus groups. In J. S. Wholey, H. P. Hatry and K. E. Newcomer, Eds., *Handbook of Practical Program Evaluation*, Second Edition. San Francisco: Jossey-Bass, pp. 340–362.

González Echeverrría, R. 1999. The Pride of Havana: A History of Cuban Baseball. New York and London: Oxford University Press.

González-Corzo, M., and Larson, S. 2007. Cuba's unique remittance landscape: A comparative perspective. *Journal of Latino-Latin American Studies* 2 (4): 47–73.

González-Pagés, J. 2003. Machismo. In L. MartínezFernández, D. J. Figueredo, L. A. Pérez, Jr. and L.González, Eds, *Encyclopedia of Cuba*, Volume 1. Westport, CT: Greenwood Press, p. 291.

Gott, R. 2004. *Cuba: A New History*. New Haven and London: Yale University Press.

Grenier, G. J., and Pérez, L. 2003. *The Legacy of Exile: Cubans in the United States*. Boston: Allyn and Bacon.

Grewal, D., and M. Levy. 2010. *Marketing*, Second Edition. New York: McGraw-Hill-Irwin.

Griffith, D., Tamer Cavusgil, S., and Xu, S. 2008. Emerging themes in international business research. *Journal of International Business Studies* 39 (7): 1220–1235.

Grupo de Estudios del Mercado. 1999. *Estudio de mercado sobre la aceptación de rermesas a través de la AIS mediante una tarjecta de débito*. Havana: CIMEX S.A.

Hastings Museum of Natural and Cultural History. 2011. Kool-Aid History. http://hastingsmuseum.org/?page_id=29, Accessed October 23, 2011.

Hechevarría, M. C. 1998. *Alicia Alonso: más allá de la técnica*. Valencia: Universidad Politécnica de Valencia.

Henken, T. 2005a. Balseros, boteros and El Bombo: Post-1995 Cuban immigration to the United States and the persistence of special treatment. *Latino Studies* 3: 3993–4016.

———.2005b. Entrepreneurship, informality, and the second economy: Cuba's underground economy in comparative perspective. In J. Pérez-López, Ed., *Cuba in Transition*, Volume 15. Washington DC: Association for the Study of the Cuban Economy, pp. 360–375.

———. 2008. *Cuba: A Global Studies Guide*. Santa Barbara, CA: ABC-CLIO.

Hernández Gómez, A. 2000. Estudio de segmentación del mercadointerno en divisas. Basado en la encuesta sobre las remesas y otros ingresos en divisas, y en monedanacional de la población de Pinar del Rio, Ciudad de la Habana, La Habana, Matanzas, Villa Clara, Camagüey, Holguín y Santiago de Cuba. Havana: Cimex (mimeo).

Hirt, S., and Scarpaci, J. L. 2007. Suburbanizing Havana and Sofia: Comparative Post-socialist peri-urban change. In J. Pérez-López, Ed. *Cuba in Transition*, Volume 17. Washington DC: Association for the Study of the Cuban Economy, pp. 288–299.

Holt, D. B. 1995. How consumers consume: A typology of consumption practices. *Journal of Consumer Research* 22: 1–16.

———. 2004. *How Brands Become Icons: The Principles of Cultural Branding*. Cambridge, MA: Harvard Business School Press.

———. 2005. How societies desire brands: Using cultural theory to explain brand symbolism. In S. Ratneshwar and D. G. Mick, Eds., *Inside Consumption: Consumer Motives, Goals and Desires*. New York and London: Routledge, pp. 273–291.

Inter-American Development Bank. 2010. *Ten Years of Innovation in Remittances: Lessons Learned and Models for the Future*. Washington DC: Inter-American Development Bank.

Iyer, E. S. 1988. The influence of verbal content and relative newness on the effectiveness of comparative advertisements. *Journal of Advertising* 17 (3): 15–21.

Jack L. Hayes International. 2010. Theft Surveys, http://www.hayesinternational.com/thft_srvys.html, Accessed June 6, 2011.

Joachmisthaler, E. and Aaker, D.A. 1997. Building brands without mass media. *Harvard Business Review* Jan.-Feb., 75(1):39–45.

Jones, R. C. 1998. Remittances and inequality: A question of migration stage and geographic scale. *Economic Geography* 74: 8–25.

Joy, A., and Wallendorf, M. 1996. The development of consumer culture in the Third World. In R. W. Belk, N. Dholakia and A. Venkatesh, Eds., *Consumption and Marketing: Maro Dimensions*. Cincinnati, OH: Southwestern, pp. 101–141.

Kapcia, A. 2005. *Havana: The Making of Cuban Culture*. Oxford and New York: Berg.

Kapur, D. and McHale, J. 2005. *Give Us Your Best and Brightest: The Global Hunt for Talent and its Impact on the Developing World*. Washington, D.C.: Center for Global Development.

Keller, K. L. 1993. Conceptualizing, measuring, and managing customer-based brand equity. *Journal of Marketing* 57: 1–29.

———. 1998. *Strategic Brand Management*. Upper Saddle River, NJ: Prentice Hall.

———. 2002. *Branding and Brand Equity*. Cambridge, MA: Marketing Science Institute Relevant Knowledge Series, 02–601.

———. 2003a. Brand synthesis: The multidimensionality of brand knowledge. *Journal of Consumer Research* 29: 595–600.

———. 2003b. *Strategic Brand Management*, Second Edition. Upper Saddle River, NJ: Prentice Hall.

Keller, M. and Vihalemm, T. 2005. Coping with consumer culture: Elderly urban consumers in post-Soviet Estonia. *Trames* 9(59/54): 69–91.

Klein, N. 2000. *No Logo*. New York: Picador.

Kool-Aid Days 2011.The history of Kool-Aid.http://www.kool-aiddays.com/index.php?option=com_content&task=view&id=91, Accessed October 23, 2011.

Kraft Foods 2011. Tang. http://www.kraftfoodscompany.com/cn/en/Brands/Powdered%20Beverage/tang.aspx, Accessed October 23, 2011.

Lee, E. 1966. A theory of migration. *Demography* 3(2): 47–57.

Lehmann, D.R. and Winer, R.S. 2002. *Analysis for Marketing Planning*. New York: McGraw-Hill Irwin.

Levi, V. G., and Heller, S. 2002. *Cuban Style: Graphics for the Golden Age of Design*. Princeton, NJ: Princeton Architectural Press.

Levine, R. *Tropical Diaspora: The Jewish Experience in Cuba*. Gainesville: University Press of Florida.

Levy, M. and Grewal, D. 2009. *Marketing*. New York: McGraw Hill Irwin.

Leyva, A. I. 2011. Incentivos a crédito para la economía cubana. *Granma*, July 30, p. 5.

Lumsden, I. 1996. *Machos, Maricones and Gays: Cuba and Homosexuality*. Philadelphia, PA: Temple University Press.

Macdonald, B. 2008. *The Bridge: The Role of Design in Marketing*. New York: Morgan James Publishing.

Macleod, C. 2011. Best Buy, Home Depot find China market a tough sell. *USA Today*, February 23, 2011, p. 5–B.

Maimbo, S. M. and D. Ratha. 2005. Eds. *Remittances: Development Impact and Future Prospects*. Washington, D.C.: The International Bank for Reconstruction and Development, The World Bank.

Martínez, I. 2011. Censo 2010: 1.8 millones de cubanos viven en EEUU. Café fuerte. Mayo 2011, http://cafefuerte.com/2011/05/27/censo-2010–1–8–millones-de-cubanos-viven-en-estados-unidos/. Accessed June 3, 2010.

Martínez-Fernández, L., Fugeredo, D.H., Pérez, L.A., and González, L. 2003. *Encyclopedia of Cuba: People, History, Culture* Volume II. Westport, Conn.: Greenwood Press.

McCullough, L., Pingali, P. L., and Stamoulis, K. 2008. *The Transformation of Agri-Food Systems: Globalization, Supply Chains, and Small-Holder Farmers*. London and Sterling, VA: Earthscan.

McDonald, H., Darbyshire, P. and Colin, J. 2000. Shop often, buy little: the Vietnamese reaction to supermarket retailing. *Journal of Global Marketing* 13:53–71.

McDonald's. 2010. McDonald's FAQs, http://www.mcdonalds.ca/en/aboutus/faq.aspx, Accessed July 12, 2010.

Morales, E. 2009. *Cuba: Tránsito Silencioso al Capitalismo?* Miami: Alexandria.

Morales, E. 2011. Cuba: menos impuestos para impulsar el trabajo privado, http://www.CafeFuerte.com, Accessed June 6, 2011.

Morales, E., and Hernández, A. 2005. Analisis de situación del Comercio minorista. Marketing Department, CIMEX, mimeo.

Morales, E., and Hernández Gómez, A. 2003. Plan de marketingoperativo 2003 (mimeo), Havana: Palmares S.A.

Morales, E., and Scarpaci, J. L. 2010a. For Cuba's savvy consumers, brand names are crucial. *Cuba News*, November, pp. 10–11.

———. 2010b. Marketing: Iconic branding: A crucial element in consumer behavior. *Cuba News*, December, p. 15.

———. 2011a. Habanos S.A. eye U.S. market. *Cuba News*, pp. 8–9.

———.2011b. Iconic brand potential: What's 'Cuban' about this product? *Cuba News*, January, p. 5.

———. 2011c. Washington and Havana line their nests with remittances. *Cuba News*, February, pp. 14–15.

Moreno Fraginals, M. 1964. *El ingenio*. Havana: Comisión Nacional Cubana de la UNESCO.

Morris, E. 2004. *From Altoids to Zim: The Surprising Stories behind 125 Famous Brand Names*. New York and London: A Fireside Book.

Múñíz, M. 2003. *La Publicidad en Cuba: Mito y Realidad*. Havana: Editorial Logos.

Muñíz, Rivero J. 1965. *Tabaco, su historia en Cuba. Desde los inicios de la segunda factoría de tabacos de La Habana, hasta medianos del sixlo XX*. Volume 2. Havana: Instituto de Historia, Academia de Ciencias de la República de Cuba.

Napcor (National Association for PT Container Resources) 2011. What is PET? http://www.napcor.com/PET/whatispet.html, Accessed October 23, 2011.

Naranjo Orovio, C. 2003. Bodegas. In Martínez-Fernández, L., Gugeredo, D.H., Pérez, L.A., and González, L., Eds., *Encyclopedia of Cuba, Volume Two: People, History, Culture*. Greenwood, CT: Greenwood Press, pp. 503–504.

Nestlé. 2011. Key figures. http://www.nestle.com/AboutUs/KeyFigures/Pages/KeyFigures.aspx, Accessed October 23, 2011.

Nye, C., Roth, M., and Shimp, T. 2008. Comparative advertising in markets where brands and comparative advertising are novel. *Journal of International Business Studies* 39 (5): 851–863.

O'Brien, E. 1995. "Waiting." In *The Best American Essays*, J. Kincaid and R. Atawan, Editors. Boston: Houghton Mifflin, 170-181.

Orozco, J. 2010. Venezuela Opens Seized Exito Stores as Bicentenario Outlets (Bloomberg) February 13, 2010, http://www.businessweek.com/news/2010–02–13/venezuela-opens-seized-exito-stores-as-bicentenario-outlets.html, Accessed December 18, 2010.

Orozco, M. 2003. *Remesas a América Latina y el Caribe, 2002*. Washington DC: Inter-American Dialogue.

———. 2006. Understanding the remittance economy in Haiti. Inter-American Dialogue. Paper commissioned by the World Bank, March 15, http://www.thedialogue.org/PublicationFiles/Understandingpercent20thepercent20remittancepercent20economypercent20inpercent20Haiti.pdf, Accessed November 26, 2010.

———. 2011. Remittance recipients and the present and future of micro entrepreneurship activities in Cuba. Washington, D.C: Inter-American Bank Development (memo), May 11.

Ortíz, F. 1995. *Cuban Counterpoint: Tobacco and Sugar*. Durham, NC: Duke University Press.

Paswan, A. K. 2004. Brand-of-country origin (COO) knowledge and COO image: Investigation in an emerging franchise market. *Journal of Product & Brand Management*. 13(3): 144–155. Doi: 10.1108/10610420410538041

Pelayo, L., Nuñez, F.A., Rojas, L., Furuseth Hansen, E., Gjerde, B., Wilke, H., Mulder, B., Robertson, L. *Giardia* infections in Cuban children: the genotypes circulating in a rural population. *Annals of Tropical Medicine and Parasitology* 102 (7): 585–595.

Pérez López, J. 1995. *Cuba's Second Economy: From Behind the Scenes to Central Stage*. New Brunswick, NJ: Transaction Books.

Pérez-López, J. 2002. The Cuban Economy in an unending Special Period. In *Cuba in Transition*, Volume 12. Washington, D.C.: Association for the Study of the Cuban Economy, p. 521.

Pernod Ricard. 2011. Spanish supreme court confirms, http://www.pernod-ricard.com/en/pages/3077/Press-releases/Spanish-Supreme-Court-confirms-the-ownership-of-Havana-Club-trademark-by-Pernod-Ricard-joint-venture.html, Accessed February 24, 2011.

Peters, P., and Scarpaci, J. L. 1998. *Cuba's New Entrepreneurs: Five Years of Small-Scale Capitalism*. Arlington, VA: Alexis de Tocqueville Institution.

Portell Vilá, H. 1939. Introduction. In F. Ortiz, Ed., *Cuban Counterpoint: Tobacco and Sugar*. Durham, NC: Duke University Press, pp. i–xix.

PR Newswire 2010. Magazines: The Power of Print. http://multivu.prnewswire.com/mnr/magazines/42679/, Accessed November 5, 2010.

Preacher, K. J. 2001. Calculation for the chi-square test: An interactive calculation tool for chi-square tests of goodness of fit and independence [Computer software], http://quantpsy.org. Accessed June 3, 2011.

Puerta, R. 2003. Remesas familiares y la política cubana, Havana. Mimeo.

Quart, A. 2003. *Branded: The Buying and Selling of Teenagers*. New York: Basic Books.

Quirk, J. 1993. *Fidel Castro*. New York: W. W. Norton.

Ransom, M. 2008. Fidel Castro—The verdict. February 27 entry of New Left blog, http://www.newint.org/blog/editors/2008/02/27/fidel-castro-the-verdict/, Accessed September 15, 2010.

Reid, S.E. 2002. Cold War in the Kitchen: Gender and the De-Stalinization of consumer taste in the Soviet Union under Khrushchev. *Slavic Review* 62(2): 211–252.

Reporters without Borders. 2011. Press Freedom Index 2010, http://en.rsf.org/press-freedom-index-2010,1034.html, Accessed March 23, 2011.

Reuters Wire Reports. 2010. Analysis: Cuba jobs reform brings opportunity and uncertainty, Tuesday, Sep 14. Marc Frank and Jeff Franks.

Ritter, A. 2010. Shifting realities in Special Period Cuba. *Latin American Research Review* 45:229–238.

Rodríguez, A. 2008. Cuba holds large gay rights rally: Raúl Castro's daughter presides at government-backed event. Associate Press Wire Report, updated May 17, 2008, http://www.msnbc.msn.com/id/24685283/ns/world_news-americas/, Accessed December 11, 2010.

Rueven International. 2011a. Rueven International. http://www.reuven.com/main.cfm, Accessed October 23, 2011.

Rueven International. 2011b. About Us. http://www.reuven.com/printerFriendly.cfm?id=534FD2FD-B6A7-8AA0-656BCA50900FC4ED, Accessed October 23, 2011.

Salgado, C. A. 1999. Hybridity in new world baroque theory. *Journal of American Folklore* 112 (445): 316–331.

Sanger, J. W. 1919. *Advertising Methods in Cuba*. Washington, DC: Department of Commerce, Bureau of Foreign and Domestic Commerce, Special Agents Series No. 178, Government Printing Office.

Sanguinetty, J.A. 1995. Evaluation of changes in economic policy in Cuba. *Cuba in Transition*, Volume 5. Washington, D.C.: Association for the Study of the Cuban Economy, pp. 31–23.

Santamaría-García, A. 2003. Sugar industry. In L. Martínez-Fernández, D. H. Gugeredo, L. A. Pérez and L. González, Eds., *Encyclopedia of Cuba*, Volume Two: People, History, Culture. Greenwood, CT: Greenwood Press, pp. 304–305.

Scarpaci, J.L. 1995. The emerging food and paladar market in Havana. *Cuba In Transition*, Volume 5. Washington, D.C.: Association for the Study of the Cuban Economy, pp. 74–84.

———. 2004. Globalization and work: Economy, remittances, and joint ventures in post-Soviet Cuba. *Transnational Law and Contemporary Problems* 14:499–516.

———. 2005. *Plazas and Barrios: Heritage Tourism and Globalization in the Latin American Centro Histórico.* Tucson and London: University of Arizona Press.

———. 2007. Globalization tourists and heritage tourists in American culture: The case of Latin American historic districts. *Material Culture* 39 (2): 1–16.

Scarpaci, J.L. and Portela, A. 2009. *Cuban Landscapes: Heritage, Memory and Place.* New York: Guilford Press.

Scarpaci, J. L, Segre, R., and Coyula, M. 2002. *Havana: Two Faces of the Antillean Metropolis.* Chapel Hill and London: University of North Carolina Press.

Schor, J. 1998. *The Overspent American.* New York: Basic.

———. 2004. *Born to Buy: The Commercialized Child and the New Consumer Culture.* New York: Scribner's.

Schwartz, B. 1974. Waiting, Exchange, and Power: The Distribution of Time in Social Systems. *American Journal of Sociology* 79:841–870.

Segre, R., Coyula, M. and Scarpaci, J.L. 1997. *Havana: Two Faces of the Antillean Metropolis.* Chichester: John Wiley and Sons.

Shanken, M. R. 1994. Cigar Aficionado, June 1, 1994 (Summer Issue), http://www.cigaraficionado.com/webfeatures/show/id/Interview-with-Fidel-Castro_7763, Accessed December 31, 2010.

Sierra Madero, A. 2006. *Del otro lado del espejo: la sexualidad en la construcción de la nación cubana.* Havana: Casa de las Américas.

Simmel, G. 1978. *The Philosophy of Money.* London: Routledge.

Simón, P. R. A. 1996. *Alicia Alonso: órbita de una leyenda.* Madrid: Autores del Siglo XX.

Skidmore, T., and Smith, P. 2004. *Modern Latin America*, Fifth Edition. New York: Oxford University Press.

Staten, Cl. 2003. *The History of Cuba.* London: Palgrave.

Stitziel, J. 2005. *Fashioning Socialism: Clothing, Politics and Consumer Culture in East Germany.* New York and Oxford: Berg.

Stratfor Global Intelligence. 2011. Venezuela: Cubans working in Exchange for oil shipments? http://www.stratfor.com/memberships/154683/sitrep/20100216_venezuela_cubans_working_exchange_oil_shipments, Accessed June 8, 2011.

Stubbs, J. 2000. Turning over a new leaf? Revisiting the Cuban cigar. *New West Indian Guide/Nieuwe West-Indische Gids* 74: 235–255.

Sujan, M. 1985. Consumer knowledge: Effects on evaluation strategies mediating consumer judgments. *Journal of Consumer Research* 12: 31–46.

Szondi, G. 2007. The role and challenges of country branding in transition countries: The Central and Eastern European experience. *Place Branding and Public Diplomacy* 3 (1): 8–20.

Tamayo, J. 2010. Cuba's Granma publishes letters critical of economy, June 1. McClatchy, http://www.mcclatchydc.com/2010/06/01/95109/cubas-granma-newspaper-publishes.html, Accessed March 23, 2011.

Taylor, H. L. 2009. *Inside El Barrio: A Bottom-up View of Neighborhood Life in Castro's Cuba.* Kumarian Press.

Terry, W. 1981. *Alicia Alonso and Her Ballet Nacional de Cuba.* Garden City, NY: Anchor.

The Havana Consulting Group. 2011. Estudio de precios de la competencia de Western Union, para los envíos de remesas al mercado cubano (July), mimeo.

The Numbers. 2011. Buena Vista Social Club gross, http://www.the-numbers.com/movies/1999/0BVSC.php, Accessed February 12, 2011.

Trip Advisor. 2010. The best customer service you'll find—can't be beat, http://www.tripadvisor.com/ShowUserReviews-g150812–d1751329–r71412492–La_Casa_del_Habano-Playa_del_Carmen_Yucatan_Peninsula.html, Accessed December 31, 2010.

Ubeda, L. (2005a) Brascuba, los próximos diez años.Opciones, SemanarioFinanciero, Comercial y Turistico de Cuba (Agosto) http://www.opciones.cu/turismo/2005-08-13/los-proximos-diez-anos/, Accessed October 30, 2011.

Ubeda, L. (2005b). Rothmans of Pall Mall, los pequeños detalles hacen una gran diferencia". *Opciones, SemanarioFinanciero, Comercial y Turistico de Cuba* (Noviembre)http://www.opciones.cu/turismo/2005-11-05/los-pequenos-detalles-hacen-una-gran-diferencia/

United Nations. 1960. *Statistical Yearbook*, 1960. New York: United Nations.

United Nations. 1964. *Demographic Yearbook*, 1964. New York: United Nations.

Valdés, Z. 1995. *La nada cotidiana.* Barcelona: Emecé Editores.

Vaynerchuck, G. 2011. *The Thank You Economy.* New York: Harper Collins.

Venard, B. and Hanafi, M. 2008. Organizational isomorphism and corruption in financial institutions: Empirical research in emerging countries. *Journal of Business Ethics* 81:481–498.

Verdecia Diez, Y. (2005). Mascalidad, prposito de Bravo S.A. *Opciones, SemanarioFinanciero, Comercial y Turistico de Cuba* (Agosto)http://www.opciones.cu/turismo/2005-08-06/mas-calidad-proposito-de-bravo-s.a/ Accessed October 30, 2011.

UNESCO. 2010. Migrant/migration, http://www.unesco.org/new/en/social-and-human-sciences/themes/social-transformations/international-migration/glossary/migrant/, Accessed November 28, 2010.

Weinreb, A. 2009. *Cuba in the Shadow of Change: Daily Life in the Twilight of the Revolution.* Gainesville: University Press of Florida.

Weissert, W. 2008. Consumerism good for Cuban communism? *Seattle Times*, April 3, http://seattletimes.nwsource.com/html/nationworld/2004324033_cuba03.html, Accessed September 15, 2010.

Wilkinson, S. 2010. David and Goliath. 100 years of Cuban independence, 200 years of US annexationism, http://www.twfabians.co.uk/cuba.html, Accessed October 11, 2010.

Women's Suffrage. 2010. A world chronology of the recognition of Women's rights to vote and to stand for election, http://www.ipu.org/wmn-e/suffrage.htm, Accessed October 11, 2010.

Woods, A. and Roberts, S. 2011. *Economic Geography: Places, Networks and Flows.* London: Routledge.

Woolworth, F. W. 1929. *1879–1929, fifty years of Woolworth: over 2100 Woolworth stores celebrate this year in 1500 cities in 5 countries of the world, the fiftieth anniversary of the F.W. Woolworth co., with amazing buying opportunities for your nickels and dimes.* New York: F. W. Woolworth.

Yadong, L., and Peng, M. W. 1999. Learning to compete in a transition economy: Experience, environment, and performance. *Journal of International Business Studies* 30 (2): 269–296.

Index

t refers to Tables, *f* refers to Figures and *n* refers to Notes

Feasible Computations and Provable Complexity Properties

JURIS HARTMANIS
Cornell University

SOCIETY for INDUSTRIAL and APPLIED MATHEMATICS • 1978

PHILADELPHIA, PENNSYLVANIA 19103

Printed by J.W. Arrowsmith Ltd., Bristol 3, England.

Library of Congress Cataloging-in-Publication Data

Hartmanis, J.
Feasible computations and provable complexity properties.

(Regional conference series in applied mathematics ; 30)
Bibliography: p.
1.Machine theory. 2. Formal languages.
3. Computationlal complexity. I. Title.
II. Series.
QA267.H35 519.4 78-14744

ISBN 0-89871-027-8